LEAVING THE BENCH

LEAVING THE BENCH

SUPREME COURT JUSTICES
AT THE END

David N. Atkinson

University Press of Kansas

© 1999 by the University Press of Kansas

Published by the University Press of Kansas (Lawrence, Kansas 66049), which was organized by the Kansas Board of Regents and is operated and funded by Emporia State University, Fort Hays State University, Kansas State University, Pittsburg State University, the University of Kansas, and Wichita State University.

Library of Congress Cataloging-in-Publication Data

Atkinson, David N. (David Neal), 1940–
     Leaving the bench : Supreme Court justices at the end / David N. Atkinson.
         p.   cm.
     Includes bibliographical references and index.
     ISBN 0-7006-0946-6 (alk. paper)
     1. United States.   Supreme Court—Biography.   2. Judges—United States—Biography.   3. Judges—United States—Retirement.
     I. Title.
     KF8744.A98   1999
     347.73′2634—dc21   98-54752
                                                                              CIP

British Library Cataloguing in Publication Data is available.

Printed in the United States of America
10 9 8 7 6 5 4 3 2 1

The paper used in this publication meets the minimum requirements of the American National Standard for Permanence of Paper for Printed Library Materials Z39.48-1984.

I gratefully dedicate this book to my parents,
two very special people,
with love and affection.

CONTENTS

PREFACE

The idea of writing a history of Supreme Court resignations, retirements, and deaths first occurred to me when Justice William O. Douglas retired. It was the most publicized, most media-covered retirement that anyone could recall at the time. Every day the reporters waited for the justice outside his home as he was taken to his car. They attempted to get him to speak, thus emphasizing his impairment, because his stroke had left him nearly inarticulate. Predictably, he responded with an attempt at bravado, but it convinced no one. The question in the public mind quickly became when he would retire, not if he would retire. So it was no surprise when even this most reluctant of retirees acquiesced to the public clamor.

This is a book of endings. There is always a paragraph or two on a justice's death, resignation, or retirement in the excellent biographical compendia providing short lives of the justices, but the detail of the research provided here in most cases goes significantly beyond what is provided in those sources alone. To achieve this result, I have culled detailed information from newspapers, biographies, memoirs, diaries, historical studies, private letters, and interviews in order to give as complete a picture as possible of how each justice left the Supreme Court. I have also tried to choose the interesting anecdote, the revealing comment, and the unusual or less frequently encountered evidence when there are the inevitable choices of material to be made. So while discussing Felix Frankfurter's last days, use has been made of Garson Kanin's memoir rather than the less flamboyant chronicles of his illness from other sources.

Admittedly, there are some justices about whom little is known beyond the bare bones of their dates of services. These are invariably nineteenth-century justices about whom little is known otherwise as well. They are, however, the exceptions. Quite a lot of material about most of the justices and how they spent their last days on the Court is available, even though—again with the nineteenth century in mind—the existing descriptions of their maladies and illnesses may be incomplete and uncertain. Doctors did not know a great deal about many illnesses during the last century, and advances in medicine were notoriously slow.[1] Medical conclusions were sometimes offered bluntly. For example, when Napoleon III's half brother, the Duc de Morny, fell ill in 1865, his physician, after all others had been asked to leave the room, told Morny—in response to a request for a frank assessment of his situation—"You're done for."[2] In the tradition of those times, Morny simply nodded and made his final arrangements while he still had the strength to do so. The nineteenth-century justices were in a similar situation; when things went wrong, there was not a whole lot that could be done about it.

The treatment of the justices is necessarily uneven; there is more material reported in the following pages about some than others. This disparity bears no relationship to their reputation in Court history. My interest here is in something very different: their health histories. Consequently, some of the more fascinating of the justices from this perspective are men such as James Wilson, Robert Grier, and Charles Whittaker, even though as justices their contributions were not as prominent as many others.

Some justices have left simply and without fanfare. Will Court papers someday tell us more about Byron White's retirement? After thirty-one years, at age seventy-five, he said it was time to step aside, and nothing more complicated than that was involved. In the absence of any evidence to the contrary, is there any reason why he should not be taken at his word? Similarly, despite the incredulity expressed by the news reporters who attended his retirement announcement, is it really remarkable that Chief Justice Warren Burger, in his seventy-ninth year, wished to put aside the burdens of office? Sometimes Court history is like that; what you see is what you get, without any hidden secrets.

---

1. The situation was much grimmer than is usually thought. As has been observed: "Unlike many aspects of daily life, medical care made no dramatic advance during the century. Nutrition was poorly understood, and physicians had very few effective ways to treat illness. Epidemic diseases swept through crowded cities. Although the bacteria that caused some of them were identified by the century's end, it would be another forty years before cures were found" (Sally Mitchell, *Daily Life in Victorian England* [Westport, Conn.: Greenwood Press, 1996], 189).
2. Rosalynd Pflaum, *The Emperor's Talisman: The Life of the Duc de Morny* (New York: Meredith Press, 1968), 252.

Some may suppose that the lives of justices who predated twentieth-century disability provisions are irrelevant to an evaluation of contemporary tenure policy. This supposition is partly true, and the inclusion of the history of those earliest justices must necessarily stand on our intrinsic interest in a part of their lives because of their general contributions to our politics. But there is something else to be considered as well. As John R. Schmidhauser has persuasively observed, more generous retirement pensions alone may not have much affected the retirement choices of many of the justices.[3] Multiple explanations for judicial behavior are more likely than not to prove compelling, and this area of judicial behavior is no exception. It is not possible to conclude with certitude that the pension reforms of 1937 have prevented future problems. Prognosticating judicial behavior is, unfortunately, not so easy as that.

My suggestions for reform are modest, although I do not think them unimportant. On the contrary, unless some changes are made, I am pessimistic about the Court's future. Relatively small changes sometimes have significant positive consequences for institutions, while inaction leads to predictable and avoidable costs.

The reader will not find here a detailed exegesis of term limits for justices. To do so would require a separate book, so fraught now is the topic with the baggage of partisan and ideological commitments.[4] For my purposes it is sufficient to note the several reasons for the present inappropriateness of term limits for the Supreme Court.

In the following pages I will explore why justices relinquish authority and also will offer views as to when they should leave government service. But in between these two concerns, as shall become evident, there is a wondrous variety in specifically how each of the justices went about—as Justice Holmes said—"bowing to the inevitable." What follows directs the reader's attention to the why (Chapter 1), how (Chapters 2–6), and when (Chapter 7) of Supreme Court departures.

I have been collecting materials on the deaths, resignations, and retirements of Supreme Court justices for twenty years. During this time, versions of some of the chapters in this book appeared in the *UMKC Law Review*, the

3. See his discussion of "Resignation and Retirement" in Kermit L. Hall, ed., *The Oxford Companion to the Supreme Court of the United States* (New York: Oxford University Press, 1992), 729–30.
4. See, e.g., George F. Will, *Restoration: Congress, Term Limits, and the Recovery of Deliberative Democracy* (New York: Free Press, 1992).

Arizona State Law Journal, and the *Drake Law Review.* My views about
Robert C. Grier's resignation first appeared in *The Supreme Court Historical
Society Quarterly.*

Interviews conducted with several of the justices in the late 1960s and
early 1970s provided material that has proved unexpectedly useful. As one
initially interested in the careers of Sherman Minton and Harold H. Burton,
I found that each of their colleagues who I asked to discuss matters of Court
history was willing to do so. In every case, the interview was sufficiently
eclectic to yield information of direct or indirect use in this book. Hugo L.
Black, William O. Douglas, Tom C. Clark, John Marshall Harlan, Stanley F.
Reed, Earl Warren, and Charles E. Whittaker all responded to my requests
for information, and I remember each of them with respect and gratitude.

Valuable information was received from Mary Anne Minton Callanan, Dr.
Sherman Minton Jr., Dr. C. Keith Whittaker, and Kent Whittaker, for which
I am thankful.

My coauthors on previous publications, Dale Neuman and Lawrence
Larsen, read the manuscript with their usual eye for detail and have saved
me from many errors. Beneficial comments on the manuscript were also received from Ross Stephens, Harris Mirkin, and Max Skidmore. At various
times, David Sprick, Jessie Jo Johnson, Cathleen Cerne, and Karen Mitchell
provided helpful assistance with research on all or parts of the manuscript.
Many people contributed valuable insights or offered suggestions. I wish
particularly to thank Dr. David Bock, George Christensen, Gerald Dunne,
Sheldon Goldman, Franz Jantzen, Peter Magrath, Jeffrey O'Connell, Stanley
Parsons, Jeffrey Segal, the late Bernard Schwartz, and Tinsley Yarbrough.

Michael Briggs and the editorial staff at the University Press of Kansas
have been a pleasure to work with during the production of this book. I
very much appreciate the enthusiasm and publishing skills they brought to
the project.

The University of Missouri supported this research through the awarding
of a Weldon Spring research grant, for which I am grateful. I am also grateful
for the opportunity to have tested parts of this material on the many able
students who I have had the pleasure to teach over the years at the University
of Missouri–Kansas City Department of Political Science and the School
of Law.

I have always held the view taken by Clark Clifford in his autobiography
that nothing undermines confidence in any book so much as factual errors,
and therefore to the extent possible they must be avoided. However impos-

sible such a task usually proves to be, I have had excellent help in striving to achieve this goal.

My principal debt is to my parents. My mother, Lena M. Atkinson, and my father, Cecil L. Atkinson, were responsible for encouraging my academic interests long ago with their confidence and support.

1

WHY DO THEY LEAVE OR STAY?

Although appointments to the United States Supreme Court have been systematically examined, there has been much less written about the historical, political, and medical circumstances of judicial deaths, resignations, and retirements.[1] The purpose of this book is to suggest why justices leave the Court and why some refuse to leave; to provide a description of how each justice left; and to ask when justices should leave. These three interrogatories—why do they leave, how do they leave, and when should they leave—are closely related. A thorough description of a justice's last days prior to his resignation will usually, although not always, reveal the reason or reasons why he voluntarily left office. Similarly, whether justices should be forced to leave before they voluntarily elect to do so depends largely, as will be seen, on how one assesses the adequacy of current retirement policy in removing justices when the reasons for their retirement outweigh the reasons for continued service.

Why Do They Leave?

Justices leave office for the following reasons: (1) the threat of impeachment; (2) an attractive pension; (3) ambition; (4) dissatisfaction or weariness; (5) poor health or declining physical energy; (6) mental decline or disability; (7) family pressure; and (8) a voluntary choice even though they remain capable of doing the work. These explanations appear repeatedly in Court history and often in combination. Some justices, like William Strong and George Shiras, chose to leave because they concluded they had served long enough, and it was important to leave office in good health and while still capable of performing at the highest level.

Supreme Court justices are appointed for life "during good Behaviour."[2]

1

As a practical matter, this provision has meant they have life tenure, because the only way to formally remove a justice is through the cumbersome impeachment process that was scathingly described by Thomas Jefferson as "a scarecrow."[3] The impeachment procedure has not yet directly resulted in the dismissal of a single justice. Very likely, James Wilson would have been removed from office had he not died just as his creditors were nearly upon him. It is also likely that an impeachment attempt would have ensued against Abe Fortas, although even Attorney General John Mitchell acknowledged Fortas had done nothing criminally wrong. In either of these cases, had the justices remained, lowered public esteem could have seriously harmed the Court, or at least Fortas expressed this concern in his case.

Impeachment has not been used successfully because Congress is reluctant to implement it. John Randolf and the Republicans did not succeed in their effort to removed Samuel Chase from the Court. The Senate failed to convict him in 1805, not only because Chase had joined those few others in risking "our Lives, our Fortunes and our sacred Honor" and had signed the Declaration of Independence, but also because President Thomas Jefferson had withdrawn his support for a conviction. Jefferson well knew what a frightening political weapon impeachment would become if it could be used to remove ideological opponents and not merely those who had committed crimes. The only crimes Chase had committed were against the British Crown. Since Jefferson was equally guilty of such crimes, Benjamin Franklin's celebrated admonishment to his fellow revolutionaries on the need to hang together or to hang separately bears a special poignancy. The consequent trial of Samuel Chase forever narrowed the scope of impeachable offenses and in the process much strengthened the independence of Supreme Court justices. *wrong & right*

Unlike the tradition in Great Britain, resignation has never become an easily accepted part of the American political tradition. This tendency has been especially so when justices did not serve long enough to qualify for a pension and lacked independent means of support. Such a combination of circumstances explained the lingering incapacitation of William Moody, who retired as soon as Congress extended full benefits to him by a special statute.

Among the early twentieth-century justices, there were few persons in public life who achieved more in a short period of years than William Moody. The former navy secretary and attorney general, a close personal friend and confidant of Theodore Roosevelt, had a brief five years on the Supreme Court before he became totally paralyzed and unable to care for himself. He was still a relatively young man when he was stricken. He has become a footnote in American history, a person of interest to period specialists, all quite contrary to the expectations his meteoric career initially suggested. Roosevelt himself, following Moody's resignation from the Court, described his departure as "a tragedy [from] the private and a real calamity from the public standpoint. He would have rendered such service as hardly any other man now in public life can hope to render."[4]

The newspapers of the day all duly reported Moody's symptoms. For seven years after his departure, he laid in bed unable to use his legs. His limbs became so progressively weakened that he could not use a pen or read a book by himself. A bachelor, Moody was dependent on his sister who nursed him until his death. Until recently, no one was very confident they knew what killed him. Acute rheumatism or infectious arthritis were usually mentioned, but some of the symptoms were atypical. Recent scholarship suggests a central nervous system disorder caused his sudden deterioration. In Moody's case the timing of his resignation was entirely dependent on the extension of pension benefits covering his sudden and unexpected decline.

The chief justices have traditionally borne the principal burden of dealing with incapacitated colleagues, which has all too frequently proved to be trying. They have been most successful when they have been able to marshal the Court in support of their effort to encourage a resignation or retirement. They have been least successful when a justice is reluctant to leave or determined to stay. Although the chief justice is primus inter pares, or first among equals, his principal power is that of persuasion.

Members of the Supreme Court were more easily persuaded to leave after Congress provided financial benefits for them. Benefits were first offered to the justices as early as 1869 by the Judiciary Act of that year.[5] Under the terms of the act, justices who served on the Supreme Court for at least ten years and who had reached the age of seventy could leave at full salary. They then continued to receive in future years the exact salary with which they resigned. The Judiciary Act of 1869 meant that disabled justices, like William Moody and Mahlon Pitney, who did not qualify for a pension required a special bill from Congress as an inducement to leave.

Technically, before the Retirement Act of 1937 either a justice resigned from the Supreme Court or died in office. No one retired, although in practice the terms "retirement" and "resignation" tended to be used loosely and interchangeably by the justices themselves in those cases where a justice was entitled to a government pension because of Court service. After the 1937 legislation, additional options became available to justices who were seventy (with ten years of federal judicial service) or sixty-five (with fifteen years of judicial service). Justices could retire (keeping the senior status of their office) rather than merely resign.

Qualifying justices could retire with senior status at the salary they were receiving for either of two reasons: age or disability. In the case of the latter, as when disability was invoked by Justice Charles E. Whittaker in 1962, the chief justice must advise the president of the disability in writing. By retiring, a justice retains a commission as a Supreme Court justice, which permits the retiree to participate in cases decided by a lower federal court. Such service is entirely elective. However, the chief justice must consent, and there is evidence in the one instance in which disability was invoked that the required consent was not forthcoming. The late federal district judge William H. Becker reported a conversation he had with Chief Justice Earl Warren about Justice Whittaker. When Whittaker wanted to try cases following his retirement and sought Warren's consent, Warren told Becker: "Tell him that I never could get him to make up his mind, and I'll be damned if I will let him do that to me again trying cases. So the answer is no."[6] In recent years some of the justices have done quite a bit of this work, often on the Court of Appeals for the District of Columbia. Justices Harold Burton, Stanley Reed, and Tom Clark all participated in lower court cases for several years following their retirements.

Since Supreme Court salaries are now controlled by legislation, they are no longer subject to civil service regulations. Previously, the pensions were subject to such fluctuations as might be mandated by the bureaucracy in control of government retirement benefits. When Oliver Wendell Holmes resigned in 1932, he received a pension of $10,000, which was only half of what he earned as a justice because the Hoover administration decided to cap federal pensions as part of an economizing plan.[7] Salaries for justices are presently fixed and are at either full or half of the original salary, depending on the justice's age or length of service. If a justice does not qualify for retirement at full salary, retirement is permitted at half salary. Quite literally, most justices retire at full pay. These pensions are adjusted upward in accordance with salaries received by active justices.[8] As long as a justice has retired to what is described as "senior status" (and thus holds a commission as a federal judge), his salary cannot constitutionally be reduced.[9] These post-1937 changes removed the need for Congress to pass special bills providing for those justices who were financially dependent on their judicial salaries, although whether and under what circumstances justices would avail themselves of these enhanced benefits remained at the time unresolved.

Federal judges sitting on legislative courts, as provided for in Article 1 of the Constitution, retain their positions for the length of time Congress prescribed at the time the court was created or as may be provided for in subsequent legislation. Congress has the power to decide, as is commonly done, upon a term of years, or it may grant tenure for "good Behaviour" or even provide for a mandatory retirement age. Similarly, Congress may reduce the salaries of these judges as it chooses, may permit the president alone to appoint judges, or may provide procedures for removal other than impeachment. No such options pertain to Supreme Court justices or the other federal judges on the district and appellate courts created under Article 3.

Ambition influenced John Jay, the first chief justice, who resigned to become governor of New York because he understandably considered the governorship to be a more important post. Arthur Goldberg was another member of the Court who succumbed to what he, incorrectly, thought at the time was a more influential position, the United Nations ambassadorship under President Lyndon B. Johnson. Dissatisfaction played a role in Benjamin Curtis's resignation from the Taney Court in order to return to his Boston law practice. He expressed concern about the salary he made as a justice, but he was also deeply troubled by the attitudes of some of his fellow justices toward the slavery issue.

Poor health accounts for most resignations and retirements. Unfortunately, sometimes the justices themselves are secretive about their health. The second John Marshall Harlan was within months of his death before the general public knew anything was seriously wrong with him. In Harlan's case, it is also true that the spinal cancer that killed him was not initially diagnosed by his doctors. That was in 1971. Scarcely any members of the general public were aware of the battery of large fluorescent floor lamps surrounding the desks of both Justices Harlan and Hugo L. Black by early 1968. Neither could see well by that time, although neither retired until near death three years later.

At present, because of the development of a full-time Supreme Court media presence, it may not be possible to entirely conceal deteriorating health from the public. Even so, the extent of the deterioration may, for reasons of personal loyalty, protectiveness, or even sentimentality, be shielded or minimized by most members of the media. Thurgood Marshall's final years provide an illustration. Few persons were quite prepared for his final press conference when his condition became a matter of public record. He was by then an exhausted, querulous man who quite literally, as he said, was "old and coming apart."[10] There was something ruthless and undignified about the harsh television closeups provided of the once confident, dapper legend of the civil rights movement. That he, like so many others in Court history, had stayed too long was shockingly apparent.

All of the reasons for leaving the Supreme Court, except ambition, dissatisfaction, and impeachment, may be related at least tangentially to the aging process. Social science, unfortunately, has had difficulty generalizing about the effects of aging on judging. Even so, there is the strong suggestion that age is important to an understanding of judicial decision making.[11] Perhaps subjective age—the way one visualizes oneself—is as important to some justices as chronological age.[12] Certainly William O. Douglas illustrates this possibility. Anyone who spent time around him in the early 1970s will remember the voice and eyes, seemingly decades younger than those of the septuagenarian he was.

Medical science will most likely continue to advance knowledge about the relationship between age and intellectual performance. Interestingly, the traditionally held belief that aging significantly diminishes all forms of human intelligence has been challenged by some researchers.[13] As long as persons remain healthy (that is, avoid diseases that affect the brain), their "crystallized intelligence" (which is the use of accumulated information to make judgments and solve problems) continues to increase steadily throughout life.[14] To the extent this may be so, age is a problem only because the frequency of age-related illnesses affecting health predictably increases.

A more recent investigation suggests the literature is less optimistic about the effects of time on the capacity to reason. Judge Richard A. Posner concludes that although crystallized intelligence—or that broad base of information people acquire—does decline with age, it does indeed decline less rapidly than "fluid intelligence," which is associated with imagination or the ability to structure problems theoretically. Unfortunately, fluid intelligence declines markedly as people age, adversely affecting the ease with which learning is acquired, since memory becomes less reliable.[15]

Until recently, biographical discretion has tended to minimize the interplay of illness and the actions of political elites. It is no surprise that the greatest interest among American scholars has been in chronicling the health of American presidents.[16] The assassination of President John F. Kennedy and the numerous health problems of Presidents Dwight D. Eisenhower and Lyndon B. Johnson led to the adoption of the Twenty-fifth Amendment in 1967. The near assassination of President Ronald Reagan and his subsequent bout with colon cancer have been more recent catalysts. The special importance of the presidency, the uncertainties of application presented by the Twenty-fifth Amendment dealing with presidential disability and death, and the wide array of "prescriptions" for even further change in the office have focused public attention as never before on age and disability among political elites. The successful effort to conceal President Franklin D. Roosevelt's declining health as he sought the presidency for the fourth time now seems even more than half a century removed, inasmuch as the ethical impropriety of public figures dissembling about their medical conditions seems well established in the public mind.[17]

Why Do They Stay?

After he retired as chief justice of the Supreme Court of Texas, Robert W. Calvert once suggested four reasons why judges are reluctant to step aside. His explanations, which on first impression may sound facetious, contain a central core of persuasiveness that can be as appropriately applied to Supreme Court justices as to other federal judges. The excuses, in order of their importance, for not retiring are:

> The judge (1) has developed no subsidiary interests and hasn't the faintest idea what he will do to occupy his time if he retires; (2) has a secret feeling that he is the indispensable man and that no successor could possibly fill his shoes; (3) wants to keep some sort of a strangle hold on the social standing his position offers him and his wife and the favors and honors which are tendered to his position rather than to him personally; and (4) isn't wanted at home by his wife because through the years she has developed her own 8 to 5 routine program and she doesn't want it interrupted.[18]

Often elements of the four excuses combine, as in the case of Chief Justice Salmon Chase. A friend of Chase once said of him, "Chase is a good man, but his theology is unsound. He thinks there is a fourth person in the Trinity."[19] His sense of indispensability was highly developed. For his energetic, socially ambitious, unhappily married daughter, Mrs. Kate Sprague, who also continually encouraged her father's presidential ambitions, resignation was out of the question. Since Chase was a widower, only the first three of the excuses applied to him.

Supreme Court justices do not voluntarily leave office for the following reasons: (1) financial considerations; (2) party or ideology;[20] (3) a determination to stay; (4) a sense of indispensability; (5) loss of status; (6) a belief they can still do the work; (7) not knowing what else to do; and (8) family pressure to stay in office. Three of these reasons—a determination to stay that usually translates into sheer stubbornness, a sense of indispensability, and a belief they can still do the work—are encouraged by the proliferation of support staff within the Supreme Court.

In fact, some believe it is now possible for a justice to merely preside over his office while a bevy of industrious clerks continues to crank out opinions that are generally consistent with his prior work.[21] The justice becomes, as a worker, superfluous. Diminished capacity under such conditions is no incentive to retire; retirement signals the end to the political and social importance that may well be what are most important to the justice or his family.

Two of the reasons why justices do not leave the bench have been effectively removed since the pension changes in 1937, although they remain prominent in Court history. Financial considerations no longer are important since a retired justice can receive the same salary as an active justice. Similarly, the concern that he would not know what to do with his time in retirement has been removed with the advent of senior status for Supreme Court justices as well as lower federal judges; a retired justice can now remain as busy as he chooses to be, as long as the chief justice is willing to provide him with assignments.

The other reasons remain very much in play. William O. Douglas and Thurgood Marshall lingered in office longer than they should have because of a determination to stay and because of ideology and party. A sense of indispensability was also evident in both cases. "Even if I'm only half alive," Douglas told a former law clerk, "I can still cast a liberal vote."[22]

Justice Douglas's wife and family did not urge him to cling to his seat following his stroke in 1975 when it became obvious he could not continue to be a productive member of the Court, but other families have responded differently. Neither Salmon P. Chase's daughter, Kate, nor Stephen J. Field's younger wife were anxious to see their father and husband leave the bench. The importance of a loss of status is more difficult to assess in any given case because it is a reason not likely to be articulated by a justice or family member. Yet, it is notable that of all the chief justices, only Charles Evans Hughes, Earl Warren, and Warren Burger retired in reasonably good health. And in each case they were quite aged.

Another reason, a sense of indispensabilty, is commonly associated with the longer tenures. Roger Brooke Taney, for example, during the Civil War acquired a sense of mission in his quarrel with Abraham Lincoln. For as long as he could still function, a resignation was not a serious possibility. Many justices have not been reluctant to insist they could still do the Court's work, even though reality indicated otherwise; the mentally impaired Robert Grier and Joseph McKenna provide tragic instances of this form of self-deception.

A Footnote on Funerals

Some of the justices who resigned or retired spent many years afterward following other pursuits or merely living in retirement. Their lives were far removed from the Court. But at their deaths, sometimes their former colleagues participated years later in funeral ceremonies. Justice Moody, for example, was attended at his funeral by William Howard Taft and his wife, along with Justices Edward Douglass White and Oliver Wendell Holmes. The practice of full Court attendance at funerals has become more common in recent years. Consequently, William O. Douglas's absence at Felix Frankfurter's funeral did not go unobserved, although intimates were well aware that their once cordial relationship during their years as law professors had become irreconcilably damaged.

Three members of the Court were present at the belated second funeral of James Wilson in November 1906.[23] Wilson, who not only served on the first Supreme Court but signed both the Declaration of Independence and the Constitution, died of stroke and fever in 1798, hounded by his creditors. He was run to ground as a debtor, in those times a serious felony, in a tavern along with his second wife (thirty-two years his junior) and their small child. Wilson was the most unfortunate of men, although much of his misfortune was indisputably of his own making. Wilson was buried where he died. Only a wooden marker acknowledged his grave in Edenton, North Carolina. Years passed until it was decided to exhume the corpse and transport it back to Philadelphia, where Wilson was given an elaborate funeral. The body lay in Independence Hall prior to the funeral, which was attended not only by all the important Pennsylvania political figures but also by Chief Justice Melville Weston Fuller and Justices Edward Douglass White and Oliver Wendell Holmes. At his second funeral Wilson received the full panoply of honors due a successful revolutionary.

One of the conservative mainstays of the 1920s and 1930s, former Utah senator George Sutherland, who has become the subject of renewed interest,[24] was moved in June 1958 from the dilapidated Abbey Mausoleum next to Arlington National Cemetery in Washington, D.C., where he had been put to rest in 1942, to another mausoleum in nearby Maryland, although this change of location was not shared with the public. At present, all of the grave sites are open to the public, although not all of them are marked in such a way as to be easily located.

2

THE ANTEBELLUM COURT, 1789–1864

Although the problem of judicial disability did not affect the work of the Supreme Court in the antebellum period as much as it did following the Civil War,[1] there were still some troublesome cases. Despite the fact that the early Supreme Court justices were young and it was not until the 1820s that the average judicial age exceeded sixty, the physical hardships incurred during the early years of circuit court riding caused numerous health problems. In fact, the toll taken by circuit court riding is a recurrent theme in the early history of the Supreme Court. Circuit court responsibilities were often neglected because of the disabilities suffered by a number of the justices, and the deliberations of the Court were even marred by instances of behavior attributed to insanity.

Of the twenty-nine justices who served through 1864, only nine resigned, and most of those resignations occurred before 1805. After that time, the only resignations were from Gabriel Duvall, then eighty-three and effectively disabled; Benjamin Curtis, who disagreed with the Court's decision in the *Dred Scott* case and also wanted to make more money as a practicing lawyer; and John Campbell, who left to join the Confederacy. In short, seldom did anyone leave voluntarily.

Of the twelve elderly justices (over age sixty-five) considered in this chapter, seven died or resigned in poor health. However, it is apparent that age is not necessarily associated with infirmity, because so many justices became ill before they reached sixty-five. Indeed, the largest category is the group in poor health who were younger than sixty-five. Of the seventeen justices who were gone from the Court before they reached sixty-five, eleven were in poor health. Moreover, there is an absence of any association between poor health and a propensity to resign. Of the eighteen who were in poor health, only five resigned, whereas four of the eleven in good health resigned.[2]

Table 2.1
Age of Death or Retirement, 1789–1864

Age	Died	Resigned
54 or younger	2	5
55–59	2	1
60–64	5	2
65–69	3	0
70–74	2	0
75–79	5	0
80 or older	1	1
Totals	20	9
Average age of those leaving the Court: 63		

Source: Elder Witt, ed., *Congressional Quarterly's Guide to the U.S. Supreme Court,* 2d ed. (Washington, D.C.: Congressional Quarterly Press, 1990).

Of this earliest group of justices, twenty died in office. Nine of those who died in office were under sixty-five, but eleven were over sixty-five, and six were over seventy-five. The pattern of not leaving the bench until necessity required it, and sometimes not even then, was established early in Court history.

John Jay (Chief Justice: 1789–1795)

In all, George Washington appointed eleven men to the Supreme Court. His first appointment was his chief justice, John Jay, who resigned on June 29, 1795, following his return from a diplomatic mission to England. Upon his arrival home, Jay learned he had been elected governor of New York. His letter of resignation contains no suggestion of regret over leaving his judicial post. Although Jay was a figure of controversy following his treaty negotiations with England, his resignation was prompted by the greater importance of the New York governorship and a lack of interest in the limited responsibilities of the Court. Jay articulated his rationale when he declined a second appointment to the chief justiceship in 1801. Jay then told President John Adams:

I left the bench perfectly convinced that under a system so defective it would not obtain the energy, weight, and dignity which was essential to its affording due support to the national government; nor acquire the public confidence and respect which, as the last resort of the justice of the nation, it should possess. Hence I am induced to doubt both the propriety and the expediency of my returning to the bench under the present system. . . . Independently of these considerations, the state of my health removes every doubt.[3]

Jay's reference to his health was probably an afterthought. He was only fifty-six when he left public life to settle into permanent retirement at his secluded farm in Bedford, New York. A devout Episcopalian, he busied himself with religious projects and was one of the founders of the American Bible Society. Actively concerned with current affairs, he opposed slavery and the War of 1812.

As the years passed, Jay "was seldom free from attacks of rheumatism, or some disorder of the liver, but the most serious ailment of all was what he termed 'the incurable' one of old age."[4] After twenty-five years of retirement, he first became seriously ill in 1827 and died two years later at the age of eighty-three. Several months before his death he found himself unable to walk unassisted. His condition rapidly deteriorated, and three days before his death on May 17, 1829, he was seized with a palsy that made it difficult for him to be understood.

John Rutledge (1789–1791; Chief Justice: 1795)

John Rutledge's decision to resign his associate justiceship on March 5, 1791, without ever having sat on the Court was also motivated by low public esteem for the Court. (He did participate in circuit court duties, however briefly.) Rutledge instead accepted the chief justiceship of the South Carolina Supreme Court, a position he considered more prestigious.

But national ambition reasserted itself, and upon learning of Jay's forthcoming resignation in 1795, Rutledge lobbied President Washington for the chief justiceship in a somewhat tactless (albeit successful) letter. He told the president he had "no objection" to taking Jay's place, and that his friends had told him he had as much "law-knowledge" as Jay "with the additional weight of much longer experience and much greater practice." When the chief justiceship became available, he felt "that the duty which I owe to my children should impel me to accept it, if offered, tho, more arduous and troublesome than my present station, because more respectable and honorable."[5] Washington gave Rutledge a recess appointment on July 1, 1795, and he presided over two cases as chief justice that summer. The Senate, however, rejected him on December 15 by a vote of 10 to 14 while he was about his circuit court duties. Although he had been confirmed previously as a member of the original Court, the Senate had since become increasingly concerned about his emotional stability. He had been extreme in his opposition to the Jay Treaty and had even said he hoped President Washington would die before he signed it.

Although opposition to the treaty was the public reason for the rejection, there was another reason as well. A rumor had long circulated that Rutledge was at least periodically insane. It was the common gist of much responsible correspondence at the time. For example, Secretary of State Edmund Randolf informed President Washington, "The conduct of the intended Chief Justice is so extraordinary that Mr. Wolcott and Col. Pickering conceive it to be a proof of the imputation of insanity."[6] The Senate rejection was not unexpected, even though Rutledge was acting as chief justice. As Attorney General William Bradford wrote to Alexander Hamilton (with reference to the attack on the Jay Treaty): "The crazy speech of Mr. Rutledge joined to certain information that he is daily sinking into debility of mind and body, will probably prevent him from receiving the appointment."[7]

Alexander Hamilton told Senator Rufus King that he would favor confirmation if only disagreement over the Jay Treaty were involved, "but if it be really true that he is sottish, or that his mind is otherwise deranged, or that he had exposed himself by improper conduct in pecuniary transactions, the basis of my judgment would be to negative."[8] Rutledge's biographer tries unsuccessfully to attribute responsibility for the rumors of insanity to Hamilton.[9] The alleged motive was Hamilton's anger at what Rutledge said about the Jay Treaty. This analysis is inconsistent with Hamilton's letter to Senator King and, in any event, Hamilton was hardly the only prominent politician who questioned Rutledge's capacity.

At home in Charleston when he heard of the Senate rejection, Rutledge shortly thereafter tried to take his life. He threw himself off a wharf into Charleston Bay and was saved from drowning only when two nearby slaves pulled him out of the water. The suicide attempt confirmed what many had suspected. As Benjamin Moodie, a Charleston lawyer, wrote Senator Jacob Read: "Poor man. I am sorry to say that my ideas were too true with respect to the deranged state of his mind as on the morning of the 26th I am credibly informed that he made an attempt to drown himself."[10] Both South Carolina senators voted in favor of Rutledge's confirmation, even though Senator Ralph Izard had written to Senator Read three years earlier following the death of Rutledge's wife that "his mind was frequently deranged so as to be in great measure deprived of his senses."[11]

John Rutledge lived another five years, during which time he suffered lapses of insanity. In May 1798 Justice James Iredell corresponded frequently with his wife about Rutledge when he was in Charleston holding court. Iredell was first given local reports that Rutledge had recovered. He then met with Rutledge and optimistically concluded, "Mr. Rutledge is perfectly recovered, and in such high spirits that he, and another gentleman, and myself, outsat all the rest of the company at a friend's house, till near 11 o'clock."[12] This was not an everyday occurrence for Rutledge, however, because the next day Iredell wrote his wife that "this week, I am told, is the first time he has broke from his retirement."[13] In fact, reports of Rutledge's recovery seem based on scant evidence, because a few days later Iredell acknowledged to his wife that Rutledge had lived as a recluse until he made the successful effort to relate to Iredell.

Rutledge also suffered from a kidney stone and Bright's disease, a kidney ailment that is often associated with hypertension. These then untreatable physical illnesses may well have contributed to the psychological difficulties to which he was already prone. Certainly he was in great periodic pain. He died at age sixty, five years after the suicide attempt, practically withdrawn from society.

Thomas Johnson (1791–1793)

Thomas Johnson had served only fourteen months when he resigned from the bench on February 1, 1793. His remains the shortest tenure in Court history. He was fifty-nine at the time and had been assigned to the southern circuit, along with Justice Iredell. The southern circuit required a justice to travel long distances over primitive roads, often in extreme heat, and with the added risk of disease, especially malaria. Although Chief Justice Jay had initially suggested that he would afford some relief, it quickly became apparent that the chief justice did not intend to rotate circuit court responsibilities. Johnson, therefore, resigned. He declined his good friend George Washington's offer to be secretary of state in 1795 but accepted a presidential appointment to the commission charged with the planning of the national capital.

Thereafter, Johnson retired to private life until his death ten days short of his eighty-seventh birthday in 1819. Although he had been frail for some years before his death and his eyesight had begun to fail, his mind remained as sharp as ever, and by his own admission his hearing remained "almost as perfect as ever and quicker now than most young people's."[14] At his death, he was eulogized in the manner of the day, which tended toward high praise or vigorous disparagement:

> His deeds are inscribed in the imperishable archives of his country; his wisdom, impartiality and integrity in the records of justice; his worth and virtues are preserved in the hearts of his countrymen; his kindness, affection and friendship in the memory of his family, relatives and friends; his trust for immortality rested in his Savior and God. Washington was his friend. Eulogium can add no more.[15]

John Blair Jr. (1789–1796)

A year after Chief Justice Jay's resignation, John Blair Jr. resigned on January 27, 1796, owing to the combined effects of ill health and the death of his wife. Like many justices, the obligatory circuit court riding proved burdensome to his health and brought on chronic headaches. After leaving the Court, he suffered from continuous indigestion and probably correctly diagnosed his problem when he told his sister he had "a good appetite and eat I believe more than is good for me; that the want of teeth to masticate my food properly are probably the cause of my malady."[16]

A year before his death, Blair described the condition, apparently a stroke, that eventually proved fatal:

> I was on 5th Nov. 1797, struck with a strange disorder to which I knew not how to give a name . . . the effects of which are to me most melancholy depriving me of nearly all the powers of mind. The effect was very sudden and instantaneous. I happened to be employed in some algebraical exercises (of which kind of amusement I was very fond) when all at once a torpid numbness seized my whole face and I found my intellectual powers much weakened and all was confusion. My tongue partook of the distress and some words I was not able to articulate distinctly and a general difficulty of remembering words at all. There are intervals when all these distresses abate considerably; but there are times when I am unable to read and am obliged to lay aside a newspaper or whatever else I may happen to be engaged in.[17]

Justice Blair never totally recovered and died on August 31, 1800, in Williamsburg, Virginia, where he lived in retirement.

James Wilson (1789–1798)

James Wilson was the first to die while still a member of the Court, although it seems likely he would have been removed had death not intervened. Born in Scotland, he was a brilliant man, renowned for his erudition and intellect, who among the early revolutionaries was a consistent democrat and may well have contributed more to the Philadelphia Convention of 1787 than anyone other than James Madison.[18] He was considered the ablest legal mind of the Washington appointees, but financial misadventures eventually ruined his private fortune, led to imprisonment for debt, and destroyed his health at an early age.[19] As his personal finances gave way to ruin because of his over-extended investments, he was not considered a suitable nominee for chief justice following Jay's resignation, despite his ability. His health thereafter rapidly deteriorated. As Justice Iredell wrote to his wife in March 1796, "Mr. Wilson has for some weeks been in very bad health."[20] When the financial crisis of 1796 deepened, Benjamin Rush found "Judge Wilson deeply distressed; his resource was reading novels constantly."[21]

Wilson's responsibilities were increased in May 1796 when his much younger second wife, Hannah, gave birth to a boy. The situation grew increasingly ominous. In August, Edward Buid wrote to Jasper Yates: "Ruin is staring in the face of the land speculators. The day of reckoning is at hand, and no prospect of disposing of their lands. There are a great number of judgments against your friend Wilson lately confessed by him. People speak very freely of the situation he is likely to be in very shortly."[22]

After riding circuit during the spring of 1797, Wilson and his wife were obliged to go into hiding to escape his creditors. But he could not avoid them. His pursuers seized him at the Morris Tavern in Bethlehem, Pennsylvania, and he found himself jailed. Wilson appealed to his son, Bird, to help him: "Bring with you shirts and stockings—I want them exceedingly—also money, as much as possible, without which I can not leave this place."[23] Wilson's son raised bail, which permitted the justice to leave for North Carolina where he hoped to spend the winter. But Pierce Butler, to whom he owed $197,000, finally caught up with him, and again Wilson was arrested and jailed for debt. He was eventually released from jail in June 1798, only to become immediately infected by malaria. With only Hannah to care for him, and without presentable clothes or even shoes, his situation shortly became entirely pathetic. When the circumstances became known to the governor of North Carolina, he wrote to Iredell:

James Wilson came to an ignoble end, hounded by creditors. (Supreme Court, Office of the Curator)

I feel very much for Judge Wilson. I hear that he has been ill. What upon earth will become of him and that unfortunate lady who has attached herself to his fortunes? He discovers no disposition to resign his office. Surely, if his feelings are not rendered altogether callous by his misfortune, he will not suffer himself to be disgraced by a conviction on an impeachment.[24]

While still living hand to mouth at the Horniblow Tavern in Edenton, North Carolina, Wilson was weakened by a stroke. Not long thereafter he died of malarial fever. Justice Iredell described Wilson's death to Mrs. Wilson's sister:

I have the pain to acquaint you that Judge Wilson died here on the night of the 21st instant, a few hours after my arrival. Though he had been at times in very bad health, evidently occasioned by distress of mind owing to his pecuniary difficulties, yet the illness of which he died was of short duration, though very sharp: the greater part of the time he was in a state of delirium, during which he would not suffer many things to be done for him which were advised, and might possibly have restored him.[25]

Justice Wilson was buried in a small cemetery in Edenton. There the body remained until November 21, 1906, when it was removed and sent to Christ Churchyard in Philadelphia for an elaborate burial attended by many dignitaries. The signer of both the Declaration of Independence and the Constitution was finally given the recognition and appreciation his improvidence had forfeited during his own lifetime.

Oliver Ellsworth (Chief Justice: 1796–1800)

After only three years on the bench, Jay's eventual successor, Oliver Ellsworth, accepted President John Adam's request that he go to France and settle the troubled diplomatic relations with the United States. Although apparently in good health at fifty-four, Ellsworth found the long transatlantic voyage was much more difficult than anticipated. He suffered greatly from sea sickness, and "his vigorous frame had already lost somewhat of its elasticity and tone from some of the infirmities of approaching age, and was not very well fortified to resist the unfavorable influences of a stormy winter's voyage."[26] During the voyage from Lisbon to L'Orient, Ellsworth's ship was stranded in a fierce gale for two weeks, and his "sufferings were extreme, and from their effects he never recovered."[27]

In a letter from France, nearly a year after he had left the United States, Ellsworth described his physical deterioration:

> Sufferings at sea, and by a winter's journey through Spain, gave me an obstinate gravel, which, by wounding the kidneys has drawn and fixed my wandering gout to those parts. My pains are constant, and, at times excruciating; they do not permit me to discharge my official duties. I have, therefore, sent my resignation of the office of Chief Justice, and shall, after spending a few weeks in England, retire for winter quarters to the south of France.[28]

He told his family, still in the United States, that he could not attempt a winter transatlantic crossing.[29] Instead, he crossed to England and took the waters at Bath. He had little hope for improvement because, as he said, his "kidneys are weakened by the constant laceration of sand." Although the waters improved his appetite, his fluid intake, and "promoted the discharge of calcareous matter," he did not believe they checked the formation of the kidney stones.[30]

Citing his declining health, Ellsworth wrote President Adams from France on October 16, 1800. He thus could not have known whether the president was likely or not to lose the election, since the only news he could have received from the United States would have arrived sometime during the late summer. There is, therefore, no evidence to indicate he resigned when he did, anticipating defeat for the Federalists at the polls, in order to provide President Adams with an opportunity to appoint a new chief justice in the final months of his presidency.[31] Thomas Jefferson, in a letter to James Madison on December 19, 1800, apparently interpreted the resignation to mean that Ellsworth anticipated an Adams victory, because otherwise the decent course of action would have been to permit the new president to make the appointment.[32]

Ellsworth returned to the United States in the spring of 1801. His remaining six years were filled with excruciating pain associated with kidney disease. In the last year of his life, he received an appointment as chief justice of the Connecticut Supreme Court, but the constant suffering made it impossible for him to accept the position. He died on November 26, 1807, at his farm near the small farming community of Windsor, Connecticut, where he had been born.

James Iredell (1790–1799)

James Iredell died at age forty-eight, exhausted from circuit court riding. Because the Supreme Court was relatively inactive, riding circuit constituted a justice's major responsibility. Iredell rode the southern circuit four times in five years. The heat and the primitive modes of conveyance combined to impair his health. Iredell's condition was apparent to his colleagues. Shortly before he died, Iredell received the following message from Justice Bushrod Washington:

> Upon my arrival at Baltimore, about the first of the month, I heard from Judge Chase, with great concern, that you were too much indisposed to attend the Supreme Court. This fatigue to which you had been exposed during the Circuit was well calculated to produce this consequence, and you would have acted imprudently, I think, to venture upon so long a journey in your then state of health. It will afford me very sincere pleasure to hear of your recovery.[33]

A prolific correspondent, much of what is known about the health of the earliest justices and the circumstances attending circuit court duties has been gathered from Justice Iredell's letters. He was stricken at the height of his powers, and his passing on October 20, 1799, was a considerable loss to the Court.

Alfred Moore (1799–1804)

Alfred Moore wrote only one opinion for the Court in five years, but as Iredell's successor he was likewise required to ride the exhausting southern circuit. This task proved too burdensome, and he resigned on January 26, 1804, giving ill health as his reason. Moore was a diminutive person, "so small in stature that at first glance he seemed only a child, for his height was about four feet five inches, and he was proportionately slender." He weighed about eighty or ninety pounds. "His head was large for his body, after the manner of dwarfs, and his face . . . was fine-featured, good-humored and dark-eyed.[34]

Moore lived another six years, remaining active as one of the developers of the University of North Carolina. He died while at the home of one of his daughters on October 15, 1810. He was only fifty-five. Of his four children, one daughter was still a minor. Although he left scarcely a trace on the

Marshall Court during his short tenure, fellow members of the North Carolina bar respected him because of his wit, humor, and sharp tongue.

William Paterson (1793–1806)

William Paterson was unable to sit during the 1804 term, also because of ill health. As with Moore and Iredell, circuit court riding had exacted its toll on Paterson's constitution since his appointment in 1793. In 1800, he had written to his wife about the condition of the roads. He was able to cover no more than a hundred miles in three days and suffered numerous injuries as a result of bolting horses and upset carriages. Moreover, Paterson often was not well received on circuit and was especially disliked by the Republicans. Jeremiah Smith of New Hampshire remarked that the Republicans hated Paterson and John Marshall "worse than they hate Chase because they are men of better character."[35]

He suffered serious injuries to his right side and shoulder when his coach went off a ten-foot embankment on October 26, 1803. Although his son escaped uninjured and his wife was merely shaken, his injuries caused him to stay at home for weeks.[36] He may never have entirely recovered. Paterson complained of pains in his chest and side while riding his circuit in 1805. By April of the next year he was unable to meet his circuit duties. Describing himself as "naturally delicate and slender," he acknowledged he was "almost worn out" by what he described as an "inflammatory fever."[37]

Acting on a premonition that his end was near, Paterson began to put his affairs in order. "A wise man," he told a friend, "ought to endeavor to arrange all his concerns, both for time and eternity, in such a manner, that, when his last hour approaches, he may have nothing to do but die."[38] Paterson decided to travel to Ballston Springs, New York, for treatment. He got only as far as his daughter's house near Albany, where he was ill a few weeks and died on September 9, 1806, while still a member of the Court. He was sixty-one when it happened, at a time when most of the other founding fathers were still living.

William Cushing (1789–1810)

When the Senate rejected John Rutledge for chief justice, President Washington first offered the chief justiceship to Patrick Henry and then to a sitting justice, William Cushing. Neither Henry nor Cushing was interested, and Oliver Ellsworth eventually accepted. The prospect of Cushing as chief justice was troublesome to many, including New Hampshire's William Plumer, who wrote that he was a man "I love and esteem . . . but Time, the enemy of man, has much impaired his mental faculties."[39]

Even though he declined the chief justiceship because of his health, Cushing not surprisingly elected to remain on the Court. Although he descended from an old and distinguished colonial Massachusetts family, he had no money and was in no position to leave the Court. As a young lawyer in Dresden, Maine, his inability to make decisions had cost him most of his law practice, and he had gravitated to public service.

As a justice, Cushing had no prospects beyond judicial office and continued on the Court despite his dislike for the obligatory circuit court riding. These duties may have weakened his health, especially as he grew older. He wrote John Jay, after the latter had been elected governor of New York, that the election "will doubtless be for the good of New York, as well of the public in general: and what is of some consequence, more for your ease and comfort than rambling in the Carolina woods in June."[40]

William Cushing died a member of the Supreme Court on September 13, 1810, at the age of seventy-eight. In his later years, there were increasing claims of substantial mental impairment. At the end he was described as "somewhat senile."[41] By the time Cushing died, at Scituate, Massachusetts, where he had been born, he was the last of Washington's original appointments still on the bench.

Samuel Chase (1796–1811)

Only one justice, Samuel Chase, has been impeached. He was not guilty of "high crimes" in any strict sense, however, and the Senate did not convict him. Nevertheless, he was one of the most difficult and disturbing persons to ever occupy a position of high authority in the government. In his youth, he had been an intense patriot and a rioter as a member of the Sons of Liberty. His early intensity attracted the attention of the mayor of Annapolis, who described him as a "busy, restless incendiary, a ringleader of mobs, a foul-mouthed and inflaming son of discord."[42] In short, Chase gave no early indication of a judicial temperament, nor, his many critics claimed, did he ever thereafter. During his impeachment proceedings he was weakened by a severe attack of gout. The disease plagued him until his death on June 19, 1811, and he was often unable to participate in deliberations. His last illness was attributed to "ossification of the heart."[43]

Henry Brockholst Livingston (1806–1823)

The Supreme Court remained unchanged for the next dozen years, until Henry Brockholst Livingston died in office of pleurisy on March 18, 1823, at the age of sixty-six. His close friend, Joseph Story, evaluated Livingston's condition: "Poor Livingston has been very ill of a peripneumony, and is still very ill; whether he will ever recover is doubtful. I rather think not. At one time he was supposed to be dying; but he has since been better, and now again has had a relapse. There is great reason to believe that he will never, even if he recovers, be a healthy man again. He is attended by his wife and daughter, and two physicians."[44]

Thomas Todd (1807–1826)

Three years later, in 1826, Thomas Todd died. He had ridden the new western circuit consisting of Tennessee, Kentucky, and Ohio since President Thomas Jefferson's appointment in 1807. The circuit court work became increasingly burdensome for him, and he had missed five entire Court terms, in 1809, 1813, 1815, 1819, and 1825, because of illness or personal business. Otherwise, he contributed a career total of only fourteen opinions, which includes his first opinion, a five-line dissent. "For some years before his death," Justice Story wrote, "he was sensible that his health was declining, and that he might soon leave the Bench."[45]

When Todd died on February 7, 1826, in Frankfort, Kentucky, he was a wealthy man. He had acquired extensive holdings in land, some 7,200 acres at the time of his death. Even after he had provided for his five children by his first wife and his three subsequent children (he had married Dolly Madison's sister, Lucy Payne, in a White House wedding after his first wife died), there was still some $70,000 left in the estate, a large sum in those years.

Robert Trimble (1826–1828)

Robert Trimble died suddenly at his home in Kentucky on August 25, 1828, after only two years of service. His death was attributed, with the medical imprecision of the age, to a "malignant bilious fever."[46] Until the sudden onset of illness, he was in excellent health and was an industrious worker. As Story concluded at the time of Trimble's death, "perhaps no man ever on the bench gained so much in so short a period of his judicial career."[47] He was only fifty-two when he died.

Bushrod Washington (1798–1829)

Bushrod Washington, President Washington's nephew, died in Philadelphia on November 26, 1829, after nearly thirty-one years of service. He had lost the vision in one eye in 1797, but he had no further difficulties with his sight. Like Trimble, who served so briefly, Washington died uneventfully and while still active on the Court. In the year of his death, as his decline became apparent to him, he left detailed instructions as to what should be done after his death, all of which were meticulously observed by his family:

> My desire is that when the Event happens, the sheet on which I am then lying may be employed as a covering sheet and at once thrown round my person and tied about my middle with a pocket hand-kerchief. The common practice of washing the body is to be avoided. My thumbs are not to be tied together nor anything put on my face or any restraint upon my person by bandages. My body is to be placed in an entirely plain coffin with a flat top and a sufficient number of holes bored through the lid and sides—particularly about the face and head to allow respiration if resuscitation should take place—and having been kept so long as to ascertain whether decay may have occurred or not, the coffin is to be closed up. My steward is to be written to immediately, on the event of despoliation, to come on, and under his care my body is to be conveyed to Virginia in the Steam Boat, by way of Baltimore, and landed directly at Mount Vernon to be buried there.[48]

Of Washington's passing, Chief Justice John Marshall remarked, "No man knew his worth better or deplores his death more than myself."[49] None could doubt the chief justice's loss. During his entire tenure, Washington disagreed with Marshall on only three occasions. Even Story, who also valued his vote, was constrained to weigh Washington's contribution in measured language: "His mind was solid, rather than brilliant; sagacious and searching, rather than quick or eager; slow, but not torpid."[50]

Others were less charitable. Abolitionists watched him, as his uncle's beneficiary following Martha Washington's death, violate his uncle's express request to free his slaves; instead, he callously disobeyed the president's instructions, sold the slaves to two Louisiana traders, and thus broke up the slave families that briefly had descended to him.[51] Few of Washington's colleagues shared Marshall's generous estimate of his ability. Justice William Johnson, who sat with him for twenty-five years, curtly observed that Bushrod Washington and Marshall "are commonly estimated as a single judge."[52]

William Johnson (1804–1834)

Ironically, William Johnson himself was next to die while still a member of the Court and under truly barbaric circumstances. He was first described by Story as "in a bad way" as early as 1831.[53] Because of his opposition to the politically tumultuous climate in the South, Johnson found it necessary to leave his home in South Carolina temporarily in the summer of 1833. He lived instead in western Pennsylvania. While there he "recontracted a bilious remittent fever from which he never entirely recovered."[54] He was able to hold circuit court in Charleston on June 13 and in Milledgeville, Georgia, as late as November 7, but over the following year his health deteriorated enormously. Johnson knew he was very seriously ill—probably of cancer of the jaw—and set out alone in July 1834 for New York, his father's birthplace. He had surgery on Monday, August 4, without anesthetics. The frightful circumstances were retold in a New York newspaper the next day:

> The Hon. Judge Johnson, of South Carolina, breathed his last, at Brooklyn, at one o'clock yesterday. He had arrived here some weeks ago, for the purpose of placing himself under the charge of an eminent medical practitioner of this city, having for some time suffered with an affection of the jaw, to eradicate which it required he should undergo the most painful surgical operation. Dr. Mott, of this city, was selected for the purpose, who expressed his opinion of the inability of the Judge to survive the operation. With a knowledge of the expression of the surgeon, he still determined upon placing himself under his hands; and without the aid of friends, or being bound, he submitted, with the utmost fortitude and calmness, to the most excruciating tortures; but in the course of half an hour after the completion of the doctor's labors, he died of exhaustion, produced by the sudden reaction of the nerves, which had been excited to their utmost power in buoying up his mind throughout the whole of the operation.[55]

Knowing the odds were against surviving the operation, he had provided for his burial arrangements beforehand. The funeral was held in a private home belonging to a New York lawyer, Zachariah Lewis. The body was then carried in a procession to St. Ann's Church, where it was deposited in one

William Johnson died in shock on an operating table. (Supreme Court, Office of the Curator)

of the vaults. The plan, also prearranged by Johnson, was for the body to then be transported back to South Carolina in the winter. When the body at last arrived in Charleston, the justice's children erected a monument honoring his memory.

Gabriel Duvall (1811–1835)

Gabriel Duvall's resignation on January 14, 1835, at the age of eighty-three relieved the Court of a major embarrassment. Shortly before Johnson's death a year earlier, a Court observer had noted that "Judge Duvall is eighty-two years old and is so deaf as to be unable to participate in conversation."[56] The practical consequence was that oral arguments before the Court were largely meaningless for him. Because of his age (he was the first justice to reach eighty), it was difficult for him to travel any distance for meetings. When Chief Justice Marshall arranged for rooms for the justices, he expressed concern that "Brother Duvall must be with us or he will be unable to attend consultations."[57]

Duvall became increasingly decrepit in the years preceding his resignation. He was, one observer said, "the oldest looking man on the bench. His head was white as a snow-bank, with a long white cue, hanging down to his waist."[58] But he was reluctant to give up his seat, fearing that a "politician" might be appointed. He was particularly determined to prevent John McLean, who eventually replaced Robert Trimble, from succeeding him.[59] In his early years as a recorder in the Annapolis mayor's court, Duvall had heard the young Roger Brooke Taney give his first speech as a lawyer. The years had not altered this first favorable impression, so when a clerk carefully leaked the information to him that President Jackson expected to nominate Taney, he resigned without further delay.

Duvall lived another nine years after his retirement, during which time he continued his interests in horses and farming.[60] He died quietly at age ninety-two on March 6, 1844, on the Maryland plantation where he had been born.

John Marshall (Chief Justice: 1801–1835)

Chief Justice John Marshall's death ended a long and rancorous legal career.[61] In 1831, at the age of seventy-six, he underwent a risky operation for the removal of bladder stones. His physician described the operation:

Gabriel Duvall stayed on long after he had become deaf and infirm. (Supreme Court, Office of the Curator)

This case was attended with singular interest, in consequence of the exalted position of the patient, at his advanced age, and the circumstances of there being upwards of one thousand calculi taken from his bladder. . . . It will be readily admitted that, in consequence of Judge Marshall's very advanced age, the hazard of attending the operation, however skillfully performed, was considerably increased. I consider it but an act of justice, due to the memory of that good and great man, to state that, in my opinion, his recovery was, in a great degree, owing to his extraordinary self-possession, and to the calm and philosophical views which he took of his case, and the various circumstances attending it. . . . [H]e did not feel the least anxiety or uneasiness respecting the operation or its result. He said that he had not the slightest desire to live, laboring under the suffering to which he was then subjected; that he was perfectly ready to take all the chances of an operation, and he knew there were many against him; and that, if he could be relieved by it, he was willing to live out his appointed time, but if not, would rather die, than hold existence accompanied with the pain and misery which he then endured.[62]

Because of his age, the extraordinary recovery that Marshall made from this operation did not last long. Chancellor James Kent of New York, long one of his admirers, reported in May 1935 that the chief justice had become "very emaciated, feeble & dangerously low."[63] Previously, Marshall had injured his back when his carriage had overturned, and, upon examination following the mishap, his physician diagnosed a diseased liver for which he could do nothing.

Marshall's close friend and supporter on the Court, Joseph Story, indicated on March 2, 1835, that there was never any evidence of intellectual decline even though the chief justice did consider resigning: "Chief Justice Marshall still possesses his intellectual powers in very high vigor. But his physical strength is manifestly on the decline; and it is now obvious, that after a year or two, he will resign, from the pressing infirmities of age. . . . What a gloom will spread over the nation when he is gone! His place will not, nay, it cannot be supplied."[64]

John Marshall died on July 6, 1835, having held the chief justiceship for thirty-four years and five months. In his final hours he was lucid and at peace. As his attending physician recalled, the chief justice was "perfectly in his senses to the last and as death approached nearer to him his pain ceased and he went off without a struggle."[65] In three months he would have reached his eightieth birthday.

In tolling his death, the Liberty Bell cracked, dramatically symbolizing the end of John Marshall's usefulness to the nation. Even so sympathetic a historian as Charles Warren recognized as much when he concluded that "a change in the leadership of the Court was possibly desirable" because Marshall at his death was "clearly out of touch with the temper of the times." He, therefore, was "less fitted to deal with the new problems of the day than with the great constitutional questions of the past."[66] Nonetheless, his countrymen mourned his passing, flags were lowered across America, and the nation's grief was profound.

The cause of Marshall's last illness was thoroughly diagnosed. His doctor described the autopsy results, which suggest cancer: "The cause of his death was a very diseased condition of the liver, which was enormously enlarged, and contained several tuberculous abscesses of great size. Its pressure upon the stomach had the effect of dislodging this organ from its natural situation, and compressing it in such a manner that for some time previous to his death it would not retain the smallest quantity of nutriment."[67]

Philip P. Barbour (1836–1841)

There were no further departures from the Court until the death of Philip P. Barbour at the age of fifty-seven from a heart attack. Barbour, who had served only five years at the time of his death on the night of February 24, 1841, had become ill in early February and returned to the Court too quickly. In a letter to his wife, Joseph Story described the situation in detail:

I now write to . . . tell you of the . . . death of Mr. Justice Barbour, which has spread a great gloom over the Court and almost disabled us from doing any business. His death was indeed awfully sudden. He was in good health and attended Court all Wednesday, and heard the extraordinary argument of Mr. Adams in the case of the Amistad; extraordinary, I say, for its power, for its bitter sarcasm, and its dealing with topics far beyond the record and points of discussion. He dined heartily, and remained with the Judges in conference until after ten o'clock in the evening, and then in a most cheerful humor. The next morning the servant went into his room between six and seven o'clock and made his fire, perceiving nothing unusual and supposing him to be asleep. About one hour afterwards the messenger with letters knocked at his door, and hearing no answer went in softly, supposing him asleep, and laid a letter upon his table and withdrew. At nine o'clock the servant called us all to breakfast, and upon going into his room, finding him still in bed, he went to him and found he could not awaken him. He was frightened, and ran into my room and told me he feared Judge Barbour was dead. I went immediately and found him lying on his left side and lifeless. His eyes were closed, his feet stretched out, and his arms in a natural position. His forehead, hands, feet and limbs were perfectly cold, but upon feeling his breast, I discovered that it was still warm. We sent immediately for Dr. Sewall, who came and said that he was indeed dead, and that he must have died of *angina pectoris*. Probably he breathed his last about daylight, and while he was yet asleep. From all appearances, he must have died without any struggle and instantaneously. We were all thrown into utter confusion, and I sat down to a most melancholy breakfast, seeing on my side the deserted chair in which he used to sit. We went down to the Court at eleven o'clock, where the Chief Justice announced the event, and the Court was at once adjourned until Monday.[68]

Smith Thompson (1823–1843)

Neither poor health nor political ambition ever affected Smith Thompson's determination to retain judicial office. At age seventy-five, he left Washington on February 6, 1843, and heard no further cases until his death on December 18, 1843, at his home in Poughkeepsie, New York. He was another justice whose unwillingness to resign left the Court shorthanded.

Earlier Thompson had declined to resign from the Court even when he had engaged in a bitter and unsuccessful race for governor of New York against his longtime political ally and supporter, Martin Van Buren. Thompson was the first justice to harbor serious presidential ambitions, though no real opportunity for him to achieve the office ever presented itself. Apparently, he did not think a judicial resignation should precede an entry into elective politics.

Henry Baldwin (1830–1844)

The mentally troubled Henry Baldwin died a year later. Soon after Baldwin joined the Court, it became obvious that President Andrew Jackson had made a major mistake in appointing him. Though the appointment was understandable since Baldwin had been one of Jackson's earliest presidential supporters, Baldwin showed signs of instability dating from his first involvement with national politics. He had entered Congress in 1817 from Pittsburgh but had resigned in 1822 for health reasons. He required two years to recover from the undisclosed illness.

On the Court, Baldwin quarreled with his colleagues, and they soon thought his behavior peculiar. Within a year he was feuding with the Court's reporter, Richard Peters, who complained of Baldwin's "malignity and injustice and baseness toward me" and wrote further about Baldwin's disruptive influence on the Court:

> I venture the assertion without fear of contradiction . . . that no one who visits the court or has an opportunity of seeing him speaks of him with respect. It is the opinion of more than the proportion I mention *that his mind is out of order.* I have heard in one day not less than five persons . . . say "he is crazy" . . . I know that some laugh at him and one of the persons whom I have named asked Dr. Hunt "if he was not out of his senses." He sits in his room for three or four hours in the dark—jumps up and runs down into the judges' consultation room in his stocking feet, and remains in that condition while they are deliberating.[69]

Within two years of the appointment, Attorney General Taney advised President Jackson that in any legal action against the Bank of the United States, Baldwin would have to preside over the trial in Philadelphia, and he could not be relied on to do so responsibly. His uncertain mental health required him to miss the entire 1833 term.

As the years passed, Baldwin's mental illness worsened. He probably suffered from obsessive-compulsive syndrome, an illness that could have been exacerbated by the financial pressures he encountered in his last years.[70] Eventually he became sometimes "violent and ungovernable in his conduct upon the bench"[71] and finally died as a result of a stroke. When he died, on April 21, 1844, Baldwin had no money. A subscription had to be raised in order to pay for his funeral.

Following his death, he was originally placed in a vault on his brother-in-law's estate. He was moved to Oak Hill Cemetery in Washington, D.C., in 1892 and according to cemetery records is still there.

Joseph Story (1811–1845)

Joseph Story survived his colleague John Marshall by a decade. Before he died in 1845, he said he looked forward to leaving the Court. As he had written the previous year, "I have done my share of the work, and have earned my title to a little indulgence."[72] Story could seldom resist expounding jeremiads. "In every way which I look to the future, I can see little or no ground of hope for our country," he wrote shortly before his death. "We are rapidly on the decline," he predicted. "Corruption and profligacy,

Henry Baldwin fought bouts of insanity. (Supreme Court, Office of the Curator)

demagogism and recklessness characterize the times, and I for one am unable to see where the thing is to end."[73] But this negative approach was nothing new for him. Ten years earlier, when he was only fifty-five years old, his lamentations following the death of Marshall were remarkable for their almost total absence of hope for the country's future.[74]

Story may or may not have resigned. He had allowed his friends to talk him out of it before. He was a confirmed workaholic and did not resign in March 1845 because there was a backlog of cases to decide in the circuit court, obviously an ever-present, all-purpose excuse for indeterminate delay. By September he still had not acted, and his health failed suddenly. He first caught a cold and was seized with a "violent stricture" closing his intestinal canal. His suffering was extreme, but his general awareness was undiminished. He told his wife, "I have no belief that I can recover; it is vain to hope for it."[75]

Shortly before he died, his thoughts turned again to his duty toward the Court, and he acknowledged that "if I were not thus ill, my letter of resignation would have been now on its way to Washington."[76] Whether or not Story would have sent the resignation had he lived—and skepticism is warranted—he never did so before he died on September 10, 1845. He survived for only eight days after he took ill; in eight more days he would have been sixty-six. His dying words praised God.[77]

Levi Woodbury (1846–1851)

Levi Woodbury, about whose health little is known, died uneventfully at the age of sixty-one on September 4, 1851, while at his home in Portsmouth, New Hampshire. A large, robust man much given to systematic hard work, he had served as a state judge on New Hampshire's highest court, as governor, as a U.S. senator, and as secretary of the navy in Andrew Jackson's cabinet until he replaced Roger Brooke Taney as treasury secretary, a position he held through Martin Van Buren's administration. He had thereafter returned to the Senate in the years before his Court appointment. One of the most political of men, at the time he took ill he was in the process of organizing an intended bid for the Democratic presidential nomination in 1852.

John McKinley (1837–1852)

Fifteen years of riding the exhausting southern circuit contributed to the death of John McKinley, who had been in poor health at least since 1842, when he suffered a paralytic attack from which he apparently never fully recovered. The former Alabama senator estimated he rode about ten thousand miles a year through Alabama, Arkansas, Louisiana, and Mississippi at a time when most of his colleagues reported a couple of thousand miles of circuit travel annually. Although he wrote ten opinions for the 1845 term, he wrote only one opinion the next term, and in 1847 he filed none. He did not attend in 1848 and delivered no opinions in 1851 and 1852. The only evidence of his participation was two dissents he joined during those last two years. Whatever the state of his health, and however diligent he may have been in the discharge of his circuit duties, the record surely is suggestive of someone who did not pull his weight as a Supreme Court justice over a considerable period of time. Nonetheless, Chief Justice Taney eulogized McKinley as "a sound lawyer, faithful and assiduous in the discharge of his duties," adding, "while his health was sufficient to undergo the labor."[78]

During his entire service, he wrote only nineteen majority opinions, four dissents, and two concurrences. However, the burdensome responsibility, not reflected in the official Supreme Court reports, of the southern circuit occupied most of his time. He died in Louisville, Kentucky, on July 19, 1852.

Benjamin R. Curtis (1851–1857)

Justice McKinley represented a pro-slavery, states' rights position on the Court, but his replacement, Benjamin R. Curtis, possessed a far different political bent. Daniel Webster, then the secretary of state and a vocal abolitionist, suggested Curtis to President Millard Fillmore. Although a compromiser who supported the Fugitive Slave Act, Curtis clashed bitterly with Chief Justice Taney over the larger issues of slavery presented by *Dred Scott v. Sandford*.[79]

Personal animosities were also involved. Several weeks after *Dred Scott* was decided, Curtis still had not seen Taney's opinion and became concerned about whether Taney was in the process of changing it. Any changes would affect his own dissent since he had keyed his writing to Taney's opinion. Taney refused to let him see the opinion (claiming Curtis only wanted to see it for purposes of partisan exploitation), and an acrimonious exchange of letters followed. Curtis was insistent he had a right to see if an opinion had been materially altered after it had been orally delivered. Taney professed personal indignation at the request, but it was clear enough that he was indeed tampering with his opinion. Taney's spitefulness was probably encouraged by Curtis's junior status and his Massachusetts origins, a state for which the chief justice had no fondness.[80]

Curtis resigned on September 30, 1857. Aside from his quarrel with Taney, he disliked riding circuit and considered his Supreme Court salary totally inadequate. Following his resignation, Curtis returned to the practice of law in Massachusetts and thereafter argued fifty-four cases before the U.S.

Supreme Court and eighty before the Supreme Judicial Court of Massachusetts. He defended President Andrew Johnson at his impeachment trial, declined the attorney generalship in 1868, and continued his lucrative law practice.

The death of a daughter in 1874, however, left him in a state of depression. While vacationing in Newport in July, his health failed. A stroke was thought imminent. Nonetheless, his doctor remained optimistic and reported confidently:

> There was every threatening of hemorrhage of the brain; but under the treatment of Dr. Gray such quiet, restful sleep has been obtained, and the other symptoms so controlled, that they say this morning they feel the crisis to have passed, and that the Judge will get well. On Thursday last they felt the greatest anxiety; . . . but he yielded to the medicines wonderfully, and all his conditions are more natural.[81]

Despite such optimism, there was no recovery, and Curtis died on September 15, 1874, in his sixty-fourth year.

Peter V. Daniel (1841–1860)

Peter V. Daniel died on May 31, 1860, at age seventy-six, after nineteen years on the Court. He apparently was in poor health during the three years prior to his death but was able to function and thus able to support the position taken by his good friend, Chief Justice Taney, in the *Dred Scott* case. A Virginian, he represented the states' rights, weak federal government, proslavery views that *Dred Scott* epitomized.

John McLean (1830–1861)

A year later, John McLean died of pneumonia, also at the age of seventy-six. The former postmaster general had vigorously dissented in *Dred Scott* and throughout his thirty-two years on the Court had flirted unsuccessfully but persistently with presidential politics. Always politically ambitious, he was even rumored to be a possibility for secretary of state in the Lincoln administration.

Accustomed to vigorous health, he felt less well in 1859 and took several weeks in late summer to vacation at Lake Pepin in Minnesota.[82] Although he seemed stronger during the following term of Court, by the winter of

1860–1861 "it was well known at that time that his friends relieved him of all labor in preparation of opinions and that he would sleep on the bench during arguments."[83] Distressed by evidence of the approaching war, distracted by the great crowds attending the inauguration of Abraham Lincoln, indifferent toward home comforts, and neglectful of his health, he had caught a violent cold by late February. On March 22, burdened with a heavy cough, he returned home to Clifton, Ohio, on the northern hills of Cincinnati. He remained active, going into the city regularly, until finally, on April 3, a physician was called early in the morning to his bedside. The diagnosis was a "pulmonary irritation." Although he seemed better during the day, he began to fail that evening. He died at nine o'clock the next day.

On the afternoon of April 6, in a downpour of rain, fifty carriages met at the Hamilton County courthouse in Cincinnati and progressed to the home, where other mourners waited to begin the funeral services. An Episcopal service was thereafter conducted at the grave. The Civil War was about to begin, and the Supreme Court had just lost one of its strongest defenders of the Union.

John A. Campbell (1853–1861)

Changes during the Civil War made possible the Republican reconstruction of the Court that followed. John A. Campbell resigned in 1861 to the scorn of both North and South. Initially, Campbell saw himself as a mediator in the confrontation over Fort Sumter, but President Lincoln and Secretary of State Seward pointedly ignored him. His own position on the pending conflict was somewhat ambivalent: he was a states' righter, but he opposed secession and was not supportive of slavery.

When he resigned, he was coldly received in the South not only because of his opposition to secession but because he had not resigned sooner. He was nearly lynched when he returned home to Mobile, Alabama. Knowing he was unsafe in Alabama, he moved to New Orleans, observing, "I did not agree to recant what I had said, or to explain what I had done; and thus, instead of appeasing my opponents, I aggravated my offenses."[84] Although he was eventually made an assistant secretary of war for the Confederacy (a relatively unimportant position), the South never created a Supreme Court because his opponents feared he might be appointed to it.

Nonetheless, his hostility toward the Lincoln administration was undoubted. To Justice Nathan Clifford, he wrote, "This administration seems determined to have a sectional war."[85] Yet, he seems to have genuinely regretted leaving the Court, "principally as it diminishes the intimacy of those relations, which have grown up, among the members of the court and from which I have derived much happiness."[86]

After the war, Campbell established a successful law practice in New Orleans, was periodically rumored as a possibility for reappointment to the Supreme Court, and later most notably appeared before the Supreme Court in the *Slaughterhouse* cases in 1873 as counsel for the butchers who lost their businesses when the state established a monopoly centralizing the slaughtering of animals.

Campbell was memorably described by a Washington reporter who observed him in his last argument before his former colleagues:

> He is a very old man. His form is thin and bent, his skin is in the parchment state, and his hair is as white as the driven snow; but a great mind looks out through his keen eye and a great soul controls his fragile body. He is a lawyer to the core—in some respects one of the wisest, broadest, deepest, and most learned in the United States. He has neither the presence, voice, nor tongue of the orator, but when he speaks in his thin, measured tones, never wasting a word, the Supreme Court of the United States listens as it listens to almost no other man.[87]

Campbell's formidable talent as an advocate caused the postwar generation of capitalists, when in conflict with government, to frequently believe that their best course of legal action was to "leave it to God and Mr. Campbell."[88] Nonetheless, when he died on March 12, 1889, in his seventy-seventh year, his passing was scarcely noticed in the national press.

Roger Brooke Taney (Chief Justice: 1836–1864)

An era ended with the death of Roger Brooke Taney. The chief justice was by then eighty-eight years old and had presided over the Court for twenty-eight years. He had been expected to die two years earlier and had even asked each of the justices to call upon him. He told them he had a premonition of death and did not expect to see them again. Still, he lingered on, and his mind remained strong and determined. By the next year his doctor thought he resembled "a disembodied spirit; for that his mind did not, in any degree, participate in the infirmities of the body."[89]

On August 6, 1863, in personal correspondence to a friend, Taney disclosed a good deal about the state of his health and his disinclination to resign:

> I have been sick, very sick, since I last wrote to you, and have recovered slowly. But I am again in my office, and feel as well as usual, but not so strong, and am obliged to confine myself to my house.
>
> During this hot season I have often thought of the pleasant days I have passed at your home, enjoying the fresh country air and walking over your grounds. But my walking days are over; and I feel that I am sick enough for a hospital, and that hospital must be my own house.
>
> Yet I hope to linger along to the next term of the Supreme Court. Very different, however, that Court will now be from the Court as I have heretofore known it. Nor do I see any ground for hope that it will ever again be restored to the authority and rank which the constitution intended to confer upon it. The supremacy of the military power over the civil seems to be established; and the public mind has acquiesced in it and sanctioned it. We can pray for better times, and submit with resignation to the chastisements which it may please God to inflict upon us.[90]

By 1864 Taney was totally enfeebled. In the spring, Attorney General Edward Bates remarked that in addition to the chief justice, Justices Wayne, Catron, and Grier were also in failing health and that if the Congress provided a retirement pension, they might be induced to resign. Congress failed to act, and there were no resignations.[91]

Finally, in the fall of 1864 Taney was stricken by a severe recurrence of a chronic intestinal disease from which he had suffered for years. As he told his daughter Anne: "My dear child, my race is run. I have no desire to stay longer in this painful world, but for my poor children."[92] The same day, October 12, the race ended. One of the women who attended him recounted what happened:

> I think it was about ten o'clock when being helped from one side to the other to relieve his pain, he suddenly raised his head, all trace of suffering gone, his eyes bright and clear, said "Lord Jesus receive my spirit," and never spoke again. He lived more than an hour afterward with the same sweet peaceful face and though we stood round his bed

Roger Brooke Taney shortly before death (the famous "old goat" portrait). (Supreme Court, Office of the Curator)

we did not know he was gone until we saw the Doctor closing his
bright uplifted eyes.[93]

Taney's body did not lie in state in the Court, nor did the government
come together to honor him at his funeral. His funeral was, however, discussed by the cabinet. The secretary of the navy, Gideon Welles, remarked
on his own mixed feelings:

> I felt little inclined to participate. I have never called upon him living,
> and while his position and office were to be respected, I had no honors
> for the deceased beyond those that were public. That he had many
> good qualities and possessed ability, I do not doubt; that he rendered
> service in Jackson's Administration is true, and during most of his po-
> litical life, he was upright and just. But the course pursued in the *Dred
> Scott* case and all the attending circumstances forfeited respect for him
> as a man or Judge . . . for I have looked on him and his Court as having
> contributed, unintentionally, perhaps, but largely, to the calamities of
> our afflicted country. They probably did not mean treason, but thought
> their wisdom and official position would give national sanction to a
> great wrong.[94]

The burial was in Frederick, Maryland, the chief justice's boyhood home.
President Lincoln, Secretary of State William Seward, and Postmaster General William Dennison attended the body while it was borne from the Taney
home to the railroad car that would carry it to Frederick. Attorney General
Bates, alone among the cabinet members, accompanied the funeral party to
the church and grave site.[95]

The Republican press was predictably hostile in its judgment, but none so
much as Massachusetts senator Charles Sumner, whose conclusion influenced
schoolroom evaluations of Taney for almost a century: "The name of Taney
is to be hooted down the page of history. Judgment is beginning now; and
an emancipated country will fasten upon him the stigma which he deserves.
. . . He administered justice at last wickedly, and degraded the judiciary of
the country, and degraded the age."[96]

The *New York Tribune,* which had criticized Taney for years, gave a more
measured, and more accurate, evaluation of his service: "He belonged to a
dispensation now happily closed; it is no more just than generous to question
his integrity, nor the sincerity, whatever we think of the quality, of his pa-
triotism. He was the product of circumstances which (we trust) will mold

the character of no future Chief Justice of the United States; but it were unjust to presume that he did not truly and earnestly seek the good of his country."[97]

Nine years passed before Congress appropriated money for a bust of Taney and his successor, Salmon Chase, for the Supreme Court. Even then, it was done quietly and without debate a month before Charles Sumner's death. In opposition, Sumner earlier told the Senate, "Taney shall not be represented as a saint by any vote of Congress, if I can help it."[98] But by then, the country—along with the Congress and the Court—had turned to more immediate concerns.

When examining health-related evidence from the antebellum period, one is confronted with the limited and impressionistic nature of so much of it. Although the general medical problem is usually understandable enough, nineteenth-century judicial biographers tended more toward eulogy than medical detail. Often the patient's own evaluation of his condition is all that has survived. Kidney or bladder stones, gout, heart disease, tumors, and stroke, rather than more exotic ailments, were recurrently diagnosed among the early justices. But there was also a troublesome incidence of mental illness, beginning with John Rutledge.

Of the nine justices who resigned, two (Jay and Rutledge) left because of ambition; three left because of dissatisfaction (Thomas Johnson, Curtis, and Campbell); and four resignations were encouraged by poor health (Blair, Ellsworth, Moore, and Duvall).

Although men were usually appointed to the Court while still middle-aged, this practice proved no guarantee against poor health. There was, in fact, a remarkable degree of poor health among the justices, which may be attributed to the unavailability of satisfactory treatment for common serious illnesses (like gout or kidney stones) that afflicted otherwise healthy individuals at an early age.

A second explanation, which the justices offered repeatedly themselves, attributes the deterioration of health to the rigors of traveling the judicial circuits by horse or carriage. Distances were great, accommodations were often primitive, local inhabitants were sometimes hostile to a stranger, roads were rough or even impassable, and the climate was inhospitable. It is not surprising, then, that riding a circuit affected the health of some justices as it did, especially as they grew older.

In addition to the arduous task of riding circuit, the courtroom the justices occupied in the basement of the Capitol prior to 1860 was decidedly unhealthy. The courtroom was either too hot or too smoky because of inadequate ventilation, or it was too chilly or too damp. The fetid air that the justices were forced to breathe caused the prominent Washington architect, Robert Mills, to say in 1850, "The death of some of our most talented jurists has been attributed to this location of the court room, and it would be but common justice in Congress to provide better accommodations for its sittings."[99]

Because in the absence of pensions so few justices resigned, and because so many were in poor health or incapacitated for long periods, the question arises why they were not removed through impeachment and conviction. The only answer is that the Congress never equated an absence of "good Behaviour" with judicial infirmity. Jefferson's curt dismissal of impeachment as an instrument of removal, following Chase's acquittal, acknowledged what became an even more pronounced pattern as the century progressed. There simply was no practical way to remove justices who were infirm and unable to responsibly perform their duties. The other justices worked around them, ignored them when necessary, and did not permit themselves to be greatly affected by them.

An evaluation of the significance of judicial infirmity during the Court's early history must reckon with the impreciseness of the medical evidence, the relative youth of the appointees, the unique burden of riding circuit court, and the absence of any practical means of removing disabled justices. Although these considerations complicate an evaluation, it still appears that constitutional arrangements worked satisfactorily from 1789 through the Civil War despite substantial evidence of infirmity among the justices.

There are two reasons why the medical history of the antebellum period did not have a more significant impact on Court performance. First, the Court had a remarkably light workload. There were not many cases decided during the period, and, moreover, Chief Justice Marshall established a pattern in which he as chief justice did most of the opinion writing. He was able to achieve this dominance because of his control over opinion assignments and because his colleagues acquiesced to the practice. Since dissents or concurrences were infrequent, most of the justices were freed from burdensome opinion-writing obligations.[100] Second, major cases usually had substantial majorities, so an incapacitated justice was seldom an important factor. Toward the end of the period, however, the *Dred Scott* case reflected the breakdown of consensus. But even then, that decision reflected the majority's tolerant attitude toward slavery, and judicial disability did not affect the outcome either way.

There is a final, albeit important, caveat about the impact of health on judicial performance. Health problems clearly did have serious adverse consequences for decision making in the circuits. When justices failed to meet their statutory circuit responsibilities, the dockets became congested and the federal judicial system functioned inadequately. Forcing the justices to ride circuit was a structural mistake in the federal judicial system, which was later corrected by statute in 1891; the increased workload assumed by the Court demanded the change. Nevertheless, with respect to the Supreme Court's own decision-making process, ill health did not substantially impair the antebellum Court's ability to deal with legal issues confronting the nation.

3

CIVIL WAR TO CENTURY'S END, 1865–1899

Too many justices held tenaciously to office between 1865–1899; of the nineteen justices considered in this chapter, twelve died in office. Even among those who eventually resigned, the circumstances often were attended by physical disability, mental decline, and even indifference toward the Court's work because of political ambition.

The years between 1865 and the end of the century constituted a period of vast industrial expansion, when a massive urbanization of the workforce occurred, and the government willingly deferred to the leaders of industry. Not surprisingly, these decades forced new pressures and obligations upon the country's democracy and thus inevitably its Supreme Court.[1] It was a time of change, of social insensitivity on an unprecedented scale, and of unregulated individualism. Watching from abroad, Thomas Carlyle characteristically observed, "In the long-run every Government is the exact symbol of its People, with their wisdom and unwisdom; we have to say, 'Like People, like Government.'"[2]

America was in social and economic ferment. But inside the Supreme Court there were striking instances of decrepitude among the justices that presented the century's strongest case for institutional reform. Only David Davis left the Court in good health and before he reached age sixty-five; the Illinois legislature in his case concluded he was more valuable in the Senate than on the Court, and he agreed.

There was more balance between deaths (nine) and resignations (six) for those over sixty-five during this period than there was on the antebellum Court. These resignations may reflect the continuing burdens of circuit riding until 1891, despite the advent of railroad travel, as the country grew larger and the workload increased.

Table 3.1
Age of Death or Retirement, 1865–1899

Age	Died	Resigned
54 or younger	0	0
55–59	0	0
60–64	3	1
65–69	2	0
70–74	3	2
75–79	4	2
80 or older	0	2
Totals	12	7

Average age of those leaving the Court: 72

Source: Elder Witt, ed., *Congressional Quarterly's Guide to the U.S. Supreme Court*, 2d ed. (Washington, D.C.: Congressional Quarterly Press, 1990).

John Catron (1837–1865)

At nearly eighty years of age (his exact date of birth is unknown), John Catron died on May 30, 1865. Like Chief Justice Roger Brooke Taney, with whom he had agreed in the *Dred Scott* case,[3] he was feeble and broken in health at the time of his death. A year earlier he had been identified by Attorney General Edward Bates as one who might be willing to resign if Congress provided an adequate pension. However, Congress remained inactive until 1869. Whether his failing health much affected the quality of his performance may be doubted. Even as of 1857, at the time of the *Dred Scott* case, one Court watcher had described him in the following terms: "Judge Catron of Tennessee is a robust, unintellectual man, advanced in years, whose judgments would be inevitably swayed by his political associations, but whose erroneous opinions would, as a general rule, more often result from obtuseness than from original sin."[4]

James M. Wayne (1835–1867)

A second southerner was taken from the Court two years later, when James M. Wayne, still vigorous of mind at age seventy-seven, though increasingly hampered by physical infirmities, died suddenly of typhoid fever on July 5, 1867, in Washington.[5] Although he too had joined with Chief Justice Taney in the *Dred Scott* case, he was generally a more substantial presence on the

Court than were many of his colleagues. Stylish and educated, he identified with the chivalric tradition of the antebellum South. At the time of his unexpected death Wayne refused to ride circuit in those southern states that were under military rule, although he indicated he had no objection to the district court judges holding court as usual in the circuit. He simply felt it was inappropriate for a Supreme Court justice to hold court in any circuit until the president ended martial law and revoked the suspension of the writ of habeas corpus.[6] He disfavored punitive retribution against the South, even though during the Civil War he, like Justice Catron, remained loyal to the Union. His death was a loss for those who favored the moderate Reconstruction measures endorsed by President Andrew Johnson.

Robert C. Grier (1846–1870)

In 1869 Congress increased the size of the Court to nine. This action was accompanied by Robert C. Grier's resignation effective February 1, 1870 (the first under the new Retirement Act of 1869), which provided President Ulysses S. Grant with two appointments. Both vacancies were defensible. The increase in the size of the Court from eight to nine made it less likely the Court would deadlock. Moreover, Grier's resignation had been strongly encouraged by his colleagues. As early as 1864, Attorney General Bates had observed that Grier was in a state of decline, which was the situation throughout the remainder of the decade. After 1862 he could perform no circuit court duties, and the simplest physical exertion became difficult for him. But he was persistent in his refusal to leave even though it was necessary to carry him onto the bench.

Grier eventually came to believe that his Court work was therapeutic, even suggesting to Chief Justice Chase in 1866 that he needed "the exercise both of *mind* and *body*—which sitting in court would afford me."[7] Yet, he could scarcely function.[8] As he acknowledged, "I can write with difficulty, even with a pencil."[9] Unfortunately, Grier's decline was mental as well as physical.[10] Justice Samuel F. Miller, who was a medical doctor before turning to the law, wrote that "Brother Grier who delivered the opinion . . . is getting a little muddy and may not have conveyed the idea clearly."[11]

With the first *Legal Tender* case[12] under consideration, it was apparent to everyone that Grier was in no condition to participate. When the case was first discussed, the result was in favor of the constitutionality of the legal tender legislation, because the Court divided evenly and the decision of the lower court remained undisturbed. But then Grier, when discussing a sub-

Robert C. Grier was the first to be asked to leave by his colleagues. (Supreme Court, Office of the Curator)

sequent case during the same conference, spoke inconsistently with how he had voted in the *Legal Tender* case. When this discrepancy was drawn to his attention, he reconsidered and changed his vote. The result was then five in favor of striking the legislation.

Pressure intensified on Grier to step aside. One of his two married daughters, Sarah Grier Beck, with whom he lived when Court was in session, wrote that "the Chief [Salmon P. Chase] and Judge [Samuel] Nelson waited on Pa this morning to ask him to resign."[13] His colleagues spent much time discussing his disability, and Justices Nelson, Davis, and Swayne were particularly loud within the counsels of the Court in hoping for his imminent resignation.[14] What exactly happened inside the Court to secure the resignation of Grier has been the subject of dispute. The evidence is subject to various interpretations.[15] Eventually Chase secured Grier's promise to resign sometime in December, although it was not to become effective until February, two months later.

However events unfolded, it is known that on January 29, 1870, two days before Grier left the bench, Chief Justice Chase got his colleagues to agree with his decision to invalidate the Legal Tender Act.[16] He had supported the legislation as Lincoln's treasury secretary, and the act was legislation that many then thought was essential to national survival during the Civil War.[17] Chase announced the result of the vote after Grier had, in fact, left the Court. He nonetheless counted Grier's crucial fifth vote in order to get the result he wanted.

On the same day, President Grant nominated for the Court both William Strong and Joseph P. Bradley, who once confirmed by the Senate voted to reinstate the Legal Tender Act within the following year and a half as a valid exercise of the congressional war power.[18] Chase's behavior has been subject to much well-deserved criticism. As Charles Fairman concluded, "The chief responsibility for [what happened] must surely be placed upon Chase."[19]

Never a strong personality, Grier had been described earlier during his participation in the *Dred Scott* case as one whose "real characteristics closely conform to his external, physiological delineations." And the observer concluded:

"He is of a soft and rosy nature. He is facile and easy of suggestion. He succumbs under touch, and returns into shape on its removal. He is ardent and impressible. He is fickle and uncertain. . . . He is impulsive and precipitate. Let Grier associate with none but honest men, and be placed in no difficult or constraining circumstances, and he would not disgrace himself or his position."[20]

As his mental health deteriorated, his indecisiveness meant much depended on with whom he last discussed an issue. His unreliability disrupted the Court's deliberative process. Following his resignation, he returned to his home in Philadelphia, where he died on September 25, 1870.

Samuel Nelson (1845–1872)

The following year President Grant appointed Samuel Nelson to a commission charged with settling certain claims by the United States against Great Britain. The claims were the result of British willingness to let Confederate ships outfit themselves in British ports during the Civil War. Justice Nelson had been on the Court since 1845. He was seventy-eight and had received relatively little national visibility except for his joint effort with Justice John Campbell to bring the North and South together shortly before the Civil War. By accepting President Grant's assignment, he hastened his own departure from the Court. He took his responsibilities with the commission very seriously. The resulting overwork, along with the insomnia from which he habitually suffered, soon took its predictable toll. He resigned from the Court the next year and died in Cooperstown, New York, eleven months later on December 13, 1873, at age eighty-one.

Salmon P. Chase (Chief Justice: 1864–1873)

Earlier, in August 1870, while returning from a western trip, Chief Justice Salmon P. Chase suffered a stroke that paralyzed his right side. He was much changed in appearance: his hair turned white and he became gaunt, even though he retained his impressiveness of presence. Following the eight months he was absent from the Court (which was the entire 1870 term), he grew a beard and mustache to disguise the "facial ravages" of his paralysis.[21] At a White House dinner, Justice David Davis's wife, Sarah, was surprised by his changed appearance: "The Chief Justice has a full pair of whiskers and a mustache, which changes his face so much that I did not recognize him until he spoke to me."[22]

The Court was without effective leadership until Chase's death three years later. He was ineligible for any retirement benefits. This consideration, added

Salmon P. Chase grew a beard after his stroke. (Supreme Court, Office of the Curator)

to his usual sense of indispensability, discouraged any thought of resignation, even though he reportedly was unable to "attempt hard and continuous labor."[23] His medical condition and his family's likely response to it were noted by Justice Miller at the time of the initial illness:

> The more recent indications are that the Chief will recover. Whether he will be able to serve efficiently may remain doubtful. But I do not think he will resign unless he is provided with something else. This is not now probable. The paralytic stroke places him out of the list of probable candidates for the Presidency, and thereby removes any inducement for Grant to propitiate him or send him to Europe which is the only alternative to his remaining a figure head to the Court. His daughters, especially Mrs. [Kate] Sprague will never consent to his retiring to private life.[24]

Accordingly, Chase participated in both the 1871 and 1872 terms, even though toward the end he was barely able to function. The 1872 term was particularly exhausting. The chief justice joined the dissenters in the *Slaughterhouse* cases,[25] decided by a 5 to 4 vote. The cases were first heard in January 1872, but since Justice Nelson was ill and did not hear oral arguments, they had to be reargued the following year and were decided on April 14, 1873. The cases pitted Justice Miller's deference toward state economic regulation against Justice Field's nationalistic laissez-faire in a conflict accompanied by strongly expressed emotions.

Chase's state of mind could not have been helped by his failure to persuade his colleagues to strike down the Louisiana law. Nor could his frustration have been abated by the willingness of his colleagues the very next day to permit, over his lone dissent, a state to deny women the right to practice law.[26] Confronted with this divisive case, involving the interpretation of the newly enacted Fourteenth Amendment, and other cases requiring written opinions from him, his decline became even more noticeable in the final days of the Court's term.

> During the last few days he sat in Court, a sudden weakness surprised him. His walk was not so firm; his breath hardly lasted the ascent of Capitol Hill, which his feet had trodden for a quarter of a century. His voice was weaker; his manner always considerate, but sometimes abrupt through nervousness or illness, became gentler and kinder every day. His very silence was benignant. On the last day Court was in session,

he relinquished his place to his venerable friend and associate, Justice Clifford, and remained seated at his side, for the first and last time of his life resting his head all day upon his hand.[27]

On May 5, Chase wrote a final letter to an old friend in Cleveland, which detailed the strain of his final days:

> Since the adjournment, which came none too soon, I have made my way to New York. . . . It seems odd to be so entirely out of the world in the midst of this great Babylon; but I am too much of an invalid to be more than a cipher. Sometimes I feel as if I were dead, though alive. I am on my way to Boston, where I am to try a treatment, from which great results are promised; but I expect little. The lapse of 65 years is hard to cure.[28]

The anticipated treatment in Boston concerned a new form of magnetism or electricity that was currently in fashion for stroke victims. Chief Justice Chase never received the anticipated treatment. The next morning his attendant found him in bed and at first thought he was asleep. But he soon became alarmed and called for a physician when it was apparent Chase was unconscious. Chase had suffered another stroke, much worse than before. As the day progressed, his labored breathing became increasingly fainter. He died the next day, at ten in the morning, without regaining consciousness.[29]

The obituary in the *New York Times* emphasized the medical deterioration that had overtaken him:

> Within the last two years he had fallen away so much in flesh that his frame presented a marked contrast with its former fullness, and his face had changed to such a degree that many of his friends who had not seen him for several months did not recognize him in company or on the street. Everybody spoke of the change in appearance of the Chief Justice, and many anticipated a sudden death. . . . He appeared to be cheerful and conversed with his usual freedom, but it was apparent that his constitution had received a shock from which he could never recover.[30]

Following a funeral in the Episcopal Church of St. George in New York City, the body was returned to Washington, D.C., for another service. The chief justice was laid in repose in the Old Senate Chambers on the same catafalque that had been used for Abraham Lincoln. He was then buried at Oak Hill Cemetery outside the capital, but in 1886 the state of Ohio asked that his remains be returned to Cincinnati, where he presently rests beside his beloved daughter, Kate.

David Davis (1862–1877)

President Lincoln's campaign manager in 1860, David Davis resigned his Supreme Court seat on March 4, 1877, to accept a seat in the U.S. Senate. He was actually elected to the Senate by the Illinois state legislature while still on the Court. Judicial work had become burdensome to him, particularly as the docket increased. At the time of his appointment in 1862, the Court met from December until March. By 1874, when he had reached his sixtieth year, the sessions began in October and continued through May. Discouraged, he concluded that "to be on a strain from 2nd Monday of October till the 1st of May is wearing to both body & mind. . . . I get so worn every Spring that I think I will never go back. . . . I ought to quit and stay at home with my wife."[31] His family agreed, and, given his extreme corpulence, there was concern he might "lose the use of his limbs" if he remained constantly at his desk.[32] He had decided to leave even before then but remained through President Grant's last term of office because of concern over the unpredictable and sometimes luckless nominations that had characterized Grant's administration.

When Davis did leave the Court, Justice Miller reacted with indignation when the suggestion reached him that John A. Campbell, who had resigned from the Court in 1861 in order to join the Confederacy, ought to be reappointed. Campbell was then sixty-five, but he had aged prematurely and appeared very old. As Miller wrote in 1877:

There is no man on the bench of the Supreme Court more interested in the character and efficiency of its personnel than I am. If I live so long, it will still be nine years before I can retire with the salary. I have already been there longer than any man but two, both of whom are over seventy.

Within five years from this time three other of the present Judges will be over seventy. Strong is now in his sixty ninth, Hunt in his sixty eighth and broken down with gout, and Bradley in feeble health and in his sixty sixth year.

In the name of God what do I and Waite and Field, all men in our

sixty first year, want of another old, old man on the bench. . . . I have
told the Attorney General that if an old man was appointed we should
have within five years a majority of old imbeciles on the bench, for in
the work we have to do no man ought to be there after he is seventy.
But they will not resign. Neither Swayne nor Clifford whose mental
failure is obvious to all the court, who have come to do nothing but
write garrulous opinions and clamor for more of that work, have any
thought of resigning.[33]

Davis never lost interest in politics. There was some talk he might be the
Democratic presidential nominee, and, as his biographer has noted, he lent
"a more or less attentive ear to the suggestions."[34] Nonetheless, he was not
given serious consideration at the convention, which nominated Samuel J.
Tilden.

Davis's subsequent election to the Senate was not without controversy,
even though he apparently did not solicit the position. He was effectively dis-
qualified as a member of the electoral commission, where he was expected to
serve. The commission had been established to determine the disputed presidential election of 1876 between Tilden and Rutherford B. Hayes. Justice
Joseph P. Bradley, a Republican, took Davis's seat on the commission and
swung the vote to Hayes. Davis later indicated he would have reached the
same conclusions, even though at the time there was speculation he would
be somewhat more independent and less inclined to vote along strict party
lines. His decision to step down from the Court was not difficult. His wife,
Sarah, had become ill, and she could no longer tolerate life in Washington.
His Senate responsibilities permitted their return to Illinois.

Davis was a strong presence in the Senate, but any presidential ambitions
had left him by 1879 when his wife died. The next year he was found to
have diabetes, but it seemed to have no debilitating effects for at least a while,
because in 1881 the Republicans unanimously elected him president pro tem
of the Senate (even though a unanimous Democratic vote in the Illinois
legislature had first sent him to the Senate). Following the assassination of
President James Garfield, Davis was next in line of succession to the presidency in the event of President Chester A. Arthur's death or resignation.
Both Republicans and Democrats during this period saw Davis as someone
who stood above party rivalry; his independence and evenhandedness were
appreciated by those who sought to encourage the mediation of differences
arising from lingering sectional animosities. Davis recognized his special
role:

The day is drawing near when I shall retire from this chamber. My only ambition, while here, is to be instrumental in bringing about perfect peace between North and South. . . . When the rude voices of faction which for fifteen years . . . have disturbed the national fellowship . . . shall be silenced, this country will bound forward in a career of grandeur and glory that will astonish mankind.[35]

After a term in the Senate, the Illinois Bar Association elected Davis its president. The next year he became ill with a carbuncle on his shoulder, an ailment associated with his diabetes. A patch of cellulitis (or erysipelas) was next discovered on his thigh. This skin infection is caused by streptococcus bacteria, which enter the body through a small cut or sore of the kind diabetics are prone to have. In the absence of antibiotics, the infection travels rapidly to the lymph glands and thereafter into the bloodstream. Blood poisoning quickly results, which in this case was accompanied by a coma.

Following Davis's death on June 26, 1886, the *New York Times* suggested that he would be best remembered as "the friend of Abraham Lincoln."[36] But more critically, the newspaper also noted that he had uncourageously shrunk from the responsibility of the electoral commission in 1877, knowing he would have been the "odd man" on the commission. The *Times* believed this reticence in the face of extreme pressure cut short his political career. Later, by not offending either party in the Senate, he commended himself to neither. But perhaps an equally persuasive argument cuts in precisely the other way: Davis's special talent for conciliation made his six years in the Senate a more significant contribution toward national reconciliation than if he had taken his seat as a partisan.

William Strong (1870–1880)

Having succeeded the incapacitated Robert C. Grier, William Strong resigned in 1880 after a decade of service while he was still recognized as one of the ablest men on the Court. He obviously hoped to set an example. The Court at the time included several people who were clearly unable to do the work but who were still reluctant to leave. Strong's daughter related the circumstances of her father's resignation as she had heard it from him:

Having reached the age of Seventy-three years, and although remarkably well preserved physically and mentally and quite as capable of efficient service as any of the other justices, he became convinced that it would be for the interest of the Court if one or two of the justices who had become enfeebled by age were to retire and their places be filled by more vigorous men. He enjoyed the position and its duties, and would not have retired at that time if the retirement of other justices could have been effected without his setting an example. This conviction led him to say to Justice Swayne, who had been on the bench a long time and was quite enfeebled, that he had in mind the strengthening of the bench by resigning, and as they had both reached the period in life when they could retire with the continuance of their salaries during life, he would offer his resignation if Mr. Justice Swayne would follow him in so doing. Justice Swayne assented to this.[37]

Justice Strong was eligible for a pension, since he had served a decade and also was over the age of seventy. But this consideration was apparently not an important one. As his daughter also said, he thought it much better to leave while people were inclined to ask, "Why does he leave?" rather than wait until they asked, "Why doesn't he leave?"[38] Justice Miller was much concerned about the resignation, writing that "the loss of Judge Strong is a heavy one to the Court, while the men occupying the other places could well be spared."[39]

Justice Strong's own father had been a Presbyterian minister, and, like him, he remained a deeply religious man. Following his resignation, Strong found himself busily engaged in religious work, serving at various times as vice president of the American Bible Society (1871–1895) and president of the American Sunday School Union (1883–1895) and the American Tract Society (1873–1895). His religious activities continued until his death on August 19, 1895, at age eighty-seven, at Lake Minnewaska, New York. At the end, he suffered a stroke after his constitution had been weakened by catarrhal fever (a medical term no longer used, but which at the time referred to an inflammation of the mucus membrane, especially of the nose and throat).

Noah H. Swayne (1862–1881)

At age seventy-seven and after nineteen years of service, Noah H. Swayne left the Court on January 25, 1881. Although Justice Strong had by words and example encouraged him to leave, it was President Rutherford B. Hayes's willingness to appoint Swayne's good friend, Stanley Matthews, that was the decisive consideration. In any event, his mental acuity and his ability to contribute had noticeably declined throughout the late 1870s.

Justice Swayne survived his resignation by three years. Although he had been reluctant to leave, he soon became converted to the pleasures of retirement. As he wrote Justice Joseph P. Bradley, who had just turned sixty-nine, about his new convictions:

> I have no doubt you will resign at the close of your seventieth year or very soon afterwards & I think you ought to. You need have no apprehension that you will not find enough to do—constantly and agreeably to employ you—nor that a moment of your time will necessarily be attended with a sense of tedium or *ennui.* You will be brighter and happier than you have been for the last five years or will be in the future while you remain on the bench.[40]

Swayne's wife died the next year, so he then moved to New York City to be with his son, Wagner Swayne, a lawyer, and remained there until his death on June 8, 1884.[41]

Nathan Clifford (1858–1881)

Nathan Clifford presented another extraordinary problem during this same period. Like Swayne, he outstayed his usefulness but remained a difficult and easily disgruntled colleague with whom it was virtually impossible to work. As John W. Wallace, the Court's reporter from 1863–1874, wrote in 1880:

> The "shorter handed" the Court is—while the observation comes from the absence of such judges as Clifford & Swayne, the more business it will do, and the better. I often used to wonder whether in the history of the whole world there ever was such a man as the first named one, *in such a place.* . . . Swayne was no worse than some other cases, but bad enough no doubt. But unless Strong has lost a good deal since I came away, his departure would, I think, be regretted. In the department of Patent Cases he was of great value on that particular bench.[42]

Justice Clifford presented a very real problem for Chief Justice Morrison R. Waite, since he had begun to mentally and physically deteriorate as early as 1874. He sometimes would reject opinion assignments, simply indicating that he did not care to write one. As he once told Waite: "I think I did not vote for the judgment. At all events I am not prepared to take the opinion."[43] He had in fact voted for the judgment in the particular case. Moreover, he was easily offended. Any perceived slight was instantly resented. "I am not willing to write an opinion on No. 93 and therefore return it," he wrote the chief justice. "If you want No. 99 for any of your friends you may have that also."[44]

Other justices had to contend with him as well. Justice Miller found himself thoroughly frustrated with what was going on: "I can't make Clifford and Swayne who are too old resign, nor keep the Chief Justice from giving them cases to write opinions in which their garrulity is often mixed with mischief."[45] Two years after Miller made this observation, Clifford was chosen, incredibly enough, to chair the electoral commission established to decide the contested presidential election of 1876. In this capacity he cast all his votes for Samuel Tilden and thereafter resolutely refused to acknowledge Hayes as president. He would neither enter the White House nor permit Hayes to appoint his successor under any circumstances.

By 1880 Justice Clifford had mentally collapsed. Justice Miller incisively reported the medical details:

Judge Clifford reached Washington on the 8th of October. . . . I saw him within three hours after his arrival, and he did not know me or any thing, and though his tongue framed words there was no sense in them.

An effort was made . . . to call it paralysis because he was taken suddenly between Boston and Washington, but there was no paralysis in the case. He remains yet about in the same condition. His general health good as usual. Able to ride out and walk about the house, but his mind is a wreck and no one believes that he will ever try another case, though the one idea which he seems to have is a desire to get to his seat in the capitol. I have seen him twice and the other judges have also. It is doubtful if he knew any of us. His wife thought I could do more to persuade him to return home than any one else and sent for me. But when I saw him I saw also that it was no use to try for he introduced me to his wife twice in ten minutes, though I have known her for eighteen years quite intimately. His work is ended though he may live for several years.[46]

Justice Clifford could have received full pay had he resigned at any time after 1873. At his death on July 25, 1881, in Cornish, Maine, he was the sole justice who had been appointed by a Democratic administration. He had barely outlived the presidency of the man he had most reviled, Rutherford B. Hayes.

Ward Hunt (1872–1882)

When he resigned in 1882, Ward Hunt was the last of a trio of incapacitated justices to leave the Court. He had been unable to serve for the previous five years. Chief Justice Waite assumed his circuit court duties for him and had hinted at the appropriateness of a resignation, but to no avail. Hunt stayed on, principally for two reasons. Like Clifford, he did not want to give President Hayes an opportunity to appoint his successor. Hunt's political sponsor, the influential Senator Roscoe Conkling of New York, had quarreled with President Hayes over reform policies, which was enough to alienate Hunt. Justice Miller confidentially confirmed Hunt's sense of indebtedness to Conkling in a letter written on December 14, 1879: "Judge Hunt would resign at once if Conkling would express his willingness. But he owed his appointment to Conkling and the latter is selfish enough to wish the chance of dictating his successor under a new administration."[47] Perhaps equally important, Hunt did not qualify for a pension. He was dependent on his salary. When Congress finally passed a special bill for him, he resigned immediately. In Congress, his cause had been effectively championed by his former colleague, Senator David Davis.

Hunt's medical difficulties became acute in 1878 when he was left speechless by a stroke. As usual, Justice Miller's summary of the situation was most perceptive:

Judge Hunt whether he shall die within the next ten days, or within the year will never return to the court. This is a great grief to me. He is a cultivated lawyer and gentleman. A warm hearted courteous man. Having no family with him but his wife, and of a sociable nature, he has made himself one of the most agreeable men on the bench.

Last winter he had three attacks of gout which is with him inherited. It enfeebled him so much that when we all adjourned it was much doubted if he would live to return. Such was also the feeling in regard to myself. He and I sympathized with each other and talked it over very freely, and I came to have a warmer affection for him than I can at my years get up for many men.[48]

Following his resignation, Hunt survived in a debilitated state for the next four years. He died in Washington on March 24, 1886.

In a little over a year, four new justices replaced Strong, Swayne, Clifford, and Hunt on the Supreme Court. Quickly the Court experienced a renewal; a period characterized by incompetence and disability was over. There were no changes during the next five years.

William B. Woods (1880–1887)

William B. Woods survived only six and a half years following his appointment. Little is known about the final illness of this Ohio man who, following the Civil War where he served as a general, stayed on in Alabama to become a successful businessman and judge. His appointment was consistent with Hayes's intention to bring the South back into the Union as quickly as possible. The *New York Times* noted that Woods had been ill for a year or more before his death. His sudden incapacitation in the spring of 1886 continued despite an extended recuperation in California.[49] He was in Washington, D.C., when he died on May 14, 1887.

Beginning in 1887 with the death of Justice Woods, the Court lost a justice each year for the next four years. Each justice died while still active.

Morrison R. Waite (Chief Justice: 1874–1888)

Prior to his death at age seventy-one after fourteen years of service, Chief Justice Morrison R. Waite had experienced only one serious ailment, which occurred in 1885 and was probably caused by overwork. He in effect suffered a nervous breakdown. Justice Miller observed what happened:

> In consequence of the illness of the Chief Justice I have had to be acting Chief Justice in his place. I always knew that he did a great deal more work than I, and had many apparently unimportant matters to look after to which the other Judges gave no time and very little attention. I find now that what I had suspected hardly came up to the draft on his time as he performed these duties. Disposition of practice cases, motions to dismiss for want to jurisdiction, reading carefully and

[word illegible] and answering letters or telling the clerk how to answer them constituted in his way of doing it a heavy load on his time and on his mind.

It is this which caused his illness. He is much broken down and if [he] does not diminish his excessive labours, he will not be capable of any work in a year or two more.

He leaves for Florida to be gone a month for recuperation.[50]

Waite's biographer remarks that the chief justice began to age rapidly. Two years after his breakdown, in a letter to his wife, Waite commented on a friend's illness in a tone mindful of his own mortality: "We can not help it darling, age has got hold of us all."[51]

Demonstrating the curious nature of causation, Chief Justice Waite's death on March 23, 1888, began with the illness of his coachman. With no coachman to drive him, Waite walked to and from a reception, which left him with a chill. In an age without antibiotics, this affliction was often the prelude to pneumonia. Even though unwell, Waite insisted on coming to Court, determined to read an opinion. But once seated on the bench he was physically unable to read his opinion, so Justice Samuel Blatchford read it for him, even though he remained while the opinion was read. People in the courtroom were shocked with his appearance. As Attorney General Alexander Garland later reported, "It was evident to the observer death had almost placed its hand upon him."[52]

Pneumonia eventually killed him, although the *New York Times* indicated he had some problems with his liver and spleen (organs that served to justify some of the more fanciful diagnostic flourishes of the day). On the day of his death, Waite awoke to the company of his nurse, said simply "I feel better," and thereupon died immediately.[53]

Morrison Waite has never ranked among the more important chief justices, but Felix Frankfurter always felt that Waite had been unfairly neglected.[54] President Hayes wrote sympathetically about him in his diary, emphasizing the human qualities he brought to public office:

He was of large and strong intellect. He was great-hearted, warm-hearted, and of generous, just and noble sentiments and feelings. He was thoroughly trained and schooled from his youth up. He was in the best sense a learned and a well educated man. He had saving common sense, untiring industry, and great energy. He was always cheerful, easily made happy by others, and with amazing powers and a never failing disposition to make others happy. He was the best beloved man that ever lived in this part of the United States.[55]

Stanley Matthews (1881–1889)

The next year Stanley Matthews died at age sixty-four after a tenure of eight years. He was incapacitated with a variety of symptoms for about a year prior to his death. He suffered from indigestion, lost a good deal of weight, and had attacks of what was described as muscular rheumatism. He tried to recuperate at his Massachusetts home, but his condition grew worse, as his rheumatism was accompanied by a high fever that confined him to bed. Matthews eventually left New England and returned to Washington, but there, racked by constant fever and chills, his suffering continued. His death occurred on March 22, 1889, reportedly because of an exhaustion of the heart and congestion of the kidneys, a generalized description that indicated the extent to which he had collapsed during the final weeks of his life.

Samuel F. Miller (1862–1890)

Before his unexpected death at age seventy-four, Samuel F. Miller was still in possession of all his considerable powers. Even though he had expressed his belief that one should leave the Supreme Court at seventy, and even though he had witnessed some of the more extraordinary instances of medical disability in Court history, he shrank from his own prescription when he turned seventy. Of course, as a physician himself, he might have acted otherwise had his own health been other than entirely robust. Certainly no one else, as his personal letters demonstrate, watched the health of others with a greater curiosity or perceptiveness. Among all the justices his interest in the health of others is rivaled only by the always observant Joseph Story.

   Although he acknowledged that judicial independence and institutional stability were important considerations, Miller nonetheless came to believe that impeachment by itself was an unsatisfactory way of removing judges who were unfit for office. As he once explained:

There are many matters which ought to be causes of removal that are neither treason, bribery, nor high crimes or misdemeanors. Physical infirmities for which a man is not to be blamed, but which may wholly unfit him for judicial duty, are of this class. Deafness, loss of sight, the decay of the faculties by reason of age, insanity, prostration by disease from which there is no hope of recovery—these should all be reasons for removal, rather than that the administration of justice should be obstructed or indefinitely postponed. . . . [A] vile and overbearing temper becomes sometimes in one long accustomed to the exercise of power unendurable to those who are subjected to its humors.[56]

A constitutional amendment would be necessary, he thought, to bring about the necessary change, although he never offered a specific draft of how it should be done.

Justice Miller's final illness was a matter of widespread national concern and interest, quite unlike the indifference often attending the final illnesses of his colleagues. On October 10, 1890, while coming home from the Court and still in the street outside his house, a stroke paralyzed his left side. Previously, a bout of dysentery (a not uncommon nineteenth-century ailment, given the state of water supplies) had somewhat weakened him that summer, but he had seemed to recover in due course. During the first day of paralysis Miller's mind remained clear, and he bantered easily with his doctors. Finally, when they told him to remain quiet because they feared he might overtax his brain, his response was, "That is a compliment for you must think that when I talk I use my brains."[57] But on the next day the paralysis of his left side deepened, and he sank into a coma. The end came as quickly and as painlessly as he might have wished for any of his own patients.

Joseph P. Bradley (1870–1892)

David Davis's replacement on the electoral commission of 1876 was Joseph P. Bradley, because he was judged to be the least partisan choice in the absence of Davis himself. He voted in favor of Rutherford B. Hayes in each case where the electoral votes were disputed, which for a while brought him a certain notoriety. He always thereafter stoutly denied any partisan motives, an assertion that was confirmed by his long and distinguished career on the Court.

Justice Bradley's work habits did not vary much over the years. He arose early and worked late. He made the following entry in his diary a year before his death. "5 1/2 a.m. My birthday. 78 years completed. Unable to work at my table last evening from somnolence. I rise early this morning to make up for lost time; as being conference time, I have many cases to master and decide. I have now been 21 years on the bench . . . and begin to be pretty tired with the awful hard work of the court."[58]

A cold weakened him the following winter, forcing him to miss frequent sessions of Court. His cold worsened, and he died on January 22, 1892, after an illness of one week.

Lucius Q. C. Lamar (1888–1893)

The next year the Court lost Lucius Q. C. Lamar, who had first had an attack of apoplexy serving in the Confederate Army encamped outside Richmond in 1861. Although his health forced him to leave the army, he soon joined the diplomatic corps and represented the Confederate cause in Europe as a special envoy to Russia. He never actually went to Russia, however, because of that government's lack of interest in his mission.

As a southerner committed to the reconciliation of the states after the Civil War, his political fortunes prospered. His health remained reasonably stable during years of elective office in both the U.S. Senate and House of Representatives, although there were reports of seizures in the 1880s when he was in the Senate and later when he was President Grover Cleveland's secretary of the interior. The nature of the "apoplexy" from which he periodically suffered strongly suggests epilepsy, but exact diagnosis remained unspecified.

Lamar's health began to fail in earnest in 1889, when he was sixty-four and had only been on the Court one year. When he did not regain his strength following an illness that winter, he wrote his sister that "two Doctors say, upon consultation, that one of the valves of my heart has ceased to act (I don't believe that)." Nonetheless, he remained very weak.[59]

He continued to do his work on the Court as best he could and even began to feel more optimistic about his health. The next winter he wrote his sister an encouraging summary of his situation:

> During the last preceding four days my health has been sensibly improving. Everyone has said all the time that I am *looking* better, but now I *feel* such a decided improvement that I have postponed my trip South until the 1st of February. Of course there is a very general protest among all my friends against this conclusion, but the work that is upon this Court is not a mere matter of sentimental duty; it is a hard reality; and if I, to give myself a respite and relief, should suspend my

share of it, I would be throwing upon my associates—some of whom are older and weaker than myself, and others more prostrated by sickness, who are staying here bravely at their post—an increase of the labor with which they are already burdened.[60]

Justice Lamar's circumstances changed dramatically between January, when he wrote to his sister, and April 3, when he wrote the following letter to President Cleveland: "I am too weak to scribble more. . . . I am sorry not to be able to give you a good account of my health. Have been down eleven days with frequent and copious hemorrhages, with no signs of an early recovery. I spend many of the silent and tedious hours of the night on my sick couch in thought of you, and in earnest aspirations for your happiness."[61]

His symptoms in the spring of 1892 suggested the possibility of tuberculosis, yet the lung hemorrhaging continued even when he went West to find drier air. His doctors failed to agree on a diagnosis. One believed his arteries and kidneys were degenerating. Another concluded he suffered from Bright's disease, a kidney ailment characterized by the presence of albumin in the urine. Whatever the correct diagnosis, Lamar clearly experienced both lung hemorrhaging and kidney difficulty.[62]

As winter approached, Lamar was discouraged about the progress he had made over the summer (as he told his sister, he had "not realized the sanguine hopes of restored health") and also about his future prospects as a member of the Court. He confided his thoughts about resignation to his sister: "I am in doubt, whether I ought to undertake that work or resign a position the duties of which I do not feel able to discharge with credit to myself and those I love, or in a manner due to the public interests concerned."[63] The matter resolved itself: Justice Lamar suffered a massive heart attack shortly before Christmas, while on a train headed for Mississippi. He was carried from the train at Atlanta and from there taken to Macon. He could go no farther; death came on January 23, 1893.

Even though he had formerly served as a soldier of the Confederacy, his commitment to the federal constitution as a jurist was unconditional, as shown by the circumstances of his funeral:

On January 27, 1893, after Justice Lucius Quintus Cincinnatus Lamar was buried on a hillcrest near the "turbid" Ocmulgee River in Macon, Georgia, the local newspaper added a poignant touch. "Justice Lamar had for many years carried in his inside vest pocket a small copy of the constitution of the United States. Next to the Bible, it was the book he loved the best, and he referred to it often. In life he was never without it, and yesterday the little book was buried with him. It lies close to the heart that loved its teachings and upheld its rights at all times."[64]

Samuel Blatchford (1882–1893)

By the following July, at the age of seventy-three, Samuel Blatchford was also dead. The scholarly and industrious Blatchford had been weakened by a series of strokes, the first occurring about a year before his death. He recovered sufficiently to resume work at the Court, but before leaving for Newport for summer vacation he had been stricken again by three smaller strokes. In this condition, his Newport holiday became a grim effort at convalescence. Three weeks before his death on July 7, 1893, he was subject to a fifth stroke. He was able to speak and maintain some mobility throughout his final ordeal.

Howell E. Jackson (1893–1895)

Howell E. Jackson experienced one of the shorter tenures in Court history. The Senate confirmed him on February 18, 1893, and he contracted tuberculosis a year later. In October 1894 he went West, hoping the drier air might improve his condition. The Supreme Court reheard the *Income Tax* case[65] in May 1895, so a very sick Jackson returned to Washington to cast his vote in favor of a national income tax statute. The vote went against him, even though his position eventually prevailed with the passage of the Sixteenth Amendment in 1913. Three months later, on August 8, 1895, he succumbed to tuberculosis at his home in Nashville, Tennessee.

Stephen J. Field (1863–1897)

The last resignation tendered in the nineteenth century was that of Stephen J. Field. Predictably, this colorful and determined personality grew more difficult and temperamental throughout his long tenure. A nagging knee injury he had suffered much earlier in life complicated his last years. The pain increased his nervous irritability, causing frequent outbursts of temper and an increased use of profanity in inappropriate situations (about which he was quite unremorseful). More practically, his game leg made it difficult for him to mount the bench. Field waved it all aside, reminding his solicitous friends that "I don't write my opinions with my leg."[66]

Rumors of Justice Field's pending resignation had swept the Court periodically over a good many years. First there was talk of resignation in 1888, but Field soon quarreled with President Cleveland, thereupon refusing to permit a president in whom he had lost confidence select his replacement. The same pattern repeated itself with President Benjamin Harrison. Then, of course, when Cleveland returned to power, Justice Field still retained his old animosity toward him. Moreover, Field had married late in life, and his wife was much younger than he was. She enjoyed the social activities in Washington and the attention she received as a justice's wife. She did not favor his resignation.

By the 1890s Field's mental condition was in noticeable decline. Once one of the workhorses of the Court, in 1895 he delivered only four opinions and had none at all the next year. Even more disturbing, it became apparent from his questions from the bench and from his conversations with the other justices that he could no longer function as he once had. He would forget how he had voted in conference and sink into long spells of lethargy.

Field's biographer tells how the justice's mind worked during these final years:

> Chief Justice Fuller sent two of his colleagues over to the Old Capitol home to present the materials which they had gathered on a case then before the Court, and to show how they arrived at the decision which they were about to adopt. They found Field in an unusually lethargic condition. He sat in a great arm chair, his head dropped forward on his breast, and his eyes closed. He stirred for a moment as he recognized his visitors, then again dropped his head and closed his eyes. Uncertain in what to do, his colleagues hesitantly took out their papers and asked if they might read them to him. Their host gave no assent nor denial, nor sign that he was any longer aware of the presence of his colleagues. Nevertheless one of them began to read the opinion which he had written. For some time Field gave no evidence that he heard. Then suddenly he raised his right hand. "Read that again," he commanded. The passage was read again. "That is not good law," he exclaimed. "You err when you say—" and here he launched into a clear and forceful argument which finally convinced his listeners that he was right. His argument completed, he lapsed into his former comatose condition. He showed no sign that he was aware when the two justices gathered up their papers and left the room.[67]

This incident was extraordinary but not unique. None can mistake the powerful lucidity of Field's concurring opinion in the first *Income Tax* case

Stephen J. Field was reluctant to leave until he set a longevity record. (Supreme Court, Office of the Curator)

of 1895.[68] It was an age when the justices wrote their own opinions, and there can be no doubt that Field was in full control of his material.

Nonetheless, as the situation continued to worsen, the other justices decided Field should be urged to resign. They requested that Justice John Marshall Harlan pay a call on Field and thereby advise him of the collective opinion of his colleagues. In such situations, diplomatic circumlocutions are not uncommon. Thus when Harlan began by cautiously reminding Field of his own visit with Justice Grier many years ago, the old gentleman roused himself one last time and spat out his memory of the occasion. "Yes!" he exclaimed. "And a dirtier day's work I never did in my life!"[69]

But time succeeded where Justice Harlan failed. The letter of resignation was finally secured in April 1897, although the resignation was not to take effect until December 1, by which time Field had served for thirty-four years, eight months, and twenty days. Justice Field attached importance to his record tenure, and it was only after he had eclipsed Chief Justice John Marshall's record of thirty-four years, five months, and five days that he was willing to seriously entertain the thought of leaving the Court.[70] He lingered on for an additional two years, until finally he took a chill while driving in the late winter air. Death came on April 9, 1899. He claimed to have seen visions shortly before he died.

From the Civil War to the end of the century the Supreme Court endured more personnel difficulty than at any other time in its history. Of the seven who resigned, only Strong did so voluntarily and in good health. Davis left exhausted and dissatisfied, Nelson, Swayne, and Hunt were in poor health, and Grier and Field suffered from mental disability. The late 1870s particularly were years when justices who were unable to adequately discharge their responsibilities were still unwilling to resign. Fortunately for the country less harm occurred than might reasonably have been anticipated, since there were relatively few cases of extraordinary constitutional importance where a disabled justice's vote was pivotal. Of course, there were some, and the first case to test the Legal Tender Acts, *Hepburn v. Griswold,*[71] is perhaps the best example. But even in that instance the other justices, knowing the importance of the case and the extent to which Justice Grier was incompetent to judge the issues, acted in a thoroughly responsible manner by rearguing the case after he was replaced.

There were many other cases in which Justices Clifford, Hunt, and Swayne participated as best they could, sometimes in a way deplored by their col-

leagues. As a practical matter, the illnesses of others placed a greater responsibility on the justices who were in good health and who were (like Miller,
Bradley, and Field) the major justices of the period. Ironically, the Court
lost so many sitting justices to ill health that the Court was renewed, much
to its advantage. In a little over a year three presidents—Hayes, Garfield,
and Arthur—appointed four remarkably able justices—William B. Woods,
Stanley Matthews, Horace Gray, and Samuel Blatchford. Justice Miller commented at the time that "the Court is as strong mentally and physically as
it ever was and is as capable of usefulness as it has ever been."[72] Academic
critics have agreed. As Charles Fairman observed from the perspective of the
1930s, "Looking back today it seems that perhaps at no other time has it
ever reached such a generally high level of distinction."[73]

There was a touch of inevitability about what happened to the Court.
Effective public pressure to which the justices might be sensitive did not
exist. Newspapers tended to ignore the personal circumstances of the justices, and medical knowledge—as witnessed by the uncertain and sometimes
fanciful diagnostic efforts of the doctors—was primitive even by the state of
knowledge at the time of the First World War.

Efforts by the other justices to encourage resignation, although the only
alternative, were also of uncertain usefulness in the absence of any focused
national attention directed toward the problem. As Chief Justice Waite discovered in the case of Justice Hunt, and as Justice Harlan learned from his
encounter with Justice Field, there is really nothing the Court collectively
can do to remove a colleague who is not amenable to peer group pressure.

Special problems arise where disabilities affect more than one justice. If a
single justice is seriously incapacitated for any length of time, the others can
absorb the workload with no institutional ill effect, at least for awhile. But
when more than one justice is disabled, their disabilities directly affect the
capacity of the institution to function as it should. In a five-justice majority,
for example, the vote of each of the prevailing justices is essential to the final
decision. When the number of participating justices declines, the degree of
responsibility is increased. It was only by chance that the justices who avoided
the most serious disabilities tended to be the ablest.

Justice Miller's concern about the practical problems of the period high-
lights the difficulty. During this time, especially, there was much to commend a constitutional amendment that would provide an alternative to
impeachment in the event of incapacitation. Something similar to the
Twenty-fifth Amendment, which presently controls presidential disability,
might have succeeded in removing disabled justices. In the nineteenth cen-

tury, such an amendment providing for a committee of physicians, selected by Congress with the concurrence of the chief justice or senior justice as the situation required, to inquire into the mental or physical health of a justice, with provision for the Congress to remove any justice if the committee's findings persuaded two-thirds of both houses of Congress that such action was appropriate, would surely have been worthy of serious consideration.

Too many nineteenth-century justices saw others with whom they worked on a daily basis stay on and on, and they too were disinclined to give up their life's work. When one searches for explanations, perhaps more striking than anything else is the strong sense of indispensability that emerges from so many of the justices. In this egoism, of course, they were far from unique; it was just that the frequency and duration of their illnesses were exceptional in the Court's history. As a famous physician of the twentieth century dispassionately concluded, "When [death] comes, you may be certain you will disappear like all the rest and that you will not be missed, nearly as much as in your sanguine moments you have been inclined to suppose."[74] The nineteenth-century justices—like most of humankind—found this truism hard to accept.

4

THE COURT IN PROSPERITY AND DEPRESSION, 1900–1936

When Justice Joseph McKenna asked Chief Justice William Howard Taft whether the Court had the authority to end his term, Taft's response was, "Of course not."[1] The other justices could only convey their view, through the chief justice, that McKenna was no longer able to do the work expected of him.

Justices who did not meet the pension requirements and who were ill, like William Moody and Mahlon Pitney, could also be encouraged to leave by Congress through the passage of a special bill. When Congress chose to extend the benefits of the Judiciary Act of 1869 in given cases, passage of the bill was always conditional on a prompt retirement. Altogether, eight of the justices who resigned from the Court between 1900 and 1937 left with pension benefits.

Only Charles Evans Hughes and John H. Clarke resigned without a pension. Hughes resigned when nominated by the Republicans to run for the presidency against Woodrow Wilson. Clarke became disenchanted with the work of the Court and left before his pension had vested. Of the other resignations, only Shiras left voluntarily; Gray, Day, Taft, and Holmes all experienced declining health.

This period was the first in Court history in which there were more resignations than deaths. Even then, for justices over the age of seventy, deaths exceeded resignations by one. Moreover, two of those resignations involved men older than eighty (McKenna and Holmes), so there was still enormous reluctance to step aside at age seventy or even seventy-five.

Although health reports were more sophisticated than they were in the nineteenth century, medical knowledge during the first third of the twentieth century was still primitive by present standards. Nonetheless, in most of the cases the medical problem is clear enough, even if few and often no useful remedy existed.

Table 4.1
Age of Death or Retirement, 1900–1936

Age	Died	Resigned
54 or younger	0	1
55–59	1	1
60–64	1	1
65–69	0	1
70–74	4	4
75–79	3	0
80 or older	0	2
Totals	9	10

Average age of those leaving the Court: 70

Source: Elder Witt, ed., *Congressional Quarterly's Guide to the U.S. Supreme Court,* 2d ed. (Washington, D.C.: Congressional Quarterly Press, 1990).

Horace Gray (1882–1902)

On July 9, 1902, at the age of seventy-four and after twenty years of service on the Supreme Court, Horace Gray informed President Theodore Roosevelt of his resignation. A bachelor most of his life, Gray married Justice Stanley Matthews's daughter when he was sixty-one.[2] Although his marriage seemed a happy one, his final decade on the Court was "spotted with illness and flagging energy."[3] Standing six feet, four inches tall, his once formidable frame became incapacitated by partial paralysis, which he had suffered some months before his resignation.

Gray resigned when it became apparent he could not recover and died shortly thereafter, on September 15, 1902, with paralysis given as the cause of death. It was reported that "Not until two years ago, when he was ill, did the regularity of his work on the bench suffer any interruption, and then he would not permit any slight indisposition to keep him from the courtroom. A few months ago he suffered a stroke of apoplexy, and from this he never sufficiently recovered to be able to resume his duties."[4]

George Shiras Jr. (1892–1903)

There was another vacancy a year later. George Shiras Jr. had determined at the time of his appointment in 1892 at the age of sixty that he would leave when he was seventy. He was one of the very few justices to make such an explicit promise. In the summer of 1902, Shiras told President Theodore

Roosevelt that he would resign early in the following year.[5] He was just past seventy-one when he left the Court. He was also one of the relatively few justices to leave in excellent health.

Shiras lived another twenty years in leisurely retirement, dying on August 2, 1924, at the age of ninety-two. He traveled frequently between homes in Florida, where he wintered, and Marquette, in northern Michigan near Lake Superior. He lived quietly and attracted little attention, with one exception. In 1913 he publicly indicated that he thought the $12,000 salary then paid to members of the Supreme Court was enough. Congress was at the time considering a pay increase for the Court that was passed despite Shiras's comments. He remained in good mental and physical health until he died of pneumonia after fracturing his leg in a fall five weeks earlier.[6]

Henry Billings Brown (1890–1906)

Henry Billings Brown, best known today as the author of the Court's opinion sustaining racial segregation in *Plessy v. Ferguson,*[7] resigned from the Court in 1906 because of neuritis (an inflammation of the nerves that, when it occurs in the eye, often leads to a degenerative condition). His vision difficulties became apparent to the public as early as December 1903, when reports appeared that he was nearly without sight in one eye and that this situation had existed for nearly two years.[8] Brown dictated all of his work, as he had accustomed himself to having his law clerk[9] and members of his family read to him. At the same time it also became known that he was expected to lose the sight of his other eye within a matter of days.[10] Nonetheless, he refused to consider leaving the Court until his retirement vested, which was another two years.

When Justice Brown did resign at age seventy in 1906, after fifteen years of service, he had recovered some of his vision. He had "placed himself under the care of expert oculists and submitted religiously to their mandate that he should not use his eyes and should remain for a certain length of time in a dark room, and after one or two operations his sight was partially restored."[11]

Ten years earlier, when Justice Stephen J. Field was still on the Court in an impaired condition, Brown had told a friend from Pittsburgh of the many difficulties Field had created by his unwillingness to step aside and concluded, "When I get to be seventy, if I don't resign from the bench, I want you to come to Washington and kick me off it." On the Friday Brown turned seventy, his friend called on him in Washington. When Brown, who was pleased but somewhat surprised to see him, asked why he was in town, his friend replied: "I have come to remind you of a conversation we had ten years ago. This is your seventieth birthday, and I have come to comply with the instructions you gave me then." Brown then recalled what he had said and reacted with good humor.[12]

In retirement Brown lived on with no impairment of his mental faculties until he died of a heart condition on September 4, 1913. His health had begun to fail during his last year or two of life, but he had not become seriously ill until two weeks before his death. He died in New York City, at the Hotel Gramatan, with his wife beside him.[13]

Rufus W. Peckham (1895–1909)

On October 24, 1909, three years after Justice Brown's resignation, Rufus W. Peckham died at age seventy-one while still a member of the Court. Death occurred at his father's country residence near Altamont, New York. The day before he died, friends reported he was able to sit up and was described as "fairly easy and comfortable," even though it was understood he was in no condition to return to the Court.[14] Peckham had suffered from heart disease for the preceding six years, and his angina pectoris was complicated by malfunctioning kidneys (Bright's disease) and hardening of the arteries.[15]

The condition of Peckham's health had not been widely known. It was not until the year of his death that Justice White had advised the attorney general, George W. Wickersham, of the situation. The attorney general thereupon sent the following information to President Taft:

> Justice White drew me aside just before the court opened this morning and told me in the strictest confidence to be shared only with you that Justice Peckham's illness is angina pectoris, and that the end may come at any time. He says that the Justice has no idea that he is seriously ill. But, he said, "the condition of this court is such that any vacancy which occurs ought to be filled at the earliest moment and I want the President to know of this impending event. So that he may have all the more time to think of a successor." He again asked me not to bring any important cause before the Court as at present constituted.[16]

The funeral was held on October 27 at St. Peter's Episcopal Church in Albany with Chief Justice Melville W. Fuller and the associate justices present as honorary pallbearers. Peckham was laid in a purple casket, surrounded by elaborate displays of flowers. There was no eulogy, only the Episcopal service for the dead. Just before the Court left together from the Ten Eyck Hotel to the church, Chief Justice Fuller said: "I am in a condition of mind that John Bright was when he rose in the House of Commons to speak in reference to the death of Mr. Cobden. He exclaimed: 'I never knew how much I loved him until I lost him.'"[17] Although the newspapers reported the fulsome eulogies delivered by colleagues and former associates, Peckham's passing seemed to leave scarcely a mark on the public consciousness and since then remarkably little has been written about him.[18]

David J. Brewer (1889–1910)

The following year, 1910, brought substantial change to the Court, with two deaths and a resignation. Justice Field's nephew, David J. Brewer, was the first to die. The seventy-three-year-old justice was in good health prior to the massive stroke (or apoplexy as it was then called) that struck him at 10:30 on the night of March 28 while he was at his Sixteenth Street home in Washington. The circumstances were as follows:

> He was preparing to retire and had disrobed. He went to the bathroom, and had been there but a moment or two when Mrs. Brewer heard the sound of a fall. She ran to the room and found her husband lying unconscious on the floor. She telephoned to Judge Ashley M. Gould of the Supreme Court of the District of Columbia, who live[ed] in the neighborhood. Judge Gould ran at once to the Brewer house and picked up the Justice and carried him to his bedroom. Justice Brewer was still breathing, but did not regain consciousness.[19]

Two doctors were summoned, but Brewer was dead before they could arrive. His death was immediately seen as unsettling, since his death so closely followed that of Peckham. And both Chief Justice Fuller and Justice John Marshall Harlan were older than seventy-seven. Moreover, since the death occurred close to the end of the term, there was speculation as to how the cases would be affected. Justice Moody had missed part of the term because of "rheumatism," leaving an eight-member Court with the possibility it might deadlock.[20] As it turned out, the *Standard Oil* case, which evoked the most concern, required reargument in the next term and was then decided by an 8 to 1 vote.[21]

Justice Brewer's remains were carried by rail back to Leavenworth, Kansas, where a service was held at the First Congregational Church. Those in attendance included the Leavenworth Bar Association, which marched together to the funeral.[22] He was buried at Mount Muncie Cemetery in nearby Lansing beside his daughter and first wife.

Melville W. Fuller (Chief Justice: 1888–1910)

Chief Justice Melville W. Fuller, at age seventy-eight, found the 1909 October term difficult to get through. Justice Moody had been incapacitated, Peckham died in October, and Brewer died the following March. For the first time, the chief justice began to show his age. He became unsteady on his feet. After Fuller's death, Justice Holmes wrote, "I never thought that the time had come when it would be wise for him to resign until this last term."[23]

Rumors about Fuller's health, quite unfounded, were widespread from about 1902, when Theodore Roosevelt may have wished to appoint Taft to the chief justiceship. During the last eight years of his life, Fuller reacted negatively to any suggestion in the newspapers that he resign. He was, he once told Holmes, "not to be paragraphed" out of his place.[24] President William Howard Taft, who was eager to have him replaced, said Fuller had confused the oath of office in 1909 and had unwittingly made him swear "to execute" the constitution instead of supporting and defending it.[25] That same year, President Taft told Judge Horace Lurton, "Really the Chief Justice is almost senile."[26]

On July 4, 1910, Chief Justice Fuller suffered a sudden heart attack while at his summer home in Sorrento, Maine. He was only able to call out to his daughter and say, "I am feeling very ill." He died before a doctor, who was three miles away, could arrive by automobile.[27] A funeral train left Boston, carrying the body back to Chicago for burial, accompanied by Justices Holmes and McKenna.[28] In Chicago, where the body was laid in repose in the Virginia Hotel for an hour, Justices Lurton, White, and Day joined the burial party.[29]

After Fuller's death, Holmes wrote about the circumstances to a friend, Baroness Moncheur: "The Chief died at just the right moment, for during the last term he had begun to show his age in his administrative work, I thought, and I was doubting whether I ought to speak to his family as they relied on me."[30] However, as Fuller's biographer emphasizes, Holmes's comment does not suggest any deficiencies in the opinions; only Fuller's administrative work was affected by his decline in vitality.

After twenty-two years as chief justice, Fuller had served in that position

longer than anyone except John Marshall and Roger Brooke Taney. Holmes
always evaluated his old friend charitably. "The Chief had outlived most of
his contemporaries," he wrote, "and I think the public will not realize what
a great man it has lost."[31]

William H. Moody (1906–1910)

That same year William H. Moody resigned from the Court. Much neglected
now, the former navy secretary and attorney general was an important and
dynamic player on the political stage in his day.[32] He was a close friend of
President Roosevelt, who had placed him on the Court when he was a vigorous fifty-three. But he stayed only four years. Of the 4,500 cases decided
during his tenure, he was able to participate in about 1,000 of them.[33] He
seemed in good health during his first two terms of service, but his affliction—described at the time as acute rheumatism but in fact probably a variant of Lou Gehrig's disease (chronic inflammatory polyneuropathy)—came
upon him slowly at first and then with debilitating suddenness.[34] It affected
his entire body, and eventually he was unable to leave his bed. He left the
Court on November 10, 1910, and was given retirement benefits by the
Congress.[35] A devastated Roosevelt called Moody's departure "a real calamity from the public standpoint."[36]

There was understandably concern and interest within the Court about
Moody's abrupt decline. The following letter from Justice John Marshall
Harlan to Justice Horace Lurton reveals much about the Court's internal
situation.

> Dear Judge:
>   A recent letter from Moody to myself contains this paragraph:
>   "As for me, the less said the better. Fourteen months on my back
> still finds me there with no improvement. The doctors promise and
> promise and apparently believe but I am sure they cannot bring me
> out a strong enough man to assume my duties within five months and
> I ought not for a moment to think of more. I should retire at the
> beginning of the October term so that the Court would no longer be
> embarrassed by my vacant seat, if it would do any good. But the Presi-
> dent would not nominate and the Senate would not recognize an ap-
> pointment made without its confirmation, so that I might as well take
> the month or so more, if I am making any progress at all, although
> hope has fled from my breast. The best that I can expect is to get up

William Moody probably had Lou Gehrig's disease. (Supreme Court, Office of the Curator)

a crippled man and perhaps with shattered health which would not enable me to do a full man's work and a man on the Supreme Court ought to be able to do a full man's work."

This is all very sad.

I earnestly hope that you will be none the worse in health for the trip to Chicago and back. My age, general condition, heat and the length of the journey absolutely forbade my going with you. My own belief is that the trip to Chicago and back to Washington, then to Sorrento, was, primarily, the cause of the Chief's sickness and death. The complimentary things said by the papers about his career and character must be gratifying to all of his friends. Perhaps, it will be best to regard what Moody says as confidential. I thought it best to let you know how he regarded his present condition and what was his purpose under the recent retirement statute.

Our regards to Mrs. Lurton and the children.

Truly yours,[37]

Moody lived on for another seven years, unable to use his limbs or even hold a book or pen. However, with the assistance of his sister, his only family, he was able to retain some of his earlier interests. "I read a great deal about public affairs," he wrote a college classmate in 1916, "all the decisions of the Supreme Court as they are delivered, much history, biography, and other literature. Or rather, all these things are read to me, for I can neither read nor write myself."[38] He lived in a state of total dependence until he mercifully died at age sixty-four on July 2, 1917, at one o'clock in the morning. Throughout the ordeal of his illness his mental powers had remained unimpaired.[39] Funeral services were held in the family home at Haverhill, Massachusetts, with President Taft (with whom Moody had served in Roosevelt's cabinet), along with Chief Justice White and Justice Holmes standing beside the casket.[40]

John Marshall Harlan (1877–1911)

John Marshall Harlan, the Court's oldest member at age seventy-eight, was reported ill with acute bronchitis on October 13, 1911. The situation was described as "grave" because of Harlan's age.[41] He had seemed in robust health, and over his lengthy career (only John Marshall and Stephen J. Field had served longer) he was seldom absent. A bout of influenza some years earlier was his only important illness.[42]

Harlan had been on the bench the previous Monday, the day the new term began. The next day, Chief Justice White, "announcing that Justice Harlan was slightly ill, asked attorneys to consider him present in spirit."[43] When his cold turned rapidly into a serious case of bronchitis, his family gathered around him during the night. He died on October 14, at 8:13 A.M.; his ambiguous last words were: "Good-by; I am sorry I kept you all waiting so long."[44] There is no record of the tone of voice in which these words were spoken.[45]

Harlan was a strong Presbyterian and had even considered leaving the Court to dedicate his efforts toward the advancement of his church.[46] Perhaps because of his fervent religiosity, the press reported the following story:

> Justice Harlan was very fond of the late Justice Peckham. The latter twitted him about his Presbyterian predilections, and in turn was twitted about being a Democrat. On one occasion Justice Harlan was explaining to his brethren on the bench that he would be forced to absent himself from court on the following day to attend a Presbyterian Conference.
>
> "You are such a good Presbyterian, Harlan," said Justice Peckham, "that I don't see why you are afraid to die."
>
> "I would not be afraid," responded Justice Harlan, "if I were sure that in the next world I would not turn up at Democratic headquarters."[47]

Only members of the immediate family and the Supreme Court attended services at the Harlan home in Washington. However, there were so many requests for a public service that the family relented and permitted a second, public service. The Court acted as pallbearers at the church. Afterward the Bible class that Justice Harlan had taught for many years escorted the casket to Rock Creek Cemetery, where he was buried.[48]

Immediately after his death, Harlan's reputation seemed secure. His contemporaries viewed him as a major jurist, although there was, perhaps, a hint of darkness in the following exchange. "I am much grieved at Harlan's death," Justice William R. Day wrote to Justice Horace H. Lurton. "Our intimacy was close and cordial and he was a friend without limits to his good will and kindness of heart. I am sorry he did some things toward the end, but this will not change the universal feeling that he was a great and good man, as indeed he was."[49]

It was, of course, not long before a more negative reaction set in. Whether it was because of the influence of conservative Court historians like Charles Warren—who disliked Harlan's views on race and monopolies—or the disparaging remarks of some of his contemporaries, most prominently Justices Holmes and Brewer (and later Justice Felix Frankfurter), it is apparent that Harlan's importance declined until the 1950s when the Warren Court encouraged a reexamination of his contemporary relevance.[50] Justice Holmes thought Harlan's mind "a powerful vise the jaws of which couldn't be got nearer than two inches to each other." He also wrote, referring to Harlan, "that sage although a man of real power, did not shine either in analysis or generalization."[51]

The death of Harlan brought to a close an extraordinary period of Court change. Beginning with Peckham's death in October 1909 and concluding with Harlan's death in October 1911, the Court had lost five justices.

Horace H. Lurton (1909–1914)

President Taft's colleague from his former years on the U.S. Court of Appeals for the Sixth Circuit, Horace H. Lurton, was only in his third term on the Court when in December 1913 he became ill with pneumonia and asthma.[52] Although he was seventy years old, he showed no interest in leaving. Instead, he took a few weeks off, went to Florida with his family, and seemed to recover. He took his seat again in April and participated fully in the Court's work.

Although no longer in the White House, Taft, his friend and patron, remained as concerned as ever about who should be on the Supreme Court. He wrote the following to Lurton and took the occasion to discourage any thoughts of resignation.

> President Wilson's control over Congress is something very wonderful. He has developed more qualities as a politician than I ever suspected he had, and he is a man of very great ability in expression and in carrying out a purpose. . . . I don't like his appointments, and I sincerely hope that there will be no vacancy on the Bench any sooner than it has to come. The influence that Bryan exerts over him in the matter of appointment is very detrimental to the interests of the Government, and no one could tell the man whom he would put on the Bench. He has not as yet shown any of the dangerous tendencies of Roosevelt with

respect to the judiciary, on general principles, but he is such an opportunist that I would be afraid to trust him were a political consideration to figure at all in either the selection of a Judge or in the treatment of a judicial decision. I would much prefer him to Roosevelt and hope that he will succeed himself unless we can get a decent Republican. I can write confidentially to you on the subject. You say that he has manifested no sort of cordiality or intimacy with the Judges of the Court. I don't think he does to anyone.[53]

Apparently Lurton seemed better that winter while vacationing in Miami, Florida. Justice Day, with whom he maintained a correspondence, wrote to him as follows:

I have been delighted with the fine reports of your progress to good health and vigor and that strength which has always been yours. I feel sure you are coming back to us in your old form and that soon. Let me, however, drop a word of caution—for you know the efficiency of a word to the wise.

It is this—don't hurry. And when you come, approach Washington by easy stages. The weather is very bad, and, my experience is that March is here, as elsewhere, a trying month.[54]

Lurton did not survive long thereafter, as the following events soon took place:

On the first of July, the Lurtons arrived in Atlantic City for another period of total relaxation. The ocean air seemed to have restorative effects, as the aging Justice enjoyed spending the long days sitting and strolling the boardwalk. After returning from his nightly walk on July 11 in excellent spirits, Lurton retired about 9 P.M., only to be awakened in great pain a few hours later. His wife immediately summoned a physician, but the cardiac damage had been severe. The death watch continued over four difficult hours before the end came at 5 A.M. on the twelfth of July, 1914.[55]

A funeral train took Lurton's body back to Clarksville, Tennessee, where, with Chief Justice White in attendance at the Episcopal Church, thousands of people paid their respects to his memory.[56]

Horace Lurton's health failed rapidly after his friend Taft appointed him. (Supreme Court, Office of the Curator)

Joseph R. Lamar (1910–1916)

A year earlier, when Joseph R. Lamar returned to Washington for the October term, persons observed that he did not seem himself. As his biographer described the situation:

> He began the winter's work with less than his usual vigor. His work no longer came to him easily, and he could not forget it during his rare hours of recreation. The eagerness with which he habitually attacked any congenial work; the careful and painstaking methods that were characteristic of him, took on a new phase. He began to drive himself to the completion of his tasks. He was feverishly anxious to do the best that was humanly possible, to put all the strength that was in him into every line that he wrote. His friends understood now what lay behind this abnormal activity, and realize that the serious affection of the heart, which was gradually sapping his strength, and which brought his life to an untimely end, was responsible . . .[57]

Lamar delivered five opinions from the bench on the last day of the 1914 term, June 21. However, Mrs. Lamar did not mention any of them in her diary; she mentioned only that her husband was very tired.[58] When the family left Washington for the summer and settled at White Sulphur Springs in Georgia, the justice seemed to improve. But when he traveled to Augusta later that same month, he returned to White Sulphur Springs exhausted.[59] It seems apparent that Lamar suffered from hypertension. He experienced his first stroke in early September while sitting on the porch of his cottage, when he found he had difficulty raising his left arm. The moment passed and he refused to send for a doctor. But when the paralysis returned, a doctor was summoned, and there was an awareness of what had taken place. The next day the fifty-seven-year-old Lamar wrote to Chief Justice White:

> I left Washington very much under the weather, and have been in the hands of the doctor all summer. I did not write you, because I did not wish to worry you. But now that I am much worse, I prefer that you should hear from me, instead of from the papers, what my condition is.
>
> When I got here, the doctor found that for years, unknown to myself, I had been suffering from considerable enlargement of the heart. That, in connection with high blood pressure, made it necessary for

me to take the baths. They seemed to benefit me very much, and to reduce the pressure. Yesterday I had what I thought was a stroke, but which he says was a clogging of some of the veins in the brain, which has resulted in a numbing or partial paralysis of the left leg and arm.

I am now in bed and suffering great inconvenience, but no acute pain. The doctor talks more encouragingly than I feel, and says that he thinks I can be up and about within a week or two. I am not so sure as he seems to be; but inexpressibly mortified at what seems to me to be helpless—and I fear will be useless—days for the remainder of a short life. Of course the prime regret is the fear that my incapacity will put more work upon others who are already carrying tremendously heavy burdens. . . .

I write with perfect frankness, because I feel that you should know the very worst, and should learn it from me, rather than from any one else. I have been silent as long as I have because I had the most encouraging reports from my doctors; and until this last incident, I myself expected to go back to Washington stronger than when I came, and as well fitted to work as ever before.[60]

Lamar was brought back to Washington. Although initially bedridden, he slowly began to recover and after awhile was able to get about with the use of a cane. Eventually, he was able to use his left arm without pain and could visit with some of his friends. His goal was to return to the Court by January 3, 1916. However, in December he contracted a severe cold and took a decided turn for the worse. He seemed to rally but then died suddenly at his home on Sunday evening, January 2. He had been fifty-eight for only a couple of months. Since he had not been eligible for retirement benefits, there had been rumors Congress might be willing to pass a private bill for him as it had for Justice Moody, but nothing ever happened.

Charles Evans Hughes (1910–1916)

That summer, on June 10 in Chicago, Charles Evans Hughes received the Republican nomination for president on the third ballot. He resigned from the Court the same day. He had completed nearly six terms of service.[61] Apparently his colleagues did not begrudge him his turn at electoral politics. As Justice Holmes wrote to him: "Your first thought was of duty. I must confess that pretty near the first with me was the loss to the Court and especially to me. I shall miss you very much in every way, so much that I wish the needs of the country could have been postponed until I am out of the business."[62]

Edward Douglass White (1894–1910; Chief Justice: 1910–1921)

When Warren G. Harding won the presidency in 1920, William Howard Taft made the trip to Marion, Ohio, along with many other job seekers, to make certain the president-elect knew of his interest in the chief justiceship.[63] Unfortunately for Taft, Edward Douglass White had not the slightest intention of retiring from the post he had held since 1910 when Taft had made the appointment. Taft was much annoyed, because he believed White had understood that the chief justiceship had been given to him provisionally until Taft could assume the position himself.[64] Whatever may have been hinted at earlier, this view clearly was not White's. However, in late 1920 Taft was told that the chief justice "looked very feeble and it seemed . . . that he might soon retire."[65] So in March 1921, Taft went to visit White in order to appraise the situation for himself. White assured him he was in excellent health except for his cataracts, but even those were not considered career-threatening. At age seventy-six, White was not budging.

But White had not been entirely truthful with Taft. In fact, he had been suffering from gall bladder disease for some time and had delayed an operation, which for a grossly overweight man of his age was not minor surgery. His voice faltered as he announced his last opinion from the bench on May 15. As it happened, he was stricken the very next day and forced to undergo an emergency operation.[66] At first it appeared he might survive it, for his pulse and temperature were normal, but he suddenly began to experience acute heart irregularities. He died three days later.[67] The way to the center chair was unexpectedly open for William Howard Taft.

John H. Clarke (1916–1922)

Three justices left the Court in 1922. The first resignation, on September 18, came as a complete surprise. Although John H. Clarke was sixty-five, he was in generally good health except for some difficulty with his hearing and was, along with Justice Louis D. Brandeis, one of the two liberal justices appointed by President Woodrow Wilson. He had served only six years. Clarke gave several reasons for leaving the Court, the principal one being his desire to work for world peace and U.S. participation in the League of

Nations. In addition, he was depressed over the death of his two sisters. A bachelor, he had been close to both. But very likely the most important consideration was that he had grown weary of the Court's work. He had increasingly come to believe much of it was of limited importance, especially when he found himself at odds with Justice Brandeis and at complete odds with President Wilson's other appointee, the irascible James C. McReynolds.[68]

Clarke communicated a sense of this frustration in a letter to Brandeis when he wrote, "I should die happier if I should do all that is possible to promote the entrance of our government into the League of Nations than if I continued to devote my time to determining whether a drunken Indian had been deprived of his land before he died or whether the digging of a ditch in Iowa was constitutional or not." The triviality of some of the cases appalled him. "Unless he sits on the bench of the Supreme Court and hears day after day the astonishing discussions and distinctions here presented," he said, "no man can fully realize the extent to which ingenuity and refinement of constitutional discussion are rapidly converting the members of our profession in this country into a group of casuists rivaling the Middle Age schoolmen in subtlety of distinction and futility of argument."[69]

McReynolds, in a display of churlishness, refused to sign Clarke's letter of tribute from the Court, just as he later was unwilling to sign similar letters when Benjamin Cardozo and Louis Brandeis resigned.[70] Clarke's letter of response to his colleagues was so frank and uninhibited about his delight in leaving that Chief Justice Taft urged him to rewrite it for the formal record.[71] He was equally impolitic when he told his successor, George Sutherland, that he was about to commence a "dog's life" as a member of the Court.[72]

Clarke had no need to work. Referring to money, he told the press that he had "attended to that long ago" when he had practiced law in Ohio for some thirty years.[73] He died in his sleep of a heart attack during the night of March 22, 1945, at the age of eighty-seven at his apartment in the El Cortez Hotel in San Diego, where he had made his retirement.[74]

His life in retirement followed a rigid pattern. He appeared for breakfast punctually at seven in the morning, with hotel personnel sounding the inevitable, "Good morning, Mr. Justice."[75] Thereafter, Clarke could be seen taking his morning walk, always wearing a dark suit, derby hat, and walking cane; this pastime would be followed by his correspondence or reading or any meeting required by his business investments. He would then dine at his luncheon club, attended by a group of men interested in reading.[76] Baseball games in the afternoons were an important part of his leisure. He ate alone in the evening and, after a game of solitaire or some more reading, would retire early.

During those twenty-three years of retirement Clarke lived mostly in political obscurity. His last public appearance was in 1937 when he made a nationwide broadcast in support of President Roosevelt's plan to add additional members to the Court.[77] He said the proposal was constitutional. That same year, when Justice Willis Van Devanter resigned, he wrote the following rather revealing letter:

My dear Judge Van Devanter:

Judging from my experience, it is wise in you to lay the burden down while you still have physical and mental strength to enjoy leisure and to reflect upon the eternal mysteries—even though insolvable—before the night comes down. The last year, with its differences upon so many questions, must have been desperately unpleasant and I have often thanked my stars, or Fate, that such an experience as you have been through was spared me.

You have forgotten it, my dear judge, but I remember it as if yesterday, how, shortly after I went to Washington, you and I were walking down from the Capitol one evening when you said, "Judge, undoubtedly your have already heard the supposed typical experience of a new member of the Court." When I said I had not, you continued, "it runs like this; that the newcomer looking about him always thinks, 'How in the world did I ever get here,' but that at the end of the first year he asks himself, 'How in the world did these other fellows ever get here.' There must have been more of reality lurking in this little bit of satire than I thought at the time, or I should not remember it at this late day.

The papers say you have purchased a farm in Virginia not far from Washington where you intend to live. I was in hopes that you would locate out here in the sunshine and that we might at least occasionally meet and renew our pleasant friendship and talk over the great adventure which life has been to both of us.

I have lived here now nearly six years and I have never once regretted what seemed at the time a somewhat radical change for one at my time of life. I have enjoyed very good health and my association, particularly with a luncheon group of lawyers and retired Army men, has been extremely pleasant. They are all reading men and the talk is often very worthwhile and usually very interesting.

No doubt with your experience of the West you have considered the question of climate as well as of associates and have decided against us, so that I must be reconciled.

Hoping that you keep well, and that you may live as long as you are physically and mentally comfortable—but not longer—believe me always,

Sincerely yours,[78]

Clarke did not live to see the creation of the United Nations the following summer, but he had become increasingly disillusioned about the prospects for world peace during the last year of his life when he also suffered increasingly from deafness and the infirmities of age. He had never joined a church, so no religious ceremonies were performed. The body was cremated, a Masonic funeral service was held, and the remains were buried in Lisbon, Ohio, where his ashes were put to rest beside his parents and his sisters. He had been as meticulous about his funeral arrangements as he had been about the routine of his daily life.[79]

William R. Day (1903–1922)

A month after Clarke resigned from the Court, William R. Day also decided to leave. The diminutive former secretary of state[80] (who had left that position to take a judgeship with Taft and Lurton on the U.S. Court of Appeals for the Sixth Circuit in 1899) had been on the Supreme Court since President Roosevelt placed him there at the age of fifty-four in 1903. In declining health, he was seventy-three years old when he left, and after twenty years the Court's workload had lost its attractiveness. He accepted President Harding's appointment to the American-German Claims Commission but found that too taxing as well and resigned in May 1923.

Day died on July 9, 1923, at 5:30 A.M. at his summer home on Mackinac Island, Michigan, where he had gone with his eldest son for the summer. He was critically ill for about ten days with lung congestion. He had suffered an attack of pneumonia in Washington three years earlier and at his age and in the absence of antibiotics had never fully recovered from the bacterial infection.[81]

Mahlon Pitney (1912–1922)

Mahlon Pitney—the sixth and last of President Taft's appointments—was the third justice to leave in 1922. While he served he was a workhorse, participating in "all but nineteen of the 2,412 decisions handed down during his service."[82] Moreover, he was almost always with the majority, with 244 Court opinions and only nineteen dissents and five concurrences.[83]

Justice Pitney suffered a severe stroke in August 1922. A month later newspapers reported he was a patient in a sanitarium in Morristown, New Jersey. Although his condition was described as serious, no details were provided.[84] By October 31 it was apparent that Pitney was in no condition to return to work. When there was no evidence of any improvement, members of Congress began to consider a private retirement bill for him, similar to the one they passed for Justice Moody. Even though he had been a justice for nearly eleven years, Pitney was only sixty-four.[85]

Although he showed some improvement and left the hospital on November 22, Congress passed the retirement bill on December 4. His doctors provided certificates that indicated he suffered from "cerebral arteria scierosis [sic] and chronic nephritis," and that he had had a mild cerebral thrombosis. Any attempt to undertake serious employment would, his family physician testified, worsen his condition.[86] President Harding signed the bill, and Pitney tendered his resignation on December 16, to become effective on January 1.[87]

Pitney lived only another year in retirement. For a time he was able, with assistance, to move about, and he remained conscious throughout. But a physical deterioration soon became apparent, and he was bedridden during the last six months of his life.[88] He died on December 9, 1924, at his Washington home.

Joseph McKenna (1898–1925)

Joseph McKenna's long tenure on the Supreme Court proved as difficult for him as was his passing from the Court. After only a year as President McKinley's attorney general, he was chosen to succeed Justice Field. He was so aware of his limitations that he voluntarily enrolled at the Columbia University Law School in New York in order to improve his legal knowledge. It was to little avail. As his biographer reports, "In his early years on the bench he was frequently irritable, nervous and rather unhappy because he was not familiar with the law nor able to construct an opinion that would adequately express the convictions of his colleagues."[89]

As McKenna neared his eightieth birthday, although his carriage remained ramrod straight, his mental alertness began to decline.[90] He sometimes missed the point of what a case was about, which caused Chief Justice Taft great consternation. Opinions had to be returned to him to be reworked, and even then they were seldom satisfactory and sometimes had to be reassigned to some other justice. As Taft wrote to his brother, "I don't know what course to take with respect to him, or what cases to assign to him. I had to take back a case from him last Saturday because he would not write it in accordance with the vote of the Court."[91]

McKenna's wife died in 1924, and his own situation worsened. His vote seemed to depend on who spoke with him last. The Court finally decided in 1924 that no case would be decided because of McKenna's vote, which had the practical effect of paralyzing the Court in 4 to 4 ties.[92]

In a confidential memorandum, Chief Justice Taft revealed the circumstances under which he had secured McKenna's promise to resign.[93] Taft first checked with McKenna's physician, who "concurred with [the Court] that his mental grasp was by no means such as it had been." Knowing he had to raise the question of resignation with McKenna, Taft tried to enlist the support of McKenna's son, Major Frank McKenna, who seemed to understand the situation and agreed to say nothing of the Court's concerns to his father. Nevertheless, shortly thereafter he apparently did take the news directly to his father, which predictably enough resulted in a telephone call in which McKenna asked for an immediate appointment with Taft.

To Taft's dismay, McKenna seemed disposed to argue the question of his ability to perform his work in an adequate fashion. Taft was diplomatic but candid with him. McKenna did say that he "thought it was a hard time to have it come to him just after his bereavement." "I concluded," Taft wrote, "it was wiser not to enter into that discussion and did not say to him, what of course is the fact, that for two years the situation has been such that we have felt it a violation of our duty not to speak earlier."[94] McKenna finally agreed to resign in January of the next year, with the understanding he would be assigned a few cases between then (November) and his resignation. Taft tried to discourage this demand but eventually yielded because he had managed, gracefully and with tact, to obtain McKenna's promise of resignation.

McKenna remained in Washington, and on November 21, 1926, the eighty-three-year-old justice passed away in his sleep at his Washington home, with his son and three daughters by his bedside.[95] He had been in failing heath for about three weeks.[96]

Edward T. Sanford (1923–1930)

Edward T. Sanford died at his Washington home on March 8, 1930, shortly after he had been carried there from his dentist's office. His death was both

A mentally impaired Joseph McKenna was asked to leave by his colleagues. (Supreme Court, Office of the Curator)

startling and unexpected. The sixty-four-year-old justice, who seemed in excellent health, had spent the previous day as usual on the bench attending to business.

Sanford's appearance of good health may have been partly illusory. He was a heavy cigarette smoker with a naturally nervous disposition. One of his law clerks described him memorably: "He was a man of highly nervous temperament, and the moment he started dictating he arose to his feet and started walking around the office, always smoking. He smoked cigars of a small size that could be consumed during a five or ten minute recess at court, but during the latter part of his tenure as a district judge, he got to smoking my cigarettes, which he always borrowed by the fives and tens and would light one from another."[97]

The day he died he decided to have a tooth pulled while on his way to the Capitol and seemed to experience no particular difficulty when it was extracted. However, as he arose from his dentist's chair he became suddenly dizzy. The dentist called a physician who examined Sanford's heart and administered a stimulant. Sanford failed to respond, lapsed into unconsciousness, and died at noon, shortly after he reached home.[98] Death was attributed to uremic poisoning,[99] which seems a curious diagnosis. More likely Sanford went into shock as a result of the extraction and suffered heart failure. In any event, his death went nearly unnoticed because his good friend, William Howard Taft, who had helped manage Sanford's appointment and with whom he usually voted, died five hours later.

William Howard Taft (Chief Justice: 1921–1930)

Chief Justice Taft did not go gently into retirement. He wrote his brother Henry the following letter in 1929:

> I am older and slower and less acute and more confused. However, as long as things continue as they are, and I am able to answer in my place, I must stay on the court in order to prevent the Bolsheviki from getting control . . . the only hope we have of keeping a consistent declaration of constitutional law is for us to live as long as we can. . . . The truth is that Hoover is a Progressive just as Stone is, and just as Brandeis is and just as Holmes is.[100]

Taft understandably had been concerned about his health for years. Although he neither smoked nor drank and did not keep late hours, he was at certain times in his life a heavy eater. He weighed 326 pounds when he became secretary of war. He was able to diet and reduce to 250 pounds with great effort, but while president he again weighed considerably more.[101] In short, during long periods of his life obesity was a serious problem for him, and it had taken its toll on his cardiovascular system. He suffered from high blood pressure at a time when this condition was not controllable and was concerned that he was affected by hardening of the arteries.[102]

The nation first learned the chief justice was ill on January 7, 1930, when newspapers reported that he was under "unusual strain" because of the Court's work, his half brother's death, and a recurrence of the bladder trouble he had experienced four years earlier.[103] He had first complained of feeling ill while returning from Cincinnati, where he had attended the funeral of his half brother Charles. While there, the seventy-three-year-old chief justice realized his own mortality and began to suffer from insomnia and extreme nervousness.

The next day, Taft checked into Garfield Hospital in Washington. While in the hospital, his physician told him to read detective stories and other lighter fare instead of his customary law books, which were left behind at home. He decided to recuperate in Asheville, North Carolina, for two or three weeks and sent word to the Court that he was feeling better already.[104] In his absence, the eighty-eight-year-old Justice Holmes presided over the Court.

Although Taft appeared to rally during the first ten days in North Carolina, taking short walks with Mrs. Taft near the Grove Park Inn where they lodged, he deteriorated markedly during the remainder of his stay and decided to return to Washington where he wished to die. He had not left his room for five days, and when he emerged supported by two attendants, reporters described his face as "white and drawn" with the "appearance of an exhausted man."[105] Attendants placed him in his car, and he proceeded directly to the railroad station.

After returning home, he resigned on February 3, 1930.[106] President Herbert Hoover appointed Charles Evans Hughes to the chief justiceship the same day, passing over Harlan Stone, which undoubtedly pleased Taft.[107] Taft had suffered from heart disease for several years and at the time of his resignation his condition was acknowledged to be far more serious than had previously been revealed. He saw no visitors and was able "only to make known his simplest needs."[108]

Little over a month later, on March 8, William Howard Taft died in the nation's capital, as he had wished, at 5:15 P.M. on the same day the Court

William Howard Taft during his presidency. (Supreme Court, Office of the Curator)

A dying William Howard Taft returns to Washington. (Supreme Court, Office of the Curator)

celebrated Justice Holmes's eighty-ninth birthday. President Hoover went immediately to the Taft home and offered the use of the East Room in the White House for the funeral. The family declined the president's gesture because Taft had requested that services be held at All Souls Unitarian Church on Sixteenth Street. Burial was in Arlington Cemetery.

Oliver Wendell Holmes Jr. (1902–1932)

On the evening of January 12, 1932, as a Court attendant helped him on with his overcoat, Oliver Wendell Holmes Jr., in his ninetieth year, was heard to remark, "I won't be down tomorrow."[109] Following a visit from Chief Justice Hughes, who had previously discussed Holmes's situation with the other justices, and with the particular agreement of Justice Brandeis, the Court decided to urge Holmes to resign.[110] He did so, gracefully and at once. As he wrote to President Hoover, "The condition of my health makes it a duty to break off connections that I cannot leave without deep regret after the affectionate relations of many years and the absorbing interests that have filled my life. But the time has come and I bow to the inevitable."[111]

Retirement rejuvenated Holmes. Freed after twenty-nine years from the burdens of the Court, he was reported to "have regained his characteristic sparkle" and was spending time reading an hour or two each day, mostly the classics in their original Greek or Latin.[112] He had frequent visitors, his law clerks read to him, and in the afternoons he liked to be driven around Washington in a rented automobile.

He lived on for another three years until, finally, he caught cold, and it quickly turned into bronchial pneumonia.[113] Holmes, though, remained cheerful and irreverent: he kidded his nurses and described the attention surrounding his final illness as "a lot of damn foolery."[114] He failed to rally however, and he was put under an oxygen tent but still seemed weaker and less lively than before.[115] At the end, his doctors gave him glucose injections in an effort to maintain his strength, but to no avail.[116] He died on March 6, 1935, two days short of his ninety-fourth birthday. Following a Unitarian service, he was buried beside his wife, Fanny, at Arlington National Cemetery.

From the turn of the century through 1936, there were several striking situations where justices who should have resigned refused to do so despite their debilitating physical conditions. The distressing facts of their various disabilities were often freely and candidly discussed among the justices them-

selves. For example, on December 25, 1903, Justice Day offered the following observations to Horace Lurton, who was close to several members of the
Court long before he was himself appointed: "Judge Harlan, I am glad to
say, keeps well. Judge Brown's eyes are in bad shape. He has not been on
the bench for some time and will probably not be able to do much this term.
Judge White asks about you often as does Judge Harlan."[117] Brown's situation is particularly interesting because, although severely impaired, he continued to participate in the Court's decisions until he reached the age of
retirement.

Brown's eye problems dated from about 1901, which meant he controlled
the decisions in *DeLima v. Bidwell*[118] and *Downes v. Bidwell,*[119] better known
as the *Insular* cases.[120] He wrote the opinion in both cases, and his vote
determined the results. His vote was also decisive in such 5 to 4 decisions as
Champion v. Ames[121] in 1903, *Northern Securities v. United States*[122] in 1904,
and *Lochner v. New York*[123] in 1905. These cases were decided at a time when
the justices did virtually all of the work themselves, aided by one law clerk
at the most. Since Brown could barely see, it is likely he worked under an
appalling handicap. Had he been able to absorb more information, it is always
possible his moderate inclinations might otherwise have asserted themselves,
especially in *Lochner.* Whether this supposition is likely must remain entirely
problematic.

Because of his obvious mental disability, it is easier to be more confident
that health played a decisive part in Justice McKenna's votes. His decline is
one of the truly unfortunate events in Court history, and there is no doubt
that his tenure was much longer than it should have been. His vote, for
example, was decisive in the Court's decision to exclude party primaries from
congressional regulation in *Newberry v. United States.*[124] The situation with
McKenna only worsened until his resignation in 1925.

Both Justices Moody and Lurton were absent for substantial periods of
time, although in the former case the incapacitation of a young and vigorous
justice could not have been anticipated. Lurton's appointment at age sixty-
five violated President Taft's customary insistence on appointing men who
were relatively young. Clearly, his personal regard for the popular Lurton
controlled his decision.[125]

While president, William Howard Taft was able to watch the Court even
more closely than usual, and his candid assessment of the situation, shared
with Horace Lurton in 1909, was less than comforting:

The condition of the Supreme Court is pitiable and yet those old fools
hold on with a tenacity that is most discouraging. Really the Chief

President Taft described the 1909 Court as "pitiable." Front row, from left: White, Harlan,
Fuller, Brewer, and Peckham. Back row: Day, McKenna, Holmes, and Moody. (Supreme
Court, Office of the Curator)

Justice is almost senile; Harlan does no work; Brewer is so deaf that
he cannot hear and has got beyond the point of commonest accuracy
in writing his opinions; Brewer and Harlan sleep almost through all
the arguments. I don't know what can be done. It is most discouraging
to the active men on the bench.[126]

There clearly were a series of troubling disability problems between 1900
and 1937. Although McKenna's lengthy decline was kept from the American
people, the newspapers reported most of the other ailments as they occurred.
People were not, for the most part, uninformed as to the state of the justices'
health. But their information was limited, since reporters during this period
were reluctant to provide more than the family made available. Aggressive
investigative reporting was never employed. Consequently, there was no particular pressure from the public for any of the disabled justices to resign
earlier than he did.

The most effective method of securing a resignation was for a chief justice
to mobilize internal agreement among the justices that it was time for one

of them to leave. Peer group pressure was used successfully in the cases of Justices McKenna and Holmes, although Taft had a much more difficult time removing McKenna than Hughes had removing Holmes. In both cases, the other justices were understandably reluctant to act until the situation had reached the point where neither McKenna nor Holmes was able to function in his customary way. Therefore, this method of removal is not likely to be employed in other than extreme situations.

Neither Fuller, Harlan, Brewer, Brown, Moody, Lurton, Lamar, or Taft was asked to leave, even though arguably they all had overstayed their usefulness. Moreover, during this period in Court history the justices did their own work; law clerks were not used to write opinions, and so those justices who were no longer able to perform at full capacity significantly burdened the remaining justices. Nevertheless, with few exceptions (most noticeably Shiras and Clarke), there was no inclination to leave the Court while in good health.

5

FROM ROOSEVELT TO WARREN, 1937–1968

No one left the Supreme Court during President Franklin D. Roosevelt's first term of office. As differences of opinion on national economic policy drew the president and the justices toward the constitutional crisis of 1937, Congress decided to legislate a retirement plan for all federal judges, which would make it more attractive for Supreme Court justices to voluntarily yield their positions. After Congress acted to permit members of the federal bench to retire at full pay at age seventy after ten years of judicial service or at age sixty-five with fifteen years of prior service, the legislation succeeded in encouraging Willis Van Devanter and George Sutherland, two elderly opponents of the administration, to leave within months of its passage. Chief Justice Hughes later concluded that if the retirement act had been passed five years earlier, Van Devanter and Sutherland would have joined Holmes in retirement at that time.[1]

Since the adoption of this legislation, there have been seven deaths in office. After mid-century, there was the unexpected death of Chief Justice Fred Vinson in 1953 and the not entirely unanticipated death of Robert Jackson in 1954. The new law made retirement a viable alternative for the justices. Between 1937 and 1969, eleven utilized the retirement provisions, with only three resignations (Roberts, Byrnes, and Goldberg).

Willis Van Devanter (1910–1937)

The retirement of Willis Van Devanter at age seventy-eight in 1937 was unexpected. In his last appearance on the bench he took half an hour to deliver an opinion; his voice was strong and clear, his arguments coherent and logical, his manner vigorous and alert.[2] Although he had written few opinions

Table 5.1
Age of Death, Resignation, or Retirement, 1937–1968

Age	Died	Resigned	Retired
54 or younger	0	0	0
55–59	2	1	0
60–64	2	1	1
65–69	1	0	2
70–74	2	1	2
75–79	0	0	5
80 or older	0	0	1
Totals	7	3	11

Average age of those leaving the Court: 69

Source: Elder Witt, ed., *Congressional Quarterly's Guide to the U.S. Supreme Court*, 2d ed. (Washington, D.C.: Congressional Quarterly Press, 1990).

during the year, he had been no less productive than usual.[3] Van Devanter's friends speculated that he would have retired earlier had the revised retirement act been in effect; he carefully worded his letter to President Roosevelt to indicate that his departure was only from "regular active service."[4]

Justice Van Devanter contended it was only "coincidental" that notice of his retirement came on the same day the Senate Judiciary Committee was scheduled to vote on President Roosevelt's "Court-packing" plan.[5] Nonetheless, it was apparent enough that the retirement was deliberately timed and that age was not a motivating consideration. As Van Devanter explained:

> I had intended first to retire five years ago but I stayed on, increasingly though I became convinced in my conclusion that I owed it to myself to quit. . . .
> I was seventy-eight and I felt at last that I owed it to myself to retire from regular active service. . . .
> It was no surprise that I did that. The surprise lay only in the time that I did it. It was a decision that was not reached overnight. . . .
> And I didn't think that I was too old for the job.[6]

Friends indicated that the justice had five years earlier changed his mind about retirement because of what he perceived to be a threat against the Constitution.[7] Also, he acknowledged he needed his judicial salary.

The political implications of Van Devanter's retirement were not unnoticed. On the day the retirement was announced, President Roosevelt was asked at a press conference if there was any special significance in the fact that a band was playing on the White House lawn. In good humor, the president responded that the point was well taken.[8]

Justice Van Devanter remained active in retirement. He accepted assignments on lower courts, where his extensive expertise in legal procedure could be utilized. He owned seven hundred acres of farmland in Maryland and a small island in the Great Lakes, where he went for relaxation.[9] He died in Washington on February 8, 1941. Burial was not in his native Wyoming, but at Rock Creek Cemetery in Washington.

Justice Van Devanter's departure marked a turning point in Court history. Within the next several years the three justices with whom Van Devanter most frequently agreed (the rigid and articulate George Sutherland, the stolid and unimaginative Pierce Butler, and the irascible and bigoted James C. McReynolds) all left the Court in rapid succession.

George Sutherland (1922–1938)

The following January, George Sutherland announced his retirement, citing his fifteen years of service and noting that he had passed his seventy-fifth year.[10] President Roosevelt offered no comment and did not immediately dispatch an acceptance letter as he had done on the occasion of Van Devanter's retirement.[11] The retirement had not come easily. As Sutherland had written to the Court: "It is very hard for me to step out of this circle, where I have taken comfort for so long. I leave the Court with keen regret. I have loved the work in which we have been engaged together; and only a definite conviction that the time has come reconciles me to the unwelcome thought of laying it down."[12]

The defeat of President Roosevelt's "Court-packing" proposal in the summer of 1937 was probably the significant catalyst in Sutherland's retirement decision, not age or length of service. He believed the institutional integrity of the Supreme Court had been preserved for the foreseeable future. So assured, he was willing to leave.[13]

Sutherland retired to Stockbridge, Massachusetts, where he died at the age of eighty on July 18, 1942, four years after his retirement. He was at first laid to rest in Abbey Mausoleum next to Arlington National Cemetery but was moved in 1958 to the Sanctuary of Truth Mausoleum at Cedar Hill Cemetery in Suitland, Maryland, a Washington suburb.

Benjamin N. Cardozo (1932–1938)

Age and ill health removed the liberal justices Benjamin N. Cardozo and Louis D. Brandeis at about the same time that their four conservative opponents retired or died. Although Cardozo's years on the Supreme Court were for him a period of physical decline, there was throughout no diminution of his extraordinary legal capabilities.[14]

Justice Cardozo suffered his first heart attack in June 1930 while on the New York Court of Appeals. He was walking on a street in Albany when he experienced this first mild attack of angina.[15] His first serious recurrence happened in the summer of 1935, and his physician then warned him to retire from the Supreme Court because failure to do so would shorten his life expectancy by two-thirds.[16] He ignored this advice. As he confided to a friend, he was

> confined to bed under the tyrannical sway of nurses and physicians. I was badly run down after the winter's work in Washington and the doctors, having put me to bed for the purposes of cure, are keeping me there, as they do hardened criminals, for the purpose of reformation. They'll have a hard time making over a tough old customer who has weathered so many years.[17]

Justice Cardozo returned to the exhausting schedule to which he always subjected himself and was able to continue until he became critically ill with the grippe (or influenza), which followed a severe cold in December 1937. At this time he was also stricken with shingles, characterized by an exceedingly painful rash brought on by the same virus that causes chickenpox. He was very uncomfortable and remarked that "the road to hell is shingled."[18] Cardiographs indicated a continuing deterioration of his heart action. Nonetheless, by January 6, 1938, he felt sufficiently recovered to journey to the home of Justice Brandeis. The next day he had another heart attack, and the following day he suffered a stroke, paralyzing his left arm, left leg, and right eye.

As the doctors struggled to save his life, they confronted the risk of pneumonia, the danger of soporific drugs needed to induce sleep, and the deep melancholia that sometimes affected Cardozo. And yet, he fought against the paralysis and did not mention the possibility of retirement. He lay immobilized, although his mind remained active. As he continued to decline

Benjamin N. Cardozo (left) with Charles Evans Hughes a year before Cardozo's death. (Supreme Court, Office of the Curator)

throughout January, it became necessary to resort to artificial feeding. He had difficulty breathing and was sometimes unconscious because of morphine injections. But in February he miraculously began to improve. By March he was able to sit in a chair, but thereafter he seemed to again lose strength and became drowsy and frequently apathetic. Chief Justice Hughes visited him as he sat in his wheelchair, and Cardozo told him, as they shook hands for the last time, "They tell me I am going to get well, but I file a dissenting opinion."[19]

In May he was taken to the Lehman home in Port Chester, New York. Judge Irving Lehman had been his good friend and colleague on the New York Court of Appeals, and he and his wife, Sissie, helped him immeasurably during his final illness. He appeared to revive, at least for a time. As he was carried by train through New York City, he asked where he was, and when told, he exclaimed, "This is the place I love. I feel better."[20] But his recovery was not to be.

On Saturday, July 9, 1938, at 6:40 in the evening, Cardozo died of a massive coronary thrombosis, a clot having formed in the blood vessels of the heart. His physician described the circumstances that preceded the end:

> It is not true that Justice Cardozo was naturally of a frail physique. He was thin and wiry. But it is remarkable that he survived as long as he did. He had been living entirely artificially. Several blood transfusions had been given and numerous injections of glucose intravenously in addition to treatment under the oxygen tent and cooling apparatus. . . .
>
> Justice Cardozo had been unable to take nourishment normally for some days and while conscious had been in a daze, from which he would arouse only after a stimulant.[21]

The final illness had so ravaged Cardozo that it was, in his physician's opinion, doubtful if he could have returned to work even if he had survived his last heart attack. Toward the end, when he became delirious, his mind retraced old cases again and again. He frequently said, "I'm sorry to be such a nuisance, but I hope if I can get well I can be of some value to my country."[22] His desire to live was linked with his capacity to work. The last thing he said was, "Thank you."[23]

Although Cardozo had shown no interest in formal religion throughout most of his adult life, an Orthodox Jewish service was held the following Monday in the early afternoon at the Lehman estate with some two hundred guests in attendance. The service was brief, lasting only ten minutes, with the Twenty-third Psalm and parts of the Book of Proverbs read in Hebrew. Cardozo had asked that there be no eulogy. The coffin lay on an altar in the library, covered with roses, with one candle burning beside it. The funeral cortege then proceeded through a light drizzle to Cypress Hills Cemetery in Queens, where the Kaddish was recited and the body was lowered into the grave.[24]

Judge Lehman described the Orthodox service as "awful" to the prominent New York lawyer Charles Burlingham. Burlingham in turn told Felix Frankfurter that "I didn't know the Sephardim were, or was, so fundamentalistic." However inconsistent the service may have been with the justice's personal beliefs, Cardozo was put to rest with all of the members of his family except for his twin sister Emily, who could not be buried in holy ground because she had married a Christian.[25]

It would be unfair to Justice Cardozo to suppose that he had intended to

Black crepe drapes Benjamin N. Cardozo's chair following his death while still in office. (Supreme Court, Office of the Curator)

cling unrealistically to power. He reportedly had sent word informally to President Roosevelt through friends of his intention to retire before his last long siege of illness. Roosevelt was said to have counseled against any precipitous action, suggesting that Cardozo ought to wait until he felt recovered and then decide whether he was physically capable of another term.[26]

Louis D. Brandeis (1916–1939)

During the same period Justice Louis D. Brandeis also began to show signs of diminished physical vigor. Although he wrote fewer opinions than was his custom during his last two full terms (1937 and 1938), there was no evidence of any intellectual decline. There had been rumors of his retirement circulating since 1936, but he had ignored them. His retirement, when it came on February 13, 1939, was both sudden and dramatically unexpected.

Brandeis had worked during the day as usual on Court business. He had been back at his desk for only a week, having just taken a month off to recover from a case of the grippe and a heart attack. His decision was conveyed to President Roosevelt in a single sentence: "Pursuant to the Act of March 1, 1937, I retire this day from regular active service on the bench."[27] He was then eighty-three years old and in good health for his age. Friends suggested that he had wanted to retire before the end of the term and had stayed on as long as he had so that Felix Frankfurter could take his seat while he was still there. Frankfurter and Brandeis served two weeks together.[28]

Justice Brandeis explained why he had retired to his sister-in-law on the same day President Roosevelt accepted his resignation: "I want you to know promptly that I am not retiring from the Court because of ill health. Mine seems to be as good as heretofore. But years have limited the quantity and intensity of work possible, and I think the time has come when a younger man should assume the burden."[29] Later there were further reports that confirmed this explanation. Brandeis had an austere attitude toward the need to do one's full share of the Court's work. When he concluded he was without sufficient strength to make his customary contribution, he promptly retired.

Only Justice McReynolds refused to sign the letter of appreciation that the other justices sent to Brandeis when he retired. (McReynolds also had previously absented himself from the memorial ceremonies held at the Supreme Court in honor of Justice Cardozo.)[30] Released from his responsibilities at the Court, Brandeis seemed to have a good deal of available energy.[31] He read, wrote letters, motored, conversed with friends, and supported Zionism.[32]

The end came easily to Brandeis. During his eighty-fifth year, on the afternoon of September 31, 1941, he became unconscious in his apartment. He never awoke, dying on October 5. A memorial service was held the next day in the apartment, where Dean Acheson spoke for his former law clerks and Felix Frankfurter told the story of the death of Mr. Valiant-for-Truth in John Bunyan's *Pilgrim's Progress*.[33] Brandeis's ashes, and those of his wife, were later interred beneath the portico of the University of Louisville Law School, in the city where his family first settled when they came to the United States.

Pierce Butler (1922–1939)

Pierce Butler, in 1939 the third oldest member of the Court, paid a courtesy call on Chief Justice Charles Evans Hughes, who was hospitalized with bleeding ulcers, before leaving for his summer vacation. Justice Butler appeared to be in superb health and, when leaving the chief justice, was heard to remark, "We'll never see the Chief again."[34] Butler's prediction was accurate, but he was the one who died, while the chief justice made a complete recovery.

He was first stricken in August with what was reported as a "minor bladder aliment" and entered Garfield Hospital in Washington.[35] Released for a short time, Butler was forced to reenter the hospital on September 21 and was reported to be seriously ill with a bladder or kidney aliment.[36] When the Court convened on October 1, he was absent, but his son, Pierce Jr., indicated that his father was improving and hoped to be back on the Court within five or six weeks.[37] Justice Butler's condition suddenly worsened, and on November 16, 1939, at 4:14 A.M., he died. He was returned to St. Paul, Minnesota, for burial.

James C. McReynolds (1914–1941)

Like Justices Van Devanter and Sutherland, James C. McReynolds retired in good health. He elected to leave on February 1, 1941, two days before his seventy-ninth birthday. His letter to President Roosevelt, whom he thoroughly disliked, was formal, referred only to the Retirement Act, and offered no explanation for his retirement.[38] McReynolds privately told friends that he had considered retirement nine years earlier but had finally decided to leave while "in full possession of my faculties and health."[39]

McReynolds died as he had lived, alone, as a result of bronchial pneumonia in a Washington hospital on August 24, 1946. No friends or family members were in attendance. His funeral, in Elkton, Kentucky, was unattended by the other justices. Only a clerk was present from the Court. Years later, "this clerk noted that in 1953, McReynolds' aged negro messenger—Harry Parker—died and the Chief Justice and four or five justices attended his funeral."[40]

To the surprise of many, McReynolds (or "Old Mac" as Justice Douglas liked to call him)—whose racist, antifeminist, and anti-Semitic views were well known to his colleagues—left his estate mostly to charities benefiting small children.

Charles Evans Hughes (Chief Justice: 1930–1941)

Charles Evans Hughes had returned to the Supreme Court as chief justice at the request of President Hoover in 1930 at the age of sixty-eight, having resigned as an associate justice in 1916 to contest for the presidency against Woodrow Wilson. The chief justice's health remained perfect until 1939. He had traveled widely during vacations and had not missed any Court sessions. And yet, the question of when to retire was one that much concerned him. Within his family, he had arranged for a secret ballot among his children should any of them fear he was becoming senile. Only the result was to be communicated to him.

Hughes first became ill about a week before a scheduled address before a joint session of Congress. The other justices had left the conference room, and as the chief justice sat alone "a gray-green pallor spread over his face." The Court's clerk helped him to a couch. Although he looked as if he might expire, he refused to permit the clerk to fetch a doctor. After awhile he felt recovered enough to make his way home; he refused to let the clerk accompany him because he feared it would excite comment. He continued to feel very weak.

On the day of his address, Hughes was so weakened that it was a struggle for him to even walk to the rostrum. Nonetheless, he braved the ordeal and then, it being Saturday, insisted that the Court meet as usual for the Saturday conference to discuss the case agenda. Justice Owen Roberts and some of the others tried to discourage him, but he was insistent; he had never postponed a conference. He presided over the conference until six o'clock, then returned home where he and Mrs. Hughes hosted a major dinner party. At the day's end he had reached his limits. On the following Monday, a physician diagnosed a bleeding duodenal ulcer. The chief justice had lost much blood.

Bedrest and diet restored his health, and he was able to return to the Court before the summer vacation.[41]

Chief Justice Hughes remained aloof from the presidential contest between Franklin Roosevelt and Wendell Willkie. However, on October 17, 1940, he received a letter from Herbert Hoover asking the chief justice to resign. Hoover admitted his suggestion was "fantastic" but justified it by his belief in a total change in administration. Chief Justice Hughes, not unexpectedly, did not formally reply to this curious suggestion but did indicate informally that such an act would be useless.[42] He obviously had no intention of ending his distinguished public career on a note of political partisanship.

The following spring, on his birthday, the following correspondence was exchanged:

> Dear Chief:
> My affectionate regard and best wishes on your Birthday. You are not a day older mentally or physically than I am—just 59!
> As ever yours,
> Franklin D. Roosevelt

> Dear Mr. President:
> Your extraordinary appraisal of my youth has almost turned my head. While I am old enough to know better, I am young enough to like it.
> Very sincerely yours,
> Charles E. Hughes[43]

Inside the Court, Justice Frank Murphy assured him it was "comforting to find you on your birthday at the very zenith of your matchless intellectual and physical powers."[44] But the reality was otherwise. The long hours and the sustained concentration he had always exacted of himself were no longer possible. If he elected to stay on the Court, he would have to content himself with a lesser burden.

Hughes described his thoughts at the time he resolved to retire: "I had criticized judges for trying to hang on after they were unable to bring full vigor to their task. As I felt that I could not keep the pace I had set for myself as Chief Justice, I decided that the time had come to follow my own advice."[45] The only chief justice to retire in good health since John Jay, his retirement took effect on July 1, 1941, at the close of the term.

Hughes was seventy-nine when he left the chief justiceship. He stayed in Washington, as dignified and distinguished in retirement as he had been in public service. He died easily of congestive heart failure while vacationing at his summer cottage on Cape Cod on August 17, 1948. When he died, it was said of Hughes that while it is next to impossible to be dignified while coming into this world or while leaving it, he came as close to leaving with dignity as is possible.

Owen J. Roberts (1930–1945)

After Hughes retired, Justice Owen J. Roberts found his own work much less satisfying. The men with whom he was most congenial were gone by the 1940s, and he did not feel comfortable with some of the new arrivals, particularly Justice Black.[46] When Roberts resigned in 1945, after fifteen years of service, he wrote with frankness to Chief Justice Hughes: "To work under you was the greatest experience and the greatest satisfaction of my life. When you left the Court, the whole picture changed. For me it would never be the same."[47]

Roberts left the Court shortly after his seventieth birthday. His friends did not believe he had given any prior thought to leaving; he was in excellent health and had not missed a Court session in a decade.[48] Unlike the others who had left after 1937, Roberts resigned rather than retire with a pension. He thereby severed all relationships with the federal judiciary, thus enabling himself to return to a private law practice in Philadelphia.[49]

Justice Roberts left the Court with full self-awareness of his place in constitutional history. "I have no illusions about my judicial career," he wrote shortly after his resignation. "But one can only do what one can. Who am I to revile the good God that he did not make me a Marshall, a Taney, a Bradley, a Holmes, a Brandeis, or a Cardozo."[50]

A year before he resigned, Roberts had become alienated from his colleagues, except for Felix Frankfurter and Robert Jackson. He apparently believed the others were scheming behind his back and releasing unfavorable comments about him to the press, all of which they denied.[51] He became thoroughly embittered. Consequently, Roberts refused to engage in the traditional handshake before the conferences by arriving late. He also refused to join the others in the robing room where he would have to greet them before going on the bench. He instead fell into line as they walked toward their seats.

Although they had once been close friends, Roberts and Hugo Black became estranged on the Supreme Court. Because of this enmity, or because of a candid assessment of Roberts's performance as a justice, Black refused to sign unless modified the letter of appreciation traditionally sent to a justice upon his resignation or retirement. More particularly, Black objected to an expression of regret from the remaining justices that Roberts was leaving and to the phrase, "You have made fidelity to principle your guide to decision."[52] Felix Frankfurter refused to agree to any modification of the original letter because to do so would make it insultingly bland, so no letter was sent at all.[53]

Roberts seemed much happier in retirement than on the Court. He busied himself in a variety of activities, which included an interest in world government as well as the presidencies of the Pennsylvania Bar Association and the American Philosophical Society. He turned a series of lectures into a book, *The Court and the Constitution,* which Harvard University Press published in 1951. He even served as the law dean at the University of Pennsylvania for three years beginning in 1948, accepting no salary for his service.[54] He died on his farm, located near Chester Springs, Pennsylvania, at age eighty on May 17, 1955.

Harlan Fiske Stone (1925–1941; Chief Justice: 1941–1946)

Harlan Fiske Stone, like Edward Douglass White before him, was elevated from within to become chief justice. Although he had no intention of continuing beyond the point at which he was able to perform with his customary vigor, he kept his time schedule indefinite. "I would be surprised," his son Marshall concluded, "if he had not thought of staying long enough for a Republican President to be able to appoint his successor."[55]

It must remain problematic as to whether Stone would have stayed on the Court too long. There was some evidence of equivocation, as when he wrote:

> Perhaps the wish is father to the thought. After one gets into his seventy-fourth year, there is a natural expectation that he will not carry for long the heavy burden that I am carrying. Sometimes I think to myself when I see the performances that go on around me, "Why subject oneself to that sort of thing?" And then I think what would happen if I weren't here, and what would I do if I didn't have this job and I conclude it is perhaps my duty to keep going.[56]

Chief Justice Stone suffered no illness, with the exception of a minor throat infection in April 1946, which only kept him in bed for half a day.

He also slipped on a piece of paper lying beside his bed, but no harm was done. "Why I didn't break my neck, I don't know," he admitted, "but as a matter of fact nothing was damaged except my temper."[57]

As he left for the Court on the morning of April 22, the day after Easter, Stone appeared healthy and in a good humor. Later in the day, as the justices sat on the bench to deliver opinions, when it came his turn to deliver three opinions, there was a silence that at once attracted attention. The next day Justice Wiley Rutledge recalled that he

> saw the Chief Justice sitting back, holding his opinions in a reading position, his right hand fumbling through the pages. Then I heard him say in a low voice something like "the case should be stayed, we decided to send this case back to conference for reconsideration." Still it did not occur to me that he was ill. I thought he had suddenly decided that a case which had been announced previously had some hitch in it and was calling a recess to go off and straighten things out. Suddenly, the gavel banged, and Black adjourned the Court until two-thirty.[58]

Justices Hugo Black and Stanley Reed carried Stone from the bench into the robing room, where he was laid on a couch at 1:45 P.M. As he lay muttering incoherently, the Court quickly reconvened in order to finalize the opinions that had been decided. No one can cast a dead man's vote; the day's business could be concluded only while Stone still lived.[59]

Chief Justice Stone never regained consciousness and was taken to his home by ambulance at about 3:30. He died in the presence of his family at 6:45 P.M. from a massive cerebral hemorrhage. With his passing, only Roosevelt appointees remained on the Supreme Court.

James F. Byrnes (1941–1942)

Barely into his first term when war broke out, James F. Byrnes was soon impatient once more to be directly involved in politics. On the Tuesday following Pearl Harbor, the Court heard arguments in a case involving the Bethlehem Shipbuilding Company.[60] He remembered telling President Roosevelt afterward:

> I must confess I found it very difficult to concentrate on the arguments this morning. . . . I've been in the middle of crises since I entered public life, but yesterday with the nation confronted with the greatest crisis in its history the best I could do was spend hours listening to argu-

ments about the payment for ships that were built twenty-three years ago. I was thinking so much about those ships sunk at Pearl Harbor that it was difficult to concentrate on arguments about ships that were built at Bethlehem in 1918.[61]

He was frankly bored at the Court. In partial jest, he observed: "Mr. President, you know, before your fight on the Supreme Court was over I had concluded you were wrong, and my service on the Court has only confirmed that view. . . . You urged that Justices be retired at seventy. From my experience, I've decided they shouldn't be appointed until they reach seventy."[62]

President Roosevelt began to call upon Byrnes for advice immediately after Pearl Harbor. The attorney general, Francis Biddle, suggested to the president that Byrnes resign, but Roosevelt resisted that suggestion. "Let's keep it open for Jimmy," the president said.[63] The matter of Byrnes's resignation was advocated again by Biddle, this time at the urging of Chief Justice Stone before the 1942 term began. Again Roosevelt resisted, asking Biddle, "Could we not appoint some 'old boy' for two or three years who would agree to retire when he reached seventy?"[64] The idea then would be to bring Byrnes back to the Court after a stint in the White House. Biddle reminded Roosevelt of his often stated desire to bring younger men onto the Supreme Court, and the matter was dropped.

When Roosevelt first suggested that Byrnes take a leave of absence from the Court in order to become director of the Office of Economic Stabilization, he declined.[65] Justice Byrnes did, however, inform Roosevelt that he would resign without hesitation if the president thought he might be of service to the war effort.[66] The distinction between a leave of absence and a resignation may have been important to Byrnes, because it was known that Chief Justice Stone strongly disapproved of the assumption of extrajudicial responsibilities by members of the Court.[67]

President Roosevelt emphasized the importance of the proposed assignment: "In these jurisdictional disputes I want you to act as a judge and I will let it be known that your decision is my decision, and that there is no appeal. For all practical purposes you will be assistant President."[68] With this understanding of his new assignment, Byrnes resigned within the hour, on October 3, 1942, in order to direct the Office of Economic Stabilization.[69] In effect, Roosevelt turned over to him the whole civilian economy.

James F. Byrnes's long and colorful political life after his sixteen months of Court service is widely known. After his White House years ended with

President Roosevelt's death, he became President Harry Truman's secretary of state until they quarreled in 1947. He practiced law for four years in Washington and then returned to his home state of South Carolina, where he reentered politics. In 1951 he became the controversial governor of South Carolina, ending his previously constructive political career by adamantly opposing racial integration of the public schools. Twenty-nine years removed from his Court service, he died of a heart attack on April 9, 1972, at the age of ninety-two.

Frank Murphy (1940–1949)

During the summer of 1949, Frank Murphy died unexpectedly, although he had been in declining health. Justice Murphy was increasingly moody during his last year on the Court; he may have felt isolated professionally, but more than likely his personal troubles also contributed to his uneasy state of mind. Some of his family, to whom he had always been generous with whatever money he had, opposed his wish to marry for the first time. Moreover, the Catholic Church was less of a comfort to him than it had been in the past.[70]

His depression was aggravated and probably related to a series of painful, annoying illnesses. Summer travel plans to Manila were canceled; he remained in a Detroit hospital and was even forced to miss the opening of the new Court term in 1948, all because of sciatic neuralgia.[71] Throughout the year he was in and out of the hospital because of shingles, which like sciatic neuralgia is a nervous disorder.

Although Murphy sometimes talked of retiring, he was not eligible for retirement benefits and had practically no money of his own beyond his salary.[72] In a conversation with his brother, he spoke despairingly: "What is the use of retiring at 70? At that date in life the Lord retires everyone anyway. It seems to me when federal service takes the best years of one's life—years you cannot recapture—the public servant should be allowed to retire without reference to disability or age."[73]

Justice Murphy's illnesses had an effect on his behavior. He relied increasingly on Justice Rutledge for information and became somewhat unpredictable, as the instability that had characterized his first term reasserted itself. Some of his colleagues may have concluded he was "burned out."[74]

Two days after the Court adjourned, Murphy entered Henry Ford Hospital in Detroit for the purpose of undergoing extensive tests. His condition was not described as serious.[75] On July 19, he died in his sleep from a sudden coronary occlusion after receiving the last rites of the Catholic Church one hour earlier. He was fifty-nine years old.

Wiley B. Rutledge (1943–1949)

Justice Wiley B. Rutledge seemed close to exhaustion physically and emotionally by the summer of 1949. The death of his good friend Frank Murphy, along with his unhappiness with many recent Court decisions, seemed to intensify his burden. His legendary capacity for hard work was taking its toll, much to the concern of his family and friends. Shortly before Rutledge's death, Irving Brant wrote: "To hell with writing opinions. . . . You are needed on the Court more now than at any previous time, but your first duty is to remain on earth."[76]

One of his colleagues described his approach to opinion writing:

> He went at writing an opinion pretty much as a law professor goes to work writing a Law Journal article. So he exhausted himself unnecessarily, doing more than deciding a particular case and trying to work out the total mosaic in which the case appeared in legal literature. His mill ground slowly and very fine. He probably put more energy and concentration into each of the several cases that came across his desk than anyone in modern history.[77]

Justice Rutledge was a perfectionist, a man haunted by the fear that whatever was done should have been done better. When his name was mentioned as a possible successor to Chief Justice Stone in 1946, he acknowledged to friends that the added work would kill him in two years.[78]

In the month following the death of Justice Murphy, Rutledge took ill while vacationing in Ogunquit, Maine. He was rushed to the hospital in York, where his illness was described as a circulatory ailment.[79] There seemed to be some improvement, but it did not last. Rutledge died of a cerebral hemorrhage on September 10, at 9:05 P.M. He was fifty-five.[80]

Fred M. Vinson (Chief Justice: 1946–1953)

Fred M. Vinson's death in Washington on September 8, 1953, was also very sudden. The chief justice was sixty-three years old and in apparent good health. He had recently returned home from the American Bar Association meetings in Boston. A physician was called to his apartment at 1:30 in the morning; forty-five minutes later, Vinson was dead, the victim of a massive heart attack.[81] Whereas his predecessors had each averaged fourteen years in office, he had been chief justice for only seven.

Chief Justice Vinson's tenure had been fraught with interpersonal controversies that he seemed unable to control. His weak leadership merely encouraged the general disrespect in which some of his colleagues held him. Conscious of Vinson's reluctance to strike at racial segregation in the states, Justice Frankfurter, when told of his death, caustically told one of his law clerks, "This is the first indication I have ever had that there is a God."

But many others were more charitable. Hundreds of mourners passed by his plain mahogany casket, unadorned with flowers, candles, or flags, as it lay before a small altar in a Washington funeral parlor.[82] The public memorial service was held at the Washington Cathedral where the Protestant Episcopal rite for the dead was observed, even though Vinson was a Methodist. The chief justice's body was dressed in the black robe of his office, and part of the coffin was covered with heavy folds of purple cloth symbolizing death. Most of the major figures from the Roosevelt and Truman years were present. President Eisenhower, Vice President Nixon, and the entire Truman family attended. President Truman, dressed in black and clearly affected by the loss of his good friend, briefly greeted President Eisenhower for the first time since the 1952 election.[83]

After the service, Vinson's remains were carried by train, with the members of the Court in attendance, to Louisa, Kentucky. There, in a town of some 2,015 people where Vinson had been born, he was buried in the family plot overlooking the Big Sandy River following a funeral service at the Louisa Southern Methodist Church.

Robert H. Jackson (1941–1954)

Robert H. Jackson likewise suffered an unexpected heart attack, on March 30, 1954. He remained hospitalized until May 17, when he went directly to the Supreme Court so as to be present when *Brown v. Board of Education*[84] was announced.

Over the summer Jackson recuperated in California. In mid-August, he interrupted his vacation to attend the American Bar Association meeting in Chicago. There he introduced his colleague from the Nuremberg trials, Sir David Maxwell Fyfe, in what was to be his last public appearance. When the fall term began in October, Justice Jackson was in his accustomed place. His response to friends who urged him to relax more and reduce his work schedule was that "he would prefer to carry out what he conceived to be his duties, even though it meant a shorter life, than to seek release from those obligations by living an easier life."[85]

A few days after the new term began, on October 9, while driving to work in his car from McLean, Virginia, Jackson suffered another heart attack. He did not survive the day.

Sherman Minton (1949–1956)

Sherman Minton's entire Supreme Court career was plagued by poor health. As a U.S. senator from Indiana (1934–1940), he had been forceful and robust, moving upward through the Senate leadership ranks more rapidly than anyone in the century except Lyndon Johnson. But when he announced he would retire from the Court effective October 15, 1956, he publicly cited poor health as the decisive consideration.[86]

He had suffered a heart attack in 1945, which required extensive hospitalization. As commonly happened in those years in the case of a serious heart attack, he never entirely recovered from the damage to his heart muscle. His elder son, Dr. Sherman A. Minton, described his father as "a cardiac invalid for the rest of life."[87] The energy and drive to exercise leadership that were displayed to such advantage in his Senate years no longer existed. Nonetheless, as one of his law clerks remembered, he was still "smart and sharp."[88]

While on the Supreme Court, Minton suffered from pernicious anemia, a circulatory ailment that results in the failure or decreased ability to absorb vitamin B_{12} from the gastrointestinal tract. As he told the press, pernicious anemia is "like diabetes—you can do something about it but you can't cure it."[89]

In Minton's case, the diagnosis was not made until his spinal column had been permanently damaged. The vitamin B_{12} therapy used now was not readily available in those years, although his son managed to obtain some for him.[90] This ailment caused him to begin using a cane during his last year on the Court. Pernicious anemia can be crippling, resulting in weakness and stiffness. Minton's knees sometimes buckled, causing him to lose his balance.

There were other considerations bearing on Minton's decision to retire. He did not particularly like work on the Supreme Court and was much happier when he had served in the Senate. Chief Justice Earl Warren thought Mrs. Minton's health may have caused him to want to return to Indiana.[91] But what influenced him most was his fear that his mental powers were failing during the 1955 term. He told one of his last law clerks that he was hav-

An ebullient Sherman Minton suffered from a damaged heart. (Supreme Court, Office of the Curator)

ing difficulty retaining arguments in his mind. This deficit too was undoubtedly related to his pernicious anemia, which can cause loss of concentration,
dullness, apathy, and irritability.[92] The law clerk thought he was overreacting
and that there was really nothing the matter with him.

But Minton's feelings of inadequacy were apparently reinforced by attitudes he sensed from some of his colleagues. He admitted to his closest
friend on the Court, Felix Frankfurter, that "when one contemplates retirement from a distance it does seem most attractive but when it comes to the
hour to go it is not easy."[93] Then, having told Frankfurter that his friendship
was one of the precious things of his life, he confided to him why he had
decided to leave: "But for my feelings of inadequacy and decrepitude and
the embarrassment which comes from the deferential treatment accorded my
'senility' I would stay on."[94]

His loyalty to his good friend President Truman caused his deepest regret
after he decided to retire. He wrote the president accordingly: "As I told you
before, I feel compelled to accept retirement, which I will do in October. I
assure you I would not take this step if I were not convinced that my condition of health compels it. It is not an easy thing to leave this attractive place
where I have served a short time with such great satisfaction, and, again,
my deepest appreciation to you for giving me this opportunity."[95] Justice
Minton felt strongly that it was improper for public persons to retain power
after they no longer could perform their duties with their accustomed ability. On this score he was even willing to criticize one of his political icons,
Franklin Roosevelt.

A fiercely partisan man (Justice Frankfurter told him in a letter that he was
"a pathological Democrat"), once Minton decided to retire he put aside all
partisan considerations, leaving on October 15, 1956, thereby giving President Eisenhower an opportunity to make an appointment in an election year.
His regret and his disappointment surfaced in his farewell remarks to the
press. "There will be more interest in who will succeed me than in my passing," he said. "I'm an echo."[96]

Minton returned home to New Albany, Indiana, where he lived another
nine years. There he continued his correspondence, watched the Court with
interest (confiding as always in Felix Frankfurter), retained his abiding interest in Democratic politics, and was a great favorite at Indiana Bar Association meetings.[97]

Late in life he converted to Catholicism, which was his wife's religion.[98]
Mrs. Minton, however, was not inclined to proselytize her religious beliefs,

according to her daughter, either with her Protestant grandchildren or her husband. On several occasions she said her husband's religious beliefs were his own business. The only comment on the topic the justice ever made in his daughter's presence was that he wondered why he had not converted years earlier.[99]

Minton was seventy-four years old when he died on April 9, 1965, in New Albany Hospital. Burial was in the Catholic cemetery there in his hometown.

Stanley F. Reed (1938–1957)

The following year Stanley F. Reed left the Court in good health. He had been thinking about retirement for about a year but decided to ask that his retirement be made effective on February 25, 1957, the nineteenth anniversary of his appointment.[100]

When Reed was asked why he decided to retire, he smiled and said, "Because I am 72 years old."[101] He then added that work on the Court necessarily involved long hours of highly concentrated effort, and "the strain of such unremitting exertion no longer seems wise."[102] There was probably another consideration as well for why he elected to leave the Court halfway through the 1956 term. Looking at the cases previously accepted to be heard, Reed "foresaw nothing but defeat and frustration to come by his participation in the significant number of major cases scheduled to be argued and decided during the balance of the term."[103]

Justice Reed and his wife, Winifred, lived for many years at the Mayflower Hotel in Washington. He owned a farm in his hometown of Maysville, Kentucky, which he visited during the summers. Although he was knowledgeable about race horses, he did not keep them. "I lose some caste not having race horses," he told a reporter, "but cows are more profitable."[104]

Following his retirement, President Eisenhower appointed Reed chairman of the Civil Rights Commission, but he soon resigned from that post. It proved to be more burdensome and time-consuming than he had anticipated, and, beyond that, he feared it would prove politically controversial. As he indicated when he left the commission, he was concerned that his participation might "lower respect for the impartiality of the Federal judiciary."[105] He did remain active in retirement by accepting assignments on the Court of Appeals and the Court of Claims, both sitting in the District of Columbia.[106] He resigned from this work in 1970, when he found himself growing increasingly forgetful.

Justice Reed lived longer than any other justice, twenty-three of those years in retirement. He was ninety-five when he died on April 2, 1980, at a nursing home on Long Island. His wife survived him at the nursing home.

Only his good friend Potter Stewart attended the funeral and spoke at the Trinity United Methodist Church in Maysville, where Reed was buried. Later Stewart recounted a story that had stayed with him. Stewart and one of the justices were with Reed when the following exchange occurred:

> Something moved the other Justice to ask what he thought was a rhetorical question: "Golly, have you ever thought what you would do if you had your life to live over?" Justice Reed's response was immediate. "I wouldn't want to live my life over again," he said. "It couldn't possibly be so good the second time." These simple words from a man in his twilight years were truly inspirational to a young newcomer to the Court, and I shall never forget them.[107]

Harold H. Burton (1945–1958)

During the spring of 1958, Harold H. Burton suffered from tremors that initially affected his left side, forcing him to cancel several speaking engagements. His difficulty was diagnosed on Saturday morning, June 7, 1958, when his physician "identified my trouble as Parkinson's disease. It is responding to treatment very well, but [the physician] advised retirement from full Court duties."[108]

"During my clerkship," one of his last clerks remembered, "he was having severe difficulty with his eyes and control of his hands, and he worked at a very slow pace."[109] Rumors about Justice Burton's health began to circulate, all of which encouraged interest from the White House. Burton described his exchange with the attorney general on June 13:

> In p.m. Attorney Gen. Wm. Rogers came to see me. He said he had heard a report that I might retire soon and he came to urge me not to do so. He said I had been an excellent justice and he did not want me to leave the Court. I explained my plans to retire Oct. 13 and to notify the President shortly after my birthday on June 22. I explained that my doctor advised such retirement and that I was taking treatment to offset Parkinson's disease that had shown up during this term. Also that although I had originally planned to serve one more year I felt it best for the Court and my family not to do so now. I felt handicapped

in doing the work of the Court, and serving at my best during a term, taking a 10 hr. day . . . 7 days a week.[110]

Attorney General Rogers and Justice Burton called on President Eisenhower on July 17. The president read Burton's letter of resignation and, after he had expressed his regret, said he was appreciative of the advance notice. The president intended to delay any announcement until a successor was selected.[111] There was no further hint of a pending retirement; Justice Burton selected his law clerks as usual for the coming year so as to avoid comment, although he had spoken to the attorney general on July 17 about providing jobs for them should that be necessary.

On September 19, Attorney General Rogers again paid a call on Justice Burton, this time to ask him if he would reconsider his decision to retire. Burton said no. The attorney general then explained that no announcement had been made concerning his retirement because the president wished to "avoid complications with the Court views as to desegregation."[112]

The members of the Court were not informed of Burton's retirement plans until the Friday conference on September 16. Justice Burton also called the attorney general on that day and suggested that his retirement should not be announced until the Court's decision in *Cooper v. Aaron*[113] was formally delivered.[114] His retirement became effective on October 13. He was seventy years old.

Justice Burton's final years were very difficult. His illness became increasingly debilitating, and there was little in those days that could be done for him. For several years, from 1958 until his condition worsened in 1962, he was able to participate occasionally on the Court of Appeals for the District of Columbia.[115] He died in Washington, at George Washington Hospital, on October 28, 1964.

Charles E. Whittaker (1957–1962)

Justice Reed was succeeded by Charles E. Whittaker, whose story of professional achievement is one of the most interesting in Court history. He made his way to Kansas City as a lad from a prairie farm in Kansas, having been tutored in a one-room schoolhouse. In the city he prospered because of his obvious ability, self-discipline, and an extraordinary work ethic, causing the law firm that he joined as an office boy to first hire him as a lawyer and then award him a partnership in the firm. His life followed verbatim the chapters in a Horatio Alger novel.

Whittaker's later rise within the judiciary was also meteoric during the Eisenhower years. First he became a federal district court judge in western Missouri for two years and then a member of the Court of Appeals for the Eighth Circuit for another year. An appointment to the Supreme Court followed logically.

But he had been on the Supreme Court only a few months when Justice Burton made an ominous observation in his diary: "Justice Whittaker has been on the edge of a nervous breakdown but hopes to finish the term and then recuperate."[116] The following years proved to be equally difficult for Whittaker, until he finally collapsed in March 1962 with what was then described as a nervous breakdown.[117]

When Whittaker first came to the Court, Justice Black at once asked him, "Well, how do you feel about being here as a justice?" Whittaker replied, "Mr. Justice, I am scared to death." Black then said reassuringly, "Well, there is no reason for that. You will find that these justices are all just boys grown tall."[118] Nonetheless, he found it impossible to adjust to life on the Court.

As a lawyer Whittaker had simply adopted his client's point of view; it usually had not been necessary for him to decide between competing positions. But as a judge, making decisions was what he had to spend much of his time doing, which was a continuous problem for him. He once said, speaking of the weekly conferences in which cases are decided, that as the junior justice he was obliged to speak last and vote first. It was an arrangement that "put the monkey on the junior's back."[119] He was very uncomfortable as the tiebreaker.

Whittaker liked to tell his law clerks that "everything you write is to be etched in marble and takes great care."[120] A clerk related that Whittaker "talked about a sentence; a five year and ten year sentence. He thought he had been sentenced [to a five year term] but then he began to lengthen it."[121]

One of his law clerks concluded that he thought "Justice Whittaker fought the job . . . instead of being able to master it he fought it and [continued] wishing and hoping it could be handled in a different way."[122] It was apparent that "what he agonized over was writing opinions. . . . Writing opinions was more of a chore for him than it need be or must be for someone who must write."[123]

Another clerk assessed Whittaker's problem in a somewhat more generalized fashion: "If he had difficulty in serving it was because of the pressures. All Justices have the same pressures but over time the others were able to adjust and adapt and accept the responsibility without continuing to feel the

Charles E. Whittaker suffered from mental illness when appointed. (Supreme Court, Office of the Curator)

burden. The responsibilities as he understood them never enabled him to make the adjustment. He worried too much."[124]

At Justice Douglas's suggestion, Whittaker entered Walter Reed Army Medical Center on March 6, 1962, although he had never previously been hospitalized. Whittaker later revealed that by "the middle of February he began to feel tired and worn out, and this condition of exhaustion became progressively worse. He had difficulty in sleeping, lost some of his appetite, began to worry and found it difficult to concentrate. 'I was burning the candle at both ends to a point where I became completely enervated,' he said."[125]

Washington, D.C., was never a congenial place for the Whittakers. He found certain of his colleagues difficult, particularly Douglas and Frankfurter. But it probably was not conflict within the Court or even the stress and uncertainty that was with him during the spring of 1962 as he struggled with *Baker v. Carr*[126] and the reapportionment issue that precipitated the breakdown.[127] According to one of the justice's three sons, Dr. C. Keith Whittaker, a neurosurgeon, it was disease—that is, the deep depression that overcame him—that caused his father's final collapse. Unknown to most people, Whittaker had suffered previously from depression. His son recalled that during the 1930s Whittaker's law firm had sent him to Arizona, by himself, for a period of recuperation while he struggled with depression.[128] Thus Whittaker came to the Supreme Court with a preexisting medical condition that in later years would have precluded his appointment altogether.

Hospitalization at Walter Reed was less than satisfactory. According to Whittaker's son, his doctors were "abysmally ignorant" as to how to treat him.[129] He was given thioridazine, which resulted in akathisia, a condition characterized by extreme restlessness.[130] He could not sit still and was continually inclined to move restlessly about. The justice's condition was more severe than the general public could have known: he became suicidal. His son was persuaded that he intended to take his life at one point and, on a Sunday morning, pleaded with him not to do so. Justice Whittaker finally promised his son he would not commit suicide.[131]

After retiring because of disability (the first justice to do so explicitly on this basis) on March 29, it took Whittaker about a year and a half to recover.[132] It was not until 1965 that he resigned from the federal judiciary to take employment with General Motors. He did not otherwise engage in the practice of law. He went to his office regularly, dined at a downtown Kansas City restaurant favored by lawyers where he held court each noon, and resumed the pattern of life he had enjoyed in his younger years.[133]

Whittaker was a small man, formal and courteous toward others, and much given to cigarettes, although the large desk in his usually empty downtown Kansas City office was generally cluttered with corncob pipes. The rapid shifting of those corncob pipes on his desk was often a sign the justice was tiring of a conversation.

Essentially a successful trial lawyer, in retirement he was still an energetic speaker. Although he apparently enjoyed public speaking and was accomplished at it, he always refused to accept an honorarium after he left the Court.[134] In 1971 he gave an address on the "The Court and the Constitution," dealing largely with the constitutional power to regulate commerce, to a packed audience of college students at the University of Missouri–Kansas City. The students enthusiastically welcomed his talk. He was obviously pleased by his reception, because he had been received less courteously at other forums where he had taken a strong law and order position on the rising wave of social protests in the late 1960s. When one of the students asked him, impressed by his performance, why he had left the Court, Whittaker answered that his doctor had put in writing his professional opinion that he would die if he did not retire.[135]

Justice Whittaker's death on November 26, 1973, at St. Luke's Hospital in Kansas City was quite unexpected. He was in good spirits, even playful, with no premonition the end was near when an undiagnosed aneurysm burst in his abdominal aorta, causing his death at two o'clock in the afternoon. His son was on staff at the hospital at the time and arrived quickly at his father's side, although nothing could be done to save him. Death had come very suddenly because the aneurysm was massive and had been unanticipated.

Whittaker had initially entered the hospital complaining of symptoms not unlike those that forced him to retire from the Court. He had again gone into serious depression. His doctors prescribed lithium, which seemed to be working very well for him. However, the situation was further complicated by urinary retention, which caused his kidneys to become dysfunctional. He then required a dialysis machine. None of these symptoms was perceived as life threatening; the real threat to his life remained undiagnosed.

Justice Whittaker's wife, Winifred, was an Irish Catholic, so their sons were reared as Catholics. Consequently, he was buried in his judicial robe next to his wife in a Catholic cemetery in Kansas City. The justice, however, retained his own religion. At about the age of fifty he had joined the Methodist Church, in large part because one of his oldest friends was a member. Formal religion never played an important part in his life, and his own father had never joined a church. Nonetheless, he was sometimes asked to speak at various church events, and he was always willing to do so. His interdenominational funeral service at Central Methodist Church in Kansas City included seven Methodist and Catholic clergymen.

Felix Frankfurter (1939–1962)

Felix Frankfurter also left the Court in 1962 in shattered health. He had been ill previously in 1958 with a minor heart attack, of which he had been unaware until he was given a routine checkup. He at once entered a hospital and said to his doctors: "Look here. I want to ask you fellows something, and I'll be guided by your opinion and advice in the matter. Do you think I should sit down right now and write out my resignation from the Court?" He was quickly assured there was no need to do that, and he made a full recovery.[136]

The illness that forced Justice Frankfurter off the Court first occurred on April 5, 1962. He was working at his desk in his Supreme Court office when he collapsed with a stroke.[137] He slumped out of his chair and fell onto the floor where he remained until his secretary found him.[138] It seemed at first that the stroke was relatively minor, and its cause had "cleared spontaneously and left no residual after effect."[139] A few days later, however, while still in the hospital, Frankfurter experienced a second, more severe stroke. This attack left his speech slightly impaired and paralyzed his left arm and leg. At the end of April, there was a hospital announcement to the effect that he could be expected back at the Court during the current term.[140]

Justice Frankfurter returned to his Georgetown home on July 14; on July 26 he received a courtesy call from President John Kennedy. Although his energy was much depleted and he tired quickly, there appeared to be no mental incapacity. He was present at a discussion between two of his doctors, and when one of them noted he had only limited use of his left arm and leg, the other replied, "No matter. The world has never counted much on this one's abilities as an athlete." The justice recounted the exchange for friends with obvious delight, tapped his forehead, and exclaimed, "Nothing wrong here, you see, nothing at all."[141] He continued to dictate his voluminous correspondence each morning as usual.

Reluctantly, but predictably, Justice Frankfurter retired on August 28, 1962. In his letter to President Kennedy, he explained, "To retain my seat on the basis of a diminished work schedule would not comport with my own philosophy or with the demands of the business of the Court."[142] He also indicated that an attempt to accelerate therapy might entail further hazards to his health. Moreover, given his penchant for interaction with counsel during oral arguments, he may have been self-conscious about his speech impairment. Certainly the actress Ruth Gordon and her husband, Garson Kanin, found him very sensitive about wearing a sling after being released from the hospital. The following exchange occurred: "His left arm is in a bandagelike sling, with an odd foam-rubber handle close to the elbow. I ask at once [said Kanin], 'What's all that?' The question, I fear, angers him. He replies snappishly, 'It's a sling! Haven't you ever seen a sling? What's so remarkable about it? You had slings when you were a boy, didn't you? Well, this is a sling.'"[143] Following the stroke, his voice began to reacquire the Viennese accents of his youth.

Less than three years remained for him. Both Frankfurter and his wife, Marion, were then confined to wheelchairs. But he attended President Kennedy's funeral nonetheless and spent more time with Marion than had been possible for many years. Every day remained a delight and something new to be experienced. As his chauffeur recalled, the elderly couple would sit holding hands, and "he'd point things out like as she were a tourist and him a guide—he'd get all excited, y'know, the way he did—all *involved*—and she'd—well, you know, she'd make all the right sounds. Some fine days, he'd be like a little boy looking things over—every time like the first time—the Justice could do that, y'know."[144]

Justice Frankfurter became ill again on February 21, 1965, at age eighty-two. He was taken to George Washington Hospital, where at a little after five o'clock in the afternoon, he spoke his last words to a Court employee who was with him. "I hope," he said, "I don't spoil your Washington's birthday."[145] He died a moment later.

A memorial service was held in the apartment where he and Marion had moved, attended by over a hundred people, including the president and the Court. There were two readings, a Jewish prayer and, as with Brandeis, the words from *Pilgrim's Progress* recording the death of Mr. Valiant-for-Truth.[146]

Arthur J. Goldberg (1962–1965)

Like Justice Byrnes, Arthur J. Goldberg resigned from the Supreme Court after a brief tenure to assume another position. On July 20, 1965, he accepted President Johnson's request, made the previous evening, that he succeed Adlai E. Stevenson as the ambassador to the United Nations. Justice

Goldberg's ambition was to be influential in the conduct of foreign policy.[147] As one of his friends told the press, "Arthur has always gone with the action."[148]

It was not long before he realized, too late, that he had yielded his justiceship for a position that carried with it little actual authority. Although Johnson later described Goldberg as "bored" on the Court in his memoirs in 1971, Goldberg responded by describing his Court years as "the culmination of a life's ambitions."[149] Goldberg's bitterness was surely aggravated by his belated awareness of Johnson's real motive, which was to open a vacancy for Abe Fortas.

Since Goldberg wrote no memoirs and was notoriously reluctant to discuss with any precision exactly what happened to cause him to leave the Court, the circumstances of his resignation are somewhat ambiguous. Nonetheless, it is possible to conclude that Johnson wanted Goldberg's seat vacant so it could be offered to his longtime friend and personal lawyer, Abe Fortas; that Johnson was willing to suggest several positions with Goldberg, including the posts of attorney general and secretary of health, education, and welfare, in addition to the UN ambassadorship; and that Goldberg did believe he was duty bound to take the United Nations position not just because it was the president who offered it to him but also because he thought his negotiating skills could make a difference in bringing about a resolution of the Vietnam conflict.[150]

President Johnson surely applied pressure to Goldberg as only he could during a flight on *Air Force One* as they traveled to Adlai Stevenson's funeral in Illinois. What transpired on that flight between the two men can never be known for certain, since only the president's account of the conversation exists. Nonetheless, the president's memory of what happened appears most likely when it is recalled that Goldberg never expressly denied he was restless and bored on the Court, and the discussion would not have progressed as it did had Goldberg firmly discouraged it, which obviously did not happen. Therefore, it is likely that Johnson did tell Goldberg he "had heard that he might step down from the Court and therefore might be available for another assignment" and that Goldberg answered that "these reports had substance."[151] It is also most likely that Johnson dangled the prospect of the vice presidency, however obliquely, before the ambitious Goldberg.[152] Ambassador Henry Cabot Lodge's vice presidential selection by Richard Nixon in 1960 was at the time very recent history.

A more controversial explanation also has been suggested: that Johnson had "a hold over Goldberg" because of a party Goldberg, as secretary of labor, had held for Vice President Johnson and a group of labor leaders that was designed to heal past disagreements between labor and the vice president.[153] The event was orchestrated by an assistant secretary of labor, Jerry Holleman, who solicited money for the party from, among others, Bill Sol Estes, who soon thereafter came under investigation for shady business dealings. When alerted as to how the money for the lavish party was obtained, Goldberg allegedly became concerned that the fund-raising could be used to discredit both himself and the Kennedy administration, so Holleman took full responsibility for the expenditures and, rather than answer further questions, resigned his post and returned to Texas.

In later years Holleman related these events and concluded that Johnson knew what had happened and that the sequence of events surrounding the party could have blocked or embarrassed Goldberg's appointment to the Court. Holleman's story is uncorroborated and was vigorously contested by Senator Daniel Patrick Moynihan when it appeared in print. Senator Moynihan, who helped Goldberg draft his Court resignation and his acceptance of the United Nations position, concluded that the basic reason Goldberg resigned was because "he did not know how to say no to a President telling him that the highest interests of the American nation were at stake."[154] Referring to Goldberg as "one of the great tacticians of his time," Moynihan considered it inconceivable to suppose that Johnson or anyone else had a "hold" on him. As an officer in the Office of Strategic Services during World War II, Goldberg had routinely dealt with spies and double agents. Consequently, Moynihan thought it most unlikely that a man of Goldberg's wide experience would have permitted a situation where he was at Johnson's mercy.

Goldberg was the fourth justice to leave the Court during this century for another position, joining Charles Evans Hughes (who left to run for president), James Byrnes (who left to become "assistant president"), and John Clarke (who left to work on behalf of world peace). After his frustrating tenure as UN ambassador, which ended in 1968 with the Johnson administration, he remained in New York, practicing law, until he ran unsuccessfully for governor of that state against Nelson A. Rockefeller in 1970 on the Liberal-Democratic ticket. As a politician he appeared stiff and formal, lacking any natural campaigning skills. Following his first and only experience with electoral politics, he moved to Washington, D.C., where he practiced law. Appointing him an ambassador-at-large, President Jimmy Carter utilized his talents as a negotiator. For his efforts, Goldberg received the Presidential Medal of Freedom in 1978.[155]

Justice Goldberg was found dead in his Washington apartment, having died during the night of January 19, 1990, of a heart attack caused by coronary artery disease. He was eighty-one years old. His daughter, Barbara Goldberg Cramer, recalled the family's reaction to his resignation from the Supreme Court. "We all felt he shouldn't have made that decision," she said, "but he felt it was the best thing to do for the nation. His thinking was, when the president asks you to do something, you respond positively."[156]

Tom C. Clark (1949–1967)

In excellent health, Tom C. Clark retired on June 12, 1967, after eighteen years of service at the relatively young age of sixty-seven. The appointment of his son, Ramsey Clark, as attorney general motivated his retirement. Justice Clark wished to avoid any possible conflict of interest. He had earlier given notice to Chief Justice Warren of his intention to retire in the event his son became attorney general.[157] President Johnson's shrewd employment of Ramsey Clark was his way of removing the senior Clark, thereby permitting the appointment of Thurgood Marshall.[158]

Justice Clark died in his sleep on June 13, 1977, while staying at his son's home in New York. He was sitting on the Court of Appeals for the Second Circuit at the time. He remained busy in retirement and was the only retired justice to have sat on all eleven circuits. The previous fall Clark had been hospitalized for four or five days for a heart condition. Only ten days before his death he explained to a reporter that he suffered from fibrillation, which is a rapid and erratic heartbeat, but said that the medication he took controlled the condition.[159]

Between 1937 and 1969, the justices for the most part did not linger long beyond their period of useful service. The illnesses of Justices Cardozo and Murphy were somewhat more extended than most of the others, but they did not continue on the Court beyond the year of their incapacitation. The Retirement Act of 1937 seemed to have had the desired initial effect: aged justices voluntarily retired from active service instead of continuing in office until they died.

There were still seven deaths (Cardozo, Butler, Stone, Murphy, Rutledge, Vinson, and Jackson). But the three resignations (Roberts, Byrnes, and Goldberg) and eleven retirements continued and emphasized an emerging twentieth-century pattern: the number of resignations and retirements began to far exceed the number of deaths in office. Some of the justices still stayed on longer than they should have. Justice Sutherland, Hugo Black recalled in later years, almost had to be led around. Justice Black told several of his clerks, with reference to Sutherland's last days, that "one of the hardest things you have to do up here is to know when to leave. If you stay too long, you impose terrible burdens on your colleagues."[160]

Nonetheless, a desirable pattern seemed to be emerging. As medical knowledge exponentially increased during the latter half of the century, it is not surprising that the justices, like many other Americans, were direct beneficiaries of the newly emerging expertise, which made it possible for them to know more clearly than before when they should step aside. When coupled with expanding press coverage and an ongoing willingness within the Court to encourage retirement when appropriate, it is apparent that the lingering tenures of disabled justices had been, for a time, successfully discouraged.

6

THE CONTEMPORARY PERIOD, 1969–1998

Even though no justice has died in office since 1954, nine of the retirements after 1969 involved men over seventy-five, most of whom suffered periodically incapacitating illnesses. During these years, the average age for retirement or resignation has increased to seventy-seven, the highest in the Court's history. Justices are living longer, but their disinclination to leave has remained unchanged.

Earl Warren (Chief Justice: 1953–1969)

Earl Warren retired as chief justice while still in good health. At the end of the term, in June 1968, he informed President Johnson that he wished to leave because of his age, which was seventy-seven.[1] His retirement was conditional; it would not be effective until his successor was confirmed by the Senate.[2] It was apparent that Warren, a Republican, wanted President Johnson, a Democrat in his last year of office, to appoint the next chief justice.[3] When Fortas's nomination for chief justice faltered in the Senate before the oncoming presidential election and was eventually withdrawn, Warren remained on the bench for an additional year, until Warren E. Burger was confirmed on June 23, 1969.

In retirement, Warren heard no cases as a federal judge. He did, however, retain chambers at the Supreme Court, keep his secretary, and select law clerks as usual, but with the understanding that they were to work only for him.[4] He wanted the staff assistance for his memoirs (the first ever written by a chief justice), speeches, and other related purposes, much as he had used staff in his California gubernatorial years. The *Memoirs,* when eventually completed, proved disappointing. They were bland, somewhat defensive, and repeated much that was common knowledge. Warren was more candid

Table 6.1
Age of Death, Resignation, or Retirement 1969–1998

Age	Died	Resigned	Retired
54 or younger	0	0	0
55–59	0	1	0
60–64	0	0	0
65–69	0	0	1
70–74	0	0	1
75–79	0	0	5
80 or older	0	0	4
Totals	0	1	11
Average age of those leaving the Court: 77			

Source: Elder Witt, ed., *Congressional Quarterly's Guide to the U.S. Supreme Court,* 2d ed. (Washington, D.C.: Congressional Quarterly Press, 1990).

with his criticism of the proposed National Court of Appeals favored by many in the Nixon administration, which would have existed between the Supreme Court and the courts of appeals to reduce the number of appeals to the high court. Warren quickly saw this proposal as a criticism of the "Warren Court," which of course it was.[5]

In 1972 Warren found he had some coronary artery occlusion with related angina pectoris, none of which immediately discomforted him.[6] He became ill with chest pains in January 1974, but after a week of hospitalization, he continued a series of speaking engagements that left him exhausted. When he returned to Washington in May, he entered Georgetown University Hospital. After his death, it was alleged that Warren's first choice was Bethesda Naval Hospital, which was free to retired Supreme Court justices with White House permission, but President Nixon—his enemy from the California political wars—refused to sign off on Warren's admission until after he was admitted to Georgetown. At this point, so the story went, Warren refused to leave.[7]

The facts, however, were otherwise, as Bernard Schwartz has revealed.[8] Actually, Warren had difficulty arranging his usual end-of-the-year checkup at Walter Reed Army Hospital and told this to Chief Justice Burger, who was himself quite upset to hear about it. Apparently, one of the military administrators had decided that "retired officers" were no longer entitled to such services and that included the Supreme Court. When Burger called the secretary of the army, Howard H. Callaway, the secretary quickly reassured Burger that "retired officers" referred only to military personnel. The secretary wrote a letter of apology to Warren and later apologized to him on the telephone. Following this action by Secretary Callaway, Warren could at any time have entered Walter Reed or any other military hospital for medical assistance. The reason he did not do so later was because his physician there had retired, and his new doctor, Oscar Mann, was affiliated with Georgetown University Hospital.

Warren recovered sufficiently to return to his apartment at the Sheraton Park Hotel. However, on July 2, he was again admitted to Georgetown with congestive heart failure. In his last week of life, he was still strongly focused on the *Watergate Tapes* case[9] then before the Supreme Court. On the day of his death, Justice Brennan came around at about 5:30 in the afternoon to his seventh floor Georgetown Hospital room to brief him as to what the Court had decided to do about the *Watergate Tapes* case. Justice Douglas, contrary to what he reported in his autobiography, *The Court Years*, was not with him. When told that the Court unanimously was opposed to Nixon's contention that he need not release the tapes to the district court, Warren was very pleased. "Thank God! Thank God! Thank God!" Warren exclaimed. "If you don't do it this way Bill, it's the end of the country as we have known it."[10] Shortly after Brennan left, Earl Warren died, at 8:10 P.M., with his wife and youngest daughter beside him.

Abe Fortas (1965–1969)

Several weeks before Warren retired, *Life* magazine published an article on May 5 that implied Abe Fortas had acted with impropriety in matters relating to the financier Louis E. Wolfson, who was under federal indictment.[11] It was Wolfson's practice to give financial assistance to people in public life in return for speeches or consulting services of use to the Wolfson Foundation. When Wolfson offered financial assistance to Arthur Goldberg, after he had gone to the United Nations, Goldberg replied that it was "my fixed rule . . . in my public career, to manage my personal affairs with my own resources."[12] Fortas's view was different; despite having made substantial sums as a lawyer, money still attracted him. Consequently, while a member of the Supreme Court, he agreed to act as a consultant to the Wolfson Foundation at a flat fee of $20,000 each year for the rest of his life. After his death, Mrs. Fortas would continue to receive the same amount.

Justice Fortas received his first check in January 1966. In June, he decided to terminate the agreement with Wolfson. His reasons were the Court's workload, which he had underestimated, and, although he did not mention it, he had learned that Wolfson's file had been turned over to the Justice Department by the Securities and Exchange Commission for possible criminal prosecution. Wolfson was indicted in September and October 1966; Fortas returned the initial check of $20,000 in December. Although Wolfson sometimes sent Fortas material relating to the legal difficulties besetting him, the justice denied he had intervened in any way on his behalf.[13]

Justice Fortas had done nothing criminal, but he had given the impression that he was an insensitive, greedy wheeler-dealer, and the Nixon administration elected to make the most of it. Attorney General John Mitchell, orchestrating the administration's response, first briefed President Nixon and then paid a call on Chief Justice Warren, likely with a copy in hand of the foundation contract the justice had signed. Warren was publicly noncommittal, but it was said that privately he strongly disapproved of Fortas's behavior. Moreover, it seemed to be the general sentiment within the Court that a resignation was the only reasonable course of action left.[14]

Nonetheless, Fortas was inclined to wait. There was the chance that public attention might unexpectedly focus elsewhere, and he particularly wanted to wait for the advice of Justice Douglas, his former professor at Yale, who at the time was in Brazil. Unfortunately, Fortas had previously agreed to a series of college lectures, which seemed to further focus national attention on his case. On Tuesday night, May 13, Fortas met with his former law partner, Paul Porter, and Justice Douglas. Although Douglas was in "a combative mood," the decision was made that evening to resign.[15]

Clark Clifford has revealed that he too had an important role in the deliberations. He tells in his autobiography that he and Douglas, over a two-day period, talked with Fortas and confirms Douglas's strong opposition to Fortas's resignation. His description of Fortas's demeanor is interesting: "Abe talked with the same calm, quiet logic and detachment with which he analyzed legal matters—it was as if he were discussing someone else. Listening to Fortas describe his own feelings, I concluded he had made up his mind before he came to see us."[16] Clifford did not know if Attorney General John Mitchell had additional evidence against Fortas, but Fortas apparently believed the Nixon administration would continue to press for his resignation and that they were inclined to bring criminal charges against him to force his removal. The Fortas resignation, Clifford concluded, was caused by President Johnson's overreaching, Fortas's bad judgment, and the Nixon administration's attacks.[17]

After the resignation, Justice Fortas explained his reasoning to Benjamin C. Bradlee of the *Washington Post:* "If I had stayed on the Court, there would

Senator Hugo L. Black in 1935. (Supreme Court, Office of the Curator)

be this constitutional confrontation that would go on for months. Hell, I feel there wasn't any choice for a man of conscience."[18] After a period of emotional recuperation, Fortas returned to the practice of law in Washington, although not with his old firm of Arnold, Fortas, and Porter. He became a solo practitioner and continued working until his death on April 5, 1982, from a ruptured aorta.[19] He frequently smoked cigarettes and suffered from a gall bladder condition, but had appeared before the Supreme Court only two weeks earlier for the first time in thirteen years, arguing with all of his former persuasiveness and brilliance.

Hugo L. Black (1937–1971)

Two years after Abe Fortas resigned, the Supreme Court lost Hugo L. Black and John Marshall Harlan in the same month. Both became terminally ill during the Court's summer recess.

In July 1971, at the age of eighty-five, about a month after he had vigorously criticized the Nixon administration in the *Pentagon Papers* case,[20] Justice Black began to physically deteriorate. He suffered from headaches and became persuaded he was going to die. When Hugo Black Jr. arrived to be with his father, he was told at once: "Son, I can't do my job, 'cause I can't see. I've got to quit" (he had already prepared his retirement letter to President Nixon). He then concluded, "I always told you I would know when I had to get off the Court—and the time has come."[21]

His condition had been diagnosed as temporal arteritis.[22] On August 28, in the pouring rain, Black was admitted to Bethesda Naval Hospital. "He still seemed clear-minded and strong-voiced," his son recalled, "and he had not insisted I send out the retirement letter."[23] In the hospital Justice Black's premonition of death intensified. The doctors were baffled: "[His] condition just defies us. There is no physical reason why he should continue to deteriorate, but he is. It's almost like the case of an aborigine who was in excellent health, but entered the hospital convinced he was going to die because someone had put a voodoo spell on him."[24]

Black was disinterested in everything. He would sometimes stare at his hands, then move his fingers, then each finger, and then a joint. When his son finally asked what he was doing, he replied, "Just checkin' to see if a stroke has hit me."[25] Even Justice Harlan, who was a patient in the same hospital, could not arouse him from his lethargy.

Upon entering the hospital, Black had insisted that his son destroy his Court papers. Although the papers were being burned, the letter was not sent. Finally, with the papers burned and the doctors dispairing of a recovery, his son told him it was probably time to send the letter. With a stricken look Black replied, "All right, son. I can't do my job. I guess it's time to send it."[26] President Nixon accepted his resignation on September 17.

Two days after his retirement, Black suffered his first stroke. A few days later, on September 25, he had a second stroke, which rendered him speechless and caused breathing difficulty. At around midnight his son was told he was dead. He ran to the room and "found him lying there, his left eye cocked open," which he closed.[27]

Justice Black was buried at Arlington National Cemetery next to his first wife, up a hill about two hundred yards from the monument to William Howard Taft. Engraved on the simple stone is "Hugo Lafayette Black, Captain, U.S. Army." A marble bench between the two grave sites is engraved with the words "Here Lies a Good Man."[28]

A still vigorous Hugo L. Black in his last years. (Supreme Court, Office of the Curator)

John Marshall Harlan (1955–1971)

Throughout most of Justice Black's final illness, John Marshall Harlan was in a nearby room. Although in pain with an undiagnosed back ailment, the seventy-four-year-old Harlan was in good humor, continued to function as a member of the Court over his bedroom telephone, and still maintained a before-dinner cocktail hour.[29]

Justice Harlan privately asked Hugo Black Jr. if his father was going to retire. When told that Black would likely retire soon, Harlan explained why he needed to know what his plans were:

> I cannot do my job any longer; I believe I have cancer of the spine and I am going to have to retire. But I do not want to do anything to detract from the attention your father's retirement will get. I don't have to tell you. He is one of the all-time greats of our Court. He has served with over one-third of the Justices who ever sat on the Court. Nobody's judgment ever exceeded his—his is just the best. . . . Holding up until your father's retirement is recognized and commented on is the right thing to do.[30]

Justice Harlan had not been well for some years. He was nearly blind and at his last public functions had been obliged to lean heavily on Chief Justice Burger's arm.[31] And yet, the quality of his Court opinions seemed miraculously to remain unaffected.

On September 16, Harlan transferred from Bethesda Naval Hospital to George Washington University Hospital because, the press reported, they specialized in back aliments.[32] That was not the reason for the transfer. A piece of Justice Harlan's spine had been surgically removed for analysis on a Friday, and over the weekend the specimen that would determine whether he had cancer was lost. On the following Monday, when informed of what had happened, the normally mannered and patrician Harlan was infuriated. "We fired a man in our firm who made a mistake of this magnitude," he said. "I am going to leave and go to George Washington Hospital."[33]

It mattered little. The cancer that was belatedly discovered was irreversible. Harlan retired in September, waiting until after Justice Black had retired. The spinal cancer continued to metastasize, paralyzing half his body and leaving his other side racked with pain.[34] He was predictably courageous as he faced death, engaging his visitors about their concerns as he always had. Only once was he heard to call out, when visited by one of his friends from his Wall Street years, "Why did this have to happen to me?"[35] But he engaged in no self-pity, despite terrible pain. He died at George Washington Hospital three months after his retirement, on December 30, 1971, surrounded by his daughter, his sisters, and his good friend Potter Stewart.

William O. Douglas (1939–1975)

While vacationing in Nassau, William O. Douglas suffered a stroke on New Year's eve, 1974. President Ford ordered a plane to bring him back to Walter Reed Army Medical Center, where he was listed as satisfactory.[36] Since 1968 Douglas had lived with a pacemaker in his chest. Given his history of heart abnormality, his physicians suspected that a clot had formed in his heart, eventually finding its way to his brain.[37]

By mid-February Douglas was working on Court business several hours a day in his hospital room, although his progress was slower than doctors had anticipated.[38] His left arm and leg remained largely useless, and his speech was impaired. In March he returned to the Court confined to a wheelchair. "Walking," he said, "has very little to do with the Court."[39] Nonetheless, he was markedly changed in appearance: "To reporters who had known him before the stroke, the Justice appeared for the first time as a frail and fragile old man, his voice thin and uncertain, his left arm hanging useless at his side, most of the remarkable vigor of the outdoorsman drained away."[40]

Although his mind at first seemed unharmed, he acknowledged that he had "been through considerable of an ordeal; there is not the same energy I had before-hand."[41] But he did not intend to yield his place, particularly to President Gerald Ford, who had led the attempt to impeach him in 1970. As he told a friend, "I won't resign while there's a breath in my body—until we get a Democratic president."[42] Instead, during the spring of 1975 he cast votes through Justice Brennan, although the Court may have counted his vote only when it was not decisive.[43] As Douglas's biographer noted:

> Douglas' mental condition deteriorated. He repeatedly addressed people at the Court by their wrong names, often uttered non sequiturs in conversation or simply stopped speaking altogether, retreating into glassy-eyed silence. On one occasion, Douglas adamantly refused to be wheeled into his own office, claiming it was the chambers of the Chief Justice.[44]

In early September, the justice held court in Yakima, Washington. He was alert, responding to questions with "short crisp phrases," but some observers

William O. Douglas ready to hike a trail. (Supreme Court, Office of the Curator)

became alarmed when for some nine and half minutes he stared motionless at his hands while shuffling his papers, saying nothing.[45] He began to discuss federalism, turning then to a comparison between the governments of the United States and Australia, before finally issuing an emergency stay in the matter before him.[46] The fact of his incapacitation had been viewed on television by millions of people.

Douglas was determined to maintain his seat. "I'm not quite ready to commit suicide," he said. "Even if I'm half dead, maybe it will make a difference about someone getting an education."[47] When he returned to the Court, he was unprepared to discuss any business, so he insisted that his clerks wheel ten carts of petitions into the conference room. He was also incontinent. His secretary followed his wheelchair, spraying Lysol unsuccessfully to mask the odor.[48]

Douglas's situation became impossible. He could use only one hand, would alternate between periods of lucidity and drowsiness caused by medication, and would leave the bench after short periods because of the constant pain that never left him. His vision was affected, making it difficult for him to read. When absent, he cast his votes through Brennan.

A fever beset him on October 17, and he was again hospitalized at Walter Reed, where doctors became anxious over the physical deterioration that had taken place since the previous spring. He was in constant pain because of an unusual nerve condition in his left side. The medical team at Walter Reed concluded that he had no hope at all for real improvement. A second opinion was sought from Dr. Howard Rusk in New York City, a rehabilitation specialist. His advice was equally guarded, but he concluded there might be some cause for hope if the justice retired from the Court.[49] So advised, Justice Douglas retired at age seventy-seven on November 12, 1975, after thirty-six years and seven months of service, the longest tenure in the Supreme Court's history.

Later that month Douglas returned to his office at the Court to find that his clerks had been reassigned. He was furious. He intended to vote on the constitutionality of the campaign finance law, since he had heard the oral arguments and no successor had been confirmed. In fact, he intended to participate in any cases accepted prior to his retirement, which was, of course, unprecedented and quite impossible. Douglas seemed unable to accept the fact of his retirement and refused Chief Justice Burger's request to move into smaller chambers available for retired justices.

When he tried to release his thirteen-page memorandum on the campaign finance law, he was ignored by his colleagues. Court officials were instructed

A much diminished William O. Douglas (right) after his stroke, seen here with Warren E. Burger. (Smithsonian Institution)

to do likewise. As Burger told one of his clerks, "Bill is like an old firehouse dog, too old to run along with the trucks, but his ears prick up just the same."[50]

Douglas lingered on, impaired and weakened, yet fiercely determined to achieve what was still possible. With law clerk assistance he completed the final volume of his autobiography before he died on January 19, 1980, at age eighty-one.[51] Services were held on a cold day at the National Presbyterian Church in Washington, after which he was buried at Arlington National Cemetery.

Potter Stewart (1958–1981)

Potter Stewart surprised many people when he retired on July 3, 1981, at the relatively youthful age of sixty-six. Five members of his Court were then older than he was. He explained that he wanted to spend more time with his family, while taking occasional assignments with lower courts. He had evidently thought of retiring a year earlier but had delayed because it was an election year and he did not want a confirmation fight over his successor. Well aware of a tendency on the part of others to stay too long in office, Stewart commented, "It's better to go too soon than to stay too long."[52] Moreover, he wished to leave the Court in good health.

He may have regretted his early retirement, because he was later heard to say (referring to part-time work on the lower courts) that it was "no fun to play in the minors after a career in the major leagues."[53] Certainly, his close friend on the Court, Lewis Powell, did believe that retirement had contributed to Stewart's relatively early death. In any event, his health soon began to fail. In 1982 he fell at his New Hampshire home, breaking several ribs and chipping his collarbone. At age seventy he suffered a massive stroke while visiting at his daughter's home in Dummerston, Vermont. He was transported to the nearby Dartmouth-Hitchcock Medical Center in Hanover, New Hampshire, in critical condition on Monday, December 2, 1985. He died five days later, at 3:20 in the afternoon. Sources who declined to be identified revealed that Stewart was suffering from Parkinson's disease, a degenerative nervous-system disorder, at the time of his death.[54]

Justice Stewart was taken from Hanover back to Washington, D.C., for the funeral, which was held at the National Cathedral. He was buried at Arlington National Cemetery.

Warren E. Burger (Chief Justice: 1969–1986)

In late May 1986, Warren E. Burger asked for an appointment with President Ronald Reagan to discuss the Commission on the Bicentennial of the U.S. Constitution, which the president had earlier asked him to chair. As the chief justice began to discuss the commission, the president and others in the room seemed to be less than totally attentive. However, that lack of interest soon changed when the seventy-nine-year-old chief justice informed Reagan that he planned to give his full time to the administration of the commission and that he was ready to leave the Court.[55] After seventeen years, the longest tenure as chief justice in this century, Burger retired "effective July 10, or as soon thereafter as my successor is qualified."[56]

Some doubted that Burger would wish to leave the Court in the absence of a more compelling reason than the chairing of the bicentennial commission. At the news conference the next day, one reporter was persistent about why he was leaving, questioning the chief justice in the following manner:

Q. Is it a matter of health, sir? I mean, people don't leave the Court except for matters of health, normally.

A. Well, you make the diagnosis. Do I look as though I'm falling apart?

Q. Well, it's not how you look, it's how you feel. I mean, was it a matter of health, sir?

A. Never felt better in my life.[57]

The only ailment Burger acknowledged, "apart from the ordinary mental deterioration that occurs after age 40,"[58] was a "polio back" caused by contracting polio at age ten.

Nor was the chief justice inclined to attach importance to deteriorating personal relationships on the Court.[59] He emphatically denied that the Court had become more sharply divided during his administration. "In the 17 years I have been there presiding over the conferences," he said, "never once, never once, has a voice been raised in any discussions." He did, however, allow that there had been "vigorous discussions, as they should be."[60]

Chief Justice Burger correctly understood the demanding requirements of the five-year bicentennial celebration over which he presided. He lived an active life—promoting the Constitution through a myriad of activities involving publications, schools, and colleges, judicial groups, and television—until shortly before his death from congestive heart failure at age eighty-seven on June 25, 1995. Like Earl Warren and Thurgood Marshall before him, his remains were taken to the Great Hall of the Supreme Court, where the flag-draped casket—resting on the bier used by Abraham Lincoln—was viewed by hundreds of mourners. An enlarged portrait of the chief justice was at the head of the coffin. The memorial service was held on June 29 at the National Presbyterian Church, where he was eulogized by Chief Justice William Rehnquist and Justice Sandra Day O'Connor. Interment was at Arlington National Cemetery.

Chief Justice Burger's uneasy relationship with the national media extended even beyond his death. Several months after his funeral the nation was told in an Associated Press release that the chief justice had left a "woefully inadequate" will covering his $1.8 million estate, which was said to leave tax liabilities estimated at $378,000 for the federal estate tax and $78,000 for the Virginia estate tax.[61] Most of this difficulty could have been avoided with a competent estate plan, according to George W. Dodge, an Arlington, Virginia, lawyer.

Apparently, following his wife's death in 1994, Burger wrote a one-page will on his personal computer, leaving one-third of his estate to his daughter and two-thirds to his son. "Executors" was misspelled, suggesting that he had not even bothered to check the document. The overall impression left with the reader was that Burger had bungled his own will, reinforcing an image of him earlier memorialized in Bob Woodward and Scott Armstrong's controversial best-seller of 1979, *The Brethren.*

As became known a week later, the national press had run with a story that was unsound and unfair. Burger's estate plan essentially depended on the provisions in his wife's will, and sizable gifts had removed much of the estate from the provisions of the chief justice's own will. James Maloney, Burger's lawyer hired not long before his death, said: "His was not the will I would have written, but he achieved what he set out to do. There was nothing incompetent about what he did."[62] Dodge eventually apologized "for any embarrassment it [his comments] caused the Burger family."[63]

Lewis F. Powell (1971–1987)

Reluctant to join the Supreme Court when nominated, Lewis F. Powell initially thought in terms of a decade of service, thus meeting President Nixon's dictum that "ten years of Lewis Powell is worth twenty years for anyone else."[64] But since his health was good at age seventy-five (a benign polyp was removed from his colon in 1979), his children urged him to remain on the Court. He still retained his usual zest for work, so he elected not to retire in 1983 even though he gave the matter serious consideration. Unexpectedly, that same year he nearly died.

While at the Mayo Clinic, doctors discovered prostate cancer, which required surgery. He nearly died from loss of blood on the operating table. When his physicians asked if he was taking any medication, Powell told them he was not. In fact, he was taking aspirin, which thins the blood and almost resulted in his death. The doctors quickly determined the problem, but it proved difficult to control and he was much weakened. He had previously experienced hemorrhages, once in 1956 following routine surgery for a bladder obstruction and again in 1974 when he had undergone a transurethral resection of the prostate.[65]

Following his recovery from prostate cancer and the accompanying blood loss, he did not again consider retirement until the end of the 1987 term. Nearly eighty years old, this time his son, on whose advice he principally relied regarding this question, did not discourage the suggestion to leave. His

Lewis Powell was appointed to the Court even though he contemplated retirement from his Richmond law firm. (Supreme Court, Office of the Curator)

son's silence, according to his biographer, and his own sense of diminishing strength explain why the decision was made.[66]

Prior to the press conference where Powell made his announcement, he had distributed a statement offering three reasons for the retirement. The first consideration was his age, since he would be eighty when the new term opened. The justice frankly concluded that in the original Constitution it would have been wise to have provided for a retirement at age seventy-five, although he stopped short of proposing that his suggestion be adopted. The second consideration was the fact that he had served five years longer than the ten years he had originally planned to serve. The third consideration was his concern that the future would unfold serious health problems for him, which could only hamper the Court's deliberations and work.

In addition to those stated reasons, he told reporters that he had been influenced by his son's comment: "Dad, it's a whole lot better to go out when some people may be sorry than it is to wait until when you decide to go out, people say, 'Thank God we got rid of the old gent.'" Looking frail on television, but mentally sharp and alert, his regret could not be contained. "Today," he said, "is one of my worst moments. I leave the Court with a great deal of sadness."[67]

On August 25, 1998, Lewis Powell died in his sleep of pneumonia at age ninety while at his home in Richmond, Virginia. Following his retirement he continued to come to his chambers in the Supreme Court, and he accepted assignments from time to time to hear cases coming before the Richmond-based U.S. Court of Appeals for the Fourth Circuit. This pattern continued until two years before his death, when bowing to declining health and the distress caused by the death of his wife, Josephine, in 1996, he formally closed his chambers and returned permanently to Richmond.

Some nine hundred people along with all the members of the Supreme Court and retired Justice Byron White attended a heavily guarded funeral service at a Presbyterian church in downtown Richmond that Powell had joined sixty years earlier. Private graveside services followed at Hollywood Cemetery, where presidents John Tyler and James Monroe are buried, as is Confederate president Jefferson Davis.

William J. Brennan Jr. (1956–1990)

Although William J. Brennan Jr. recovered from throat cancer in 1978 when his tumor was treated by radiation therapy, the next year he suffered a stroke that left his right arm and hand partially paralyzed.[68] He remained in relatively good health until two years before his retirement in 1990, rising at five in the morning and regularly working out on an exercise bike for half an hour (or sometimes less) each day. Following this regimen, he was still able to arrive at the Supreme Court between 7:30 and 7:45 each morning.[69]

In 1988 he underwent surgery for prostate cancer at the Mayo Clinic. The next year he was admitted to Bethesda Naval Hospital for pneumonia and not long thereafter had his gall bladder removed. Nonetheless, Brennan seldom missed a day at the Court, and by the end of the 1989–1990 term he again had managed to forge controlling coalitions around controversial issues, including affirmative action and flag burning cases.[70] Despite his eighty-four years, there was no reason to suppose his time as the Court's "play maker" was ended. In fact, shortly before his birthday in April, he indicated he had no intention of retiring unless his health required it.[71]

There were others who were aware of his deteriorating health. Jim Mann, who had covered the Supreme Court for the *Los Angeles Times* from 1976 through 1984, returned to the Court in April to interview Brennan. The booming gravelly voice Mann remembered was now low and less audible. He had lost weight. "Quite evidently failing," Brennan was very much aware of his own situation and, perhaps surprisingly, willing to discuss it with some candor.[72] His doctor had urged him to cancel all public speeches and other activities. "I came back from Israel a couple of years ago with a terrible case of shingles, really a miserable case of shingles," he said. "Then I had a serious reaction only last fall to antibiotics that I was taking for influenza . . . at about that time. And I'm not out of that yet. . . . It was the reaction to those things that prompted my doctor to say that you just better slow down."[73]

At the end of the term in July, Justice Brennan and his wife, Mary, booked a two-week North Sea cruise, with stopovers in several Scandinavian countries. As he boarded the plane at Newark International Airport, he fell; during the cruise he suffered from dizziness and memory loss. When he returned home, his doctors diagnosed a minor stroke. He acted immediately, with the thought of Justice Douglas's difficult and demeaning last days, as he told his wife, very much on his mind. He faxed a letter to President Bush on board *Air Force One*, dated July 20, 1990, which said: "The strenuous demands of Court work and its related duties required or expected of a justice appear at this time to be incompatible with my advancing age and medical condition. I, therefore, retire effective immediately as an associate justice of the Supreme Court of the United States."[74] He had served nearly thirty-four years on the Court.

Justice Brennan died of pneumonia seven years later on July 15, 1997, at age 91, while at an Arlington, Virginia, nursing home where he was under-going rehabilitation after hip replacement surgery, having previously broken his hip in a fall. His body was placed on view to the public in the Supreme Court building, the coffin resting on the same catafalque used for Abraham Lincoln in 1865.[75] The funeral was held four days later. At St. Matthew's Cathedral in Washington, a church named after the patron saint of public servants, an audience of nearly 1,200, including President Clinton, attended the ninety-minute service. Outside a lone protester employed a bull-horn to attack the justice's participation in the 1973 abortion decision, *Roe v. Wade.*[76] Borne on a military caisson, followed by a riderless horse, to Arlington National Cemetery, Brennan was buried on a knoll not far from the grave of his close friend, Thurgood Marshall.[77]

Thurgood Marshall (1967–1991)

Thurgood Marshall announced his retirement on Thursday, June 28, 1991, at the age of eighty-two. He cited his "advancing age and medical condition" in his letter to President Bush, advising the president he would leave when his successor was "qualified."[78] He was reported to be both angry and discouraged with the more conservative direction the Court had taken.

Marshall's actual retirement did not become effective until October 1, when he wrote the president a note, which said: "I now request that my retirement become effective as of this date."[79] A month earlier, while still a justice, he had entered the National Naval Medical Center at Bethesda complaining of light-headedness and had a pacemaker implanted to correct an abnormally slow heart rate. A hospital spokesperson told the press that Marshall had remained "awake during the procedure and tolerated it well."[80]

Justice Marshall had suffered from poor health for many years. He had left the Court visibly shaken after the death penalty was restored in *Gregg v. Georgia*[81] in 1976. Nearly sixty-eight years old, he experienced a mild heart attack that evening. He seemed to become more irritable after the heart attack, inasmuch as his substantial drinking (Wild Turkey whiskey), smoking (three packs of Winston cigarettes a day), and eating habits were all curtailed. Also, the reduced oxygen his heart was able to pump through his body may have caused his limbs and joints to ache.[82]

Because of his emphysema Marshall was subject to recurrent attacks of pneumonia and viral bronchitis. He took a bad fall on the Capitol's steps in October 1979, which resulted in a fractured right wrist and a lacerated forehead. In August 1990 he fell in the lobby of Chicago's Hyatt Regency Hotel

Thurgood Marshall during his years as counsel for the NAACP. (Supreme Court, Office of the Curator)

while attending the American Bar Association's annual convention and required hospitalization. His eyes were impaired by glaucoma, and he required a hearing aid. Obesity made walking difficult. Despite these maladies, Marshall was reluctant to retire because, as he often said, "I was appointed to a life term, and I intend to serve it."[83] Nonetheless, by the time of his retirement he had become increasingly intransigent about his well-being. The following observations were no secret in Washington:

> Marshall was an angry and sick old man by the time he announced his retirement, five days before his eighty-third birthday. He had had a heart attack, his eyes were glazed with glaucoma, his two ears worked only with the help of hearing aids. He had fought pneumonia and bronchitis and a life-threatening blood clot in his foot. As his health deteriorated he had refused entreaties from his doctors and friends to take care of himself, to stop eating, drinking, and smoking. His always large, six-foot-two inch frame had ballooned out to two hundred and fifty pounds. He was killing himself, and he knew it.[84]

His televised press conference was quite remarkable. The camera followed him into the room, walking very slowly, using a cane. As his biographers described his appearance, "His tie, loosely knotted, was pulled to one side, and his pants were hitched up over his spreading belly, displaying the white surgical socks he wore to prevent a recurrence of the blood clot that had formed in his right leg several years earlier."[85] He was very different in appearance from the carefully dressed civil rights lawyer known to students from the pictures in civics books. He was also irritable and short-tempered with the deferential reporters who stood while he entered the room. When asked what was "wrong" with him, he shot back, incredulous that such a question needed to be asked, "I'm old. I'm getting old and coming apart."[86]

When asked if the *New York Times* editorial, which had suggested he was leaving in anger or frustration, was correct, he responded with unvarnished irritation: "That's a double-barreled lie. My doctor and my wife and I have been discussing this for the past six months or more. And we all eventually agreed, all three of us, that this was it, and this is it."[87] This observation was most unfortunate because it was known to be false. As Carl Rowan, a confidant and friend, well knew, Marshall "damaged his credibility and his image a bit in that press conference by denying what his friends and foes knew was the truth."[88] His denial is more understandable when it is remembered that

An elderly Thurgood Marshall became dependent on his law clerks. (Supreme Court, Office of the Curator)

Marshall retired rather than resigned and consequently would still be interacting with other justices at the Supreme Court on a daily basis.

Just prior to the news conference the Court had handed down *Payne v. Tennessee,*[89] which permitted the use of victim impact statements in capital cases. *Payne* overruled the contrary position favored by Justice Marshall, so just as in 1976 when he suffered his heart attack he had reason to be distressed. He stayed on the bench only a year longer than his close friend, William Brennan. Not only had he voted with Brennan in nearly all major cases, but he even used the same language and reasons in his letter to President Bush (i.e., "advancing age and medical condition").

Justice Marshall lived a year longer, dying of heart failure at 2 P.M. on Monday, January 25, 1993, at Bethesda Naval Medical Center. On the prior Wednesday he had been scheduled to administer the oath of office to Vice President Al Gore, but his health had forced him to cancel.[90] Many mourners passed by his casket as he lay in repose in the Great Hall of the Supreme Court, the first associate justice to be so honored.

He had provided his own epitaph at his last press conference when the columnist Clarence Page asked him how he wanted to be remembered. "Squinting in my direction," Page recalled, "the old curmudgeon appeared to be at once amused and irritated as he reflected for a microsecond, then muttered in his gravelly voice: 'That he did what he could with what he had.'"[91]

Byron R. White (1962–1993)

"After 31 years," said Byron R. White, "I think that someone else should be permitted to have (the) experience."[92] He was the only sitting justice appointed by a Democratic president (John Kennedy) and was seventy-five years old when he announced his intention to retire at the end of the 1992 term. He was in good health, but rumors circulated that he was bored with the Court's work after so many years of service and was more than willing to step aside if a Democratic president could appoint his successor.[93]

Justice White had two rules about retirement. He did not favor a retirement during an election year because the vacancy would inevitably become excessively politicized. His second concern was with dual vacancies; he felt there should only be one vacancy at a time. Both conditions were met at the end of the 1992 term.[94]

Events soon thereafter confirmed his sense that it was time to retire. During the summer he told a friend he had made the right choice because he found, while fly fishing, that he "could not easily tie a number 18 Adams on a standard tippit."[95] White, the most athletic of men, would not have trivialized the importance of such personally disturbing evidence of aging. If he could not perform physically to his own satisfaction, it was time to leave the field.

Unlike his predecessors in retirement, Justices Powell and Marshall, he predictably held no news conference. Nor was he feted at the White House, as was the next retiree, Justice Blackmun. The justice, always brusque, noncommital, and even dismissive toward the national media, received only measured words acknowledging his retirement from President Clinton and the press. It did not appear to bother him in the least.

Having completed the fourth longest tenure of the century, White became the first justice to move out of the Supreme Court building since it was built in 1935. He instead took an office in the Federal Judicial Center.

Harry A. Blackmun (1970–1994)

In 1977 Harry A. Blackmun underwent a radical prostatectomy at the Mayo Clinic, a procedure in which the cancerous prostate is removed along with the surrounding tissue. The cancer recurred ten years later in the justice's seventy-eighth year and was described by a Mayo Clinic spokesperson as a "small and localized recurrence."[96] The cancer was discovered after he entered the clinic for a hernia operation. He was treated as an outpatient and was not incapacitated for any length of time. His office downplayed the event. A former law clerk reported that "my impression is that it's a minor thing," and another former clerk, after breakfast with the justice, concluded that "he seemed alert and spry and healthy." On a more sobering note, the clerk then acknowledged that "at his age, you're never really sure."[97]

Although he appeared somewhat frail, Blackmun proved resilient despite his ongoing prostate difficulties and did not retire until the end of the 1993–1994 term at age eighty-five. He gave no hint about his plans when the term started. Each summer he returned to the Mayo Clinic, which he had represented as its general counsel in the 1950s, for an annual physical examination. That November he was amazed to discover he was the fourth oldest person to serve on the Supreme Court (only Taney, Holmes, and Black had been older).

He remained active throughout his tenure, lecturing at universities and interacting with diverse groups of citizens during his summers. His interest in public affairs never waned. He and Justice White joked with each other about who should retire first, causing Blackmun to admit: "White beat me to the punch. We'd pass each other in the hall, and he'd ask, 'Have you retired yet?' I'd say, 'Nope, have you?' I still enjoy the job. I don't know what I'll do when I retire."[98]

In his televised press conference on April 6, Blackmun explained why it was time for him to retire. He first noted his age, although he had said earlier in the year, "One is as old as he feels, and I feel pretty well."[99] He next indicated that he did not want to wait until, like Justice Holmes, his colleagues should find it necessary to call upon him to retire. He declared he was "still feeling all right" and that "my work output is still acceptable." And when he was asked whether debate and controversy within the Court about the death penalty, causing him to declare in his last term his unalterable opposition to it, was a factor in his retirement, he said the issue did not weigh on his decision to retire.

Justice Blackmun and his wife, Dottie, were friends of President and Mrs. Clinton before they reached the White House. Accordingly, the president declared April 7 "Justice Blackmun's day," thanking him in a public ceremony for "his humanity and sense of justice."[100] Responding to the president's praise, Blackmun said: "It hasn't been much fun on most occasions, but it's a fantastic experience, which few lawyers are privileged to have. It's not easy to step aside, but I know what the numbers are, and it's time."[101]

Only infrequently during the contemporary period have all nine justices failed to participate in the more publicized cases. But this circumstance can be deceiving. Conference items and oral arguments can be rescheduled in major cases so as to minimize the importance of an absence, concealing consequences affecting litigants, sometimes in life-and-death situations. When Justice Powell was at the Mayo Clinic about to undergo surgery for prostate cancer, the first federal habeas corpus petition from one Roosevelt Green Jr. came before the Supreme Court. Green was a black man convicted of murdering a white woman. His petition claimed discrimination, based on statistical evidence of disparities between blacks and whites in the application of the death penalty.

The Court deadlocked 4 to 4, with Justices Brennan, Marshall, Blackmun, and Stevens in favor of granting the petition, thereby permitting the Court of Appeals to make an inquiry into the question of whether racial discrimination was present. The remaining justices, Burger, White, Rehnquist, and O'Connor, disagreed and voted against granting habeas. The result was that the Court deadlocked, and the lower court decision remained unchanged. Roosevelt Green Jr. was then electrocuted in Georgia on January 9, 1985. No one can be certain how Justice Powell would have voted had he been able to participate, but Green's habeas corpus appeal was his first, and Powell was more likely to vote in favor of a first appeal than for a subsequent habeas appeal. It is possible and even likely he might have voted with the Brennan group had he been present.[102]

Not participating, as in Powell's case, most obviously means a vote is lost, which can control the result. Beyond that, an absent justice can neither influence colleagues nor be influenced by them either in public during oral argument, where counsel may also affect a vote, or privately in the conference. Oral argument ordinarily may not sway many votes, but it can happen on occasion when a lawyer presents an imaginative and persuasive argument. Justice Stanley Reed once recalled that he had seen it done by John W.

Davis, when the former solicitor general and 1924 Democratic presidential candidate was practicing on Wall Street.[103] The justices had gone into the oral arguments persuaded on the basis of the briefs that Davis's client had the weaker case. But Davis's impressive oral presentation of the case soon changed their minds. Conversely, a lawyer can also lose a case during oral argument, usually by adopting an unnecessarily inflexible position that alienates one or more of the justices.[104]

An absent justice also affects the conference in two ways: at any time a justice may influence others or be influenced by the views of others. The former consideration is especially important if internal leaders like Justices Brennan or Powell were absent. Among the chief justices, only John Marshall and, to a lesser extent, William Howard Taft have carried their Courts with them,[105] which suggests that most Courts have been divided by factions, with a corresponding fragmentation of leadership. When a Court leader, like Brennan or Powell, is unable to participate, his absence becomes magnified.

Too many of the justices have held to their offices beyond their period of capable service. Hugo Black experienced no debilitating health problems, apart from failing eyesight, until 1969, when he suffered a mild stroke while playing tennis. His doctor gave him a 90 percent chance of recovering, and his mind seemed to clear, although his wife noticed he had become forgetful while telling stories at parties.[106] Shortly thereafter his wife concluded that she had a "gnawing conviction that Hugo must get off the Court."[107] Although he remained reluctant to retire, his deterioration became increasingly evident to onlookers when he required physical assistance from Chief Justice Burger as he left the bench for the last time following the delivery of the opinions in the *Pentagon Papers* case.[108]

As early as April 1970, Justice Douglas described John Marshall Harlan as "blind in one eye and only able to see three inches away from the other."[109] But Harlan was also reluctant to leave, even after he knew he was grievously ill. The following description provides a distressing scene:

Harlan continued to run his chambers from his hospital bed. Nearly blind, he could not even see the ash from his own cigarette, but he doggedly prepared for the coming term. One day a clerk brought in an emergency petition. Harlan remained in bed as he discussed the case with the clerk. They agreed that the petition should be denied. Harlan bent down, his eyes virtually to the paper, wrote his name, and handed the paper to his clerk. The clerk saw no signature. He looked over at Harlan.

"Justice Harlan, you just denied your sheet," the clerk said, gently pointing to the scrawl on the linen. Harlan smiled and tried again, signing the paper this time.[110]

Following his stroke, William O. Douglas tenaciously held to office, even though he showed signs of the paranoia that frequently afflicts stroke victims. He soon began to believe that people were plotting to remove him from the Court or even to kill him.[111]

Despite being beset with the inevitable illnesses of advancing age, there has been no shortage of justices willing to persuade themselves of their indispensability, at least for a little while longer. But younger justices can also be incapacitated, as was the case with William H. Rehnquist at age fifty-seven in 1982, when an incident raised questions about balancing a justice's privacy in matters of personal health and the public's right to know the facts about the condition of public officials.

Justice Rehnquist had experienced severe lower back pain for many years. In 1981 lawyers before the Court began to notice that his speech was slurred and he had difficulty pronouncing longer words, although his questions still seemed appropriate. He thereafter was hospitalized and experienced a drug withdrawal reaction lasting about two hours during which time he experienced "disturbances" and "distortions" in mental clarity.[112] Rehnquist was unwilling to discuss his situation, remarking only, "I'm leaving it to my doctor to deal with the media."[113] The doctor in turn refused to elaborate about the hospital incident. There was no information provided about the effect of the drug on the justice prior to hospitalization, although it was later revealed to be the prescription hypnotic Placidyl, which normally should be taken only for short periods at a time.[114]

Justice Rehnquist's excessive use of Placidyl was eventually revealed to the public by reporters, but only with difficulty. In fact, most of the justices have been less than forthcoming in volunteering information about their health, even though that information may be relevant and bear on their work as public officials. When Charles Whittaker was nominated to the Supreme Court in 1956, for example, no mention was made of his past history of depression. It was not a topic that anyone discussed. More so than is usually acknowledged, the same reticence about personal health records has continued throughout the contemporary period.

In recent years, the law clerks have played an ever larger role in protecting disabled justices from unfavorable public attention. This development may be because as a group they have become more important, and, since there are more of them, they are able to form an effective cordon around their justice.[115] Thurgood Marshall's disabilities were skillfully camouflaged by dutiful clerks so that the general public was unaware of the state of his physical and mental health. When he became confused and voted for the first time in favor of the death penalty in conference, his law clerks rectified the situation for him, quickly changing his vote the next day.[116]

More so than at any time since 1900–1937, justices have been reluctant to leave the Court. Some of the best known of them have continued to serve long past their most productive years, relying increasingly on law clerk assistance, the advantages of the computer revolution, the protectiveness of judicial anonymity, and somewhat more friendly media coverage than can be found on most other public policy assignments.

These recent developments suggest the possibility of a reemergence of the difficulties of earlier decades. Because of this tendency, the contemporary record, despite the relatively few difficulties encountered since 1937, provides sufficient evidence to justify a reconsideration of current retirement practices.

7
WHEN SHOULD JUSTICES LEAVE?

Does the colorful and sometimes tragic chronicle of Supreme Court departures justify a change in retirement practices? Although constitutional change is improbable as a practical matter in the absence of a crisis drawing public attention to the issue, there is a strong likelihood that the pattern of recent years will continue—with justices becoming more and more reluctant to retire, despite infirmities and advanced age. If so, the case for change could become stronger, and if the Court continues to assert itself aggressively into the major social issues of American life, the required political momentum for change may well develop.

Although there is indeed some evidence that people become more "conservative" as they age, it is even more probable that they tend to reflect the ideas and attitudes they developed in their formative years; in that sense, aging justices may be said to represent the past rather than the present, as was so clearly the case earlier in the twentieth century.[1] On the contrary, if the Court becomes less involved in controversial issues and more deferential to popular political decision making, there will be less pressure for change as the justices become less relevant to public concerns. In short, the collective role that the justices assume for themselves carries major implications for how their institution will be perceived by the American public and, consequently, how that public will respond to their behavior.[2]

In any discussion of aging and disability there is a special caveat to bear in mind: aging alone, unless associated with disability or various forms of mental or emotional illness, may be only one of any number of factors influencing decision making and may not even be an important consideration in any given situation. All too easily age can become a scapegoat for ideological disagreement, with judicial decisions sometimes spawning the most intense recriminations from critics. For example, in 1970 a prominent political scientist concluded that Justice Hugo Black had become a "rigid, crotchety, dogmatic old man" based on a CBS interview aired in 1968 with Eric Sevareid and Martin Agronsky as the interviewers.[3] Black was described as "too old for the job" and ironically identified as one of those, along with Felix Frankfurter, who was expressly put on the Supreme Court to "break the grip of gerontocracy" and ended up as a supporter of a conservatism at odds with the spirit of the New Deal.[4] Others who saw Justice Black during that time had very different impressions.[5] Had the aging process changed him into a nearly senile old man or had the issues changed, as others believed?[6] Justice Black himself thought the Supreme Court had changed.[7]

Constitutional issues sometimes become reconfigured and may not seem identical or even similar to what they were earlier. Every generation, as Holmes noted, rewrites its law. Issues do change or vary, eliciting different responses. Public officials do not live in a social vacuum; they are subject to the same cacophony of diverse social and political impressions that cause others to change their minds, sometimes inconsistently over a lifetime. Justices too respond with change, sometimes imperceptibly and sometimes more noticeably, to the inevitable accumulation of experiences that affect everyone else. Some critics will be displeased with or unsympathetic toward any change. And, as a last consideration, the personal chemistry of the Court should not be discounted, for it also changes—however imperceptibly—with each new appointment.[8] Some justices may be inclined to take cues from others, either positively or negatively.[9] When justices join or leave a small group like the Court these relationships are unavoidably affected. Black's long tenure suggests that all of these considerations—quite apart from his age—may consciously or unconsciously have influenced his voting behavior.

A Defense of the Status Quo

Although it happened often enough during the nineteenth century, there have been no recent instances of justices clinging to their seats for years after falling into decrepitude, despite relatively short-term disabilities. There are several reasons at present, which were previously absent or less important, that justify life tenure during good behavior.

First, the changes in the retirement law passed in 1937 make it more attractive for elderly justices of no personal fortune to retire with dignity. Second, there are important internal mechanisms, however informal, that have come to bear increasingly on retirement. Peer group pressure may well be exerted on a justice who is incapable of performing satisfactorily. This behavior may be characterized by an unaccustomed deference, like Justice Minton thought was accorded to him shortly before his retirement. Moreover, should a justice be reluctant to retire, it is possible to carry cases over to the next term if the vote of an incapacitated justice may be decisive, which was apparently what happened during the spring of 1975 with Justice Douglas. The Court is patient with its members but not endlessly so. There are several instances prior to 1937 when another justice or group of justices was obliged to call upon a senior member of the Court and inform him that a consensus had formed among the other justices in favor of his retirement.[10]

A third consideration making it unlikely that a permanently disabled justice would try to retain his or her seat against all advice to the contrary is the current pressure exercised by the mass media over all government officials. The mass media are important in two ways: initially, it is virtually impossible to completely conceal physical or mental decrepitude within the Court at the present time. Furthermore, adverse media coverage is itself an inducement to leave, as in the case of Justice Fortas. Justice Douglas was relentlessly pursued, questioned, or indeed interrogated about his retirement plans throughout his illness. The issue of one's incapacitation is given urgency that neither the justice nor the public is likely to ignore. Consequently, because of the improved retirement benefits, peer group pressures that now are somewhat formalized by historical precedent, and the role of the modern mass media, life tenure during good behavior does not present the same risks to the institutional competency of the Court that were present at an earlier time.

Nonetheless, life tenure has been frequently criticized. It has been suggested, for example, that an age limit might be advisable. But as Charles Evans Hughes has indicated:

> I agree that the importance in the Supreme Court of avoiding the risk of having judges who are unable properly to do their work and yet insist on remaining on the bench, is too great to permit the chances to be taken, and at any age selected must be somewhat arbitrary as the time of the failing in mental power differs widely. The exigency to be thought of is not illness but decrepitude.[11]

An argument, therefore, over whether a justice should retire at age sixty-five or seventy or seventy-five does not satisfactorily resolve the basic issue of competence. As the review of recent Court retirements indicates, some of the ablest justices have performed at advanced ages. And as has been suggested, the danger of extended service on the part of a decrepit justice is today less than in the earlier periods of Court history.

There remains, of course, the problem of total disability that insofar as the presidency is concerned has been constitutionally resolved by the adoption of the Twenty-fifth Amendment, which provides a mechanism for the removal of a president incapacitated by mental illness, prolonged unconsciousness, or total paralysis. Although a similar provision could be made applicable to Supreme Court justices by constitutional amendment, their status is more analogous to members of the Congress than to a president. A disabled justice would not paralyze the work of the Court in the same way that a disabled president would affect the executive branch or in fact the nation. In a word, justices lack the indispensable centrality of presidents.

Critics of the status quo are inclined to attack the basic concept of life tenure and defend limited terms of service. Life tenure is sometimes thought to encourage outmoded judicial attitudes. As Theodore L. Becker has noted, "There are potentially fine and active and creative men and women in their thirties and forties who never get a chance because of the temptation for the older person to hang on and on."[12] Nonetheless, the abolition of life tenure would not necessarily cause an increase in the appointment of younger justices, because presidents are already free to appoint younger persons to the bench if they choose to do so. To some extent this tendency has already occurred, as presidents have hoped to extend their influence over Court policies into the indefinite future. Those hopes, however, are not infrequently disappointed, since presidents have proven to be no more prescient than the rest of us about how justices will respond once they have donned the robes of office.

As Edward S. Corwin has observed, judicial review is "American [d]emocracy's way of hedging its bet."[13] Judicial independence, essential to the maintenance of judicial review, depends upon life tenure for the justices. Either an election or an appointment for a term of years would threaten that independence. It is important to distinguish between the Supreme Court and all other courts. Some of the states have fared well under the policy of elected judges, but the visibility of the lower court judges is not high and it may in fact make little difference whether they are appointed or elected.[14]

With the Supreme Court, however, it is an entirely different matter. Complex civil liberties questions—often involving questions relating to minority rights—could become the object of majoritarian demagoguery, particularly during presidential campaigns. Prospective justices would, before elected, be pressured to offer informal advisory opinions (which have never been permitted even formally in the federal courts) or else, if appointed for a term of years, have to confront the question of their future prospects when their term expired if they had made unpopular decisions while in office. However, it is sometimes denied that the Court has acted to protect minority rights in a meaningful way, at least on the national level.[15] And yet, a contrary view may also be advanced, using data involving the Supreme Court and federal legislation between 1958 and 1974:

> With the exception of *Oregon v. Mitchell,* all of the 28 decisions were based upon provisions of the Bill of Rights (primarily the First and Fifth Amendments) and the Fourteenth Amendment. In addition to furthering the interests of all in the society in greater freedom of expression, equal application of the laws, and procedural fairness, the decisions had special impact upon such groups as aliens, communists and other alleged subversives, criminal defendants, war protesters, and poor people. The Court attempted to extend to these groups rights and privileges that law-making majorities had not chosen to extend.[16]

The necessity of an independent Supreme Court is also apparent when conflict arises over boundaries of political authority. In fact, some argue that "even more acutely than when only rights of private citizens or groups are at issue, boundary definitions are likely to engender resistance."[17]

Over a century ago Alexis de Tocqueville wrote that the justices "are the all-powerful guardians of a people which respects law," but he also cautioned that "they would be impotent against popular neglect or popular contempt."[18] Even the Court's severest critics recognize its indispensability to the American system of government,[19] but there has sometimes been a reluctance to admit that a less independent Court—a more politicized Court— would be less likely to function as a guarantor of the continuing integrity of constitutional freedoms.

Hamilton's Objection to an Age Limit

A strong reluctance to tamper with life tenure was expressed by Alexander Hamilton in *Federalist* 79. The framers of the Constitution were much concerned about providing for the independence of the Supreme Court and the federal judiciary. Hamilton identified independence with a secured salary, which explains the provision in the Constitution providing that judicial salaries may not be diminished while in office. Although he does not explicitly identify judicial independence with life tenure, he assumes life tenure is what the Constitution provides for federal judges.

Hamilton directly addressed the absence of a provision "for removing the judges on account of inability."[20] The reason why there is no disability provision is that it would either be ignored in practice or, if used, be subject to partisan abuse. "The mensuration of the faculties of the mind has," Hamilton believed, "no place in the catalogue of known arts." He did not have confidence in the ability of decision makers to always determine between ability and disability, because so many cases are indeterminate or uncertain. But he assumed that clear cases of insanity would "be a virtual disqualification."[21]

Presumably, Hamilton meant that someone who is thought to be insane would not be appointed or confirmed (as in the case of John Rutledge for chief justice). His argument otherwise contained no provision, except impeachment, for the removal of one who later becomes insane. Whether that would be an appropriate exercise of the impeachment clause in the context of the Supreme Court remains untested. Samuel Chase, although zealous and far from ordinary in his behavior, was clearly not insane.

Dr. Johnson's Arguments for Term Limits

"There is no reason why a Judge should hold his office for life, more than any other person in publick trust," Samuel Johnson told James Boswell.[22] Dr. Johnson offered four reasons for his conclusion. First, a justice may become "partial," either toward government or the people. In the first instance, a justice is no sure protector of the civil liberties of the people; in the second, he panders to the changing perception of what is merely popular.

Second, "a Judge may become corrupt, and yet there may not be legal evidence against him." In such situations, there is no sure way to remove a justice. The impeachment and conviction trials of federal judges Harry E. Claiborne of Nevada and Alcee L. Hastings of Florida have illustrated how difficult it is to remove judges even when overwhelming incriminating evidence is available. Would it prove any less arduous to remove a justice from the Supreme Court if he or she resisted all entreaties to leave?

Third, Dr. Johnson thought a justice might become "froward"—or disposed to opposition—from age. William Howard Taft's lament that "the old men of the Court seldom die and never retire" at least emphasizes their unwillingness to voluntarily yield judicial power.[23]

Fourth, since a judge can grow unfit in many ways, it is "desirable that there should be a possibility of being delivered from him" by a new chief executive who has come to office. This countermeasure avoids the anomalous situation where the "dead hand of the past" reaches forward to control the present. Appointed by President Roosevelt in the 1930s, both Black and Douglas sat into the 1970s. Clarence Thomas, appointed by George Bush in 1991, has repeatedly expressed his intention to sit for as long as possible in order to confound his critics.[24]

Mandating Retirement by Constitutional Amendment

Some have suggested that Congress could simply pass a mandatory retirement statute.[25] This argument is logical enough, since there is nothing in Article 3 of the Constitution that would bar such a statute, and mandatory retirement would not necessarily pose a threat to judicial independence, the core interest protected by Article 3. The principal constitutional risk such a statute would encounter would occur when and if Congress attempted to change the retirement age.[26]

Nonetheless, any attempt to enforce by statute a mandatory retirement for Supreme Court justices almost certainly would meet with resistance from the Court and very probably would be invalidated by it, because the matter has been long settled by our political history and traditions, just as Congress could not now entirely remove the appellate jurisdiction of the Supreme Court. A constitutional amendment, specifically limited to the Supreme Court, would be the only viable alternative available.

A constitutional amendment mandating retirement at age seventy or seventy-five was suggested many years ago by Justice Owen J. Roberts.[27] The matter of determining the appropriate age of retirement would be left to the judgment of Congress. If adopted, the amendment would protect the Court against the charge that aged justices were clinging to power when they were no longer able to perform their work. It also would increase the likelihood that every administration would have the opportunity to appoint persons to the Court, thus minimizing the conflicts between the justices and the elected branches of government that so characterized government between 1900 and 1937. The phrase "the old Court" used by its opponents in the "Court-packing" proposal of 1937 suggests both of Justice Roberts's concerns. Such a constitutional amendment would ensure the independence of the judiciary, supporters contend, while at the same time removing aged justices who may more accurately reflect the past than the present in their decisions.

Other reasons are sometimes advanced in favor of a mandatory retirement provision in the Constitution. Most of the men and women who become Supreme Court justices have extraordinary stamina; otherwise they would not have achieved the visibility needed to secure a nomination in the first place. Many elderly persons retain a high degree of stamina, but at some point it is lost or noticeably decreases. When this diminishment occurs, one of two things will happen. Either there will be a reduced contribution to the final product of the Court from that justice, or there will be an increased delegation to the law clerks, with the justice assuming a lesser role in what is contributed from his or her office. Given the importance of many policy decisions made by any justice, either alternative is inimical to the country's best interests.

It is not uncommon for chief executive officers of major American businesses to leave their positions at age sixty-five, regardless of their health or ability. This pattern merely reflects the observation that the energy, fresh ideas, and enthusiasm that young people often bring to a task are desirable traits, and that at a certain age decline is imminent and likely to prove eventually dysfunctional. This analogy is perhaps more persuasive in the context of the American presidency because of the individualized responsibility assumed by executives. Nonetheless, given the importance of individual justices in split decisions affecting matters of large national concern in this century, it is clearly a mistake to discount too much the importance of each justice.[28]

No one seriously disputes that elderly justices have more health problems than their younger associates. Exceptions such as Justice Holmes do not disprove the general rule; they merely confirm it, although even Holmes failed at the end and was asked to leave. It remains highly problematic that an elderly justice, weakened by bouts of ill health, is as able to withstand internal opposition to his viewpoint. Like Grier or McKenna, he is likely to vacillate and be uncertain or simply to rely on that person with whom he is most comfortable, as Holmes relied on Brandeis and Thurgood Marshall relied on Brennan in their final years.

As justices grow older their mental acuity declines, as it does with everyone. Sometimes this deficit is important, sometimes it is not. Much depends on the cognitive skills with which a justice began, and much depends on the nature of the intellectual decline. Alzheimer's disease (or some form of senility) is not usually a condition that strikes with suddenness, but when it does it will affect the capacity to exercise judgment. Although individual cases vary considerably, this risk is clearly greater as one ages.

Nor can the public assume that justices who are noticeably disabled by the aging process will evidence self-awareness of their incapacity. Some of the justices, like Hughes and Blackmun, were sensitive to the problem and had asked others to deal frankly with them should a decline become apparent. Most of the justices, however, have shown no interest in receiving outside advice as to when they should leave. A sense of indispensability is not unusual among highly successful people; it would be surprising if it were otherwise.

For all of these reasons, some have argued, a policy of mandatory retirement would be in the national interest. Such a policy would correct the problems life tenure has caused while still preserving the judicial independence a term of years might well threaten.

Nonetheless, it remains that disability prior to an agreed-upon retirement age would not be affected by a mandatory retirement age, and the most elderly have sometimes been among the most astute and productive members of the Court. Wisdom in a judge is usually identified with a "mature professional judgment," which can only be obtained through experience.[29] It is in this sense that the brilliance of a judge differs from the brilliance of a scientist, many of whom do their best work while still quite young. The improved pension arrangements, the internal mechanisms, including the chief justice's power of assignment and his administrative influence over the others, combined with the power of the media are sufficient safeguards against extended disability.

The chief justice's special role in encouraging the resignation or retirement of the truly disabled justices has been fully documented. William Howard Taft's encouragement of McKenna's resignation illustrates how effective procedural pressure exerted by a chief justice can be. With the concurrence of his colleagues, Taft was able to steer important opinions away from McKenna until he was able to persuade him to leave.[30] Similarly, Warren Burger was able to secure agreement to suspend the usual certiorari procedure, which requires four votes to hear a case, when the fourth vote was cast by Justice Douglas. Also, Douglas's vote was not allowed to be decisive on any important issue.[31] When he was the deciding vote in 5 to 4 decisions, the case was simply put over for reargument. Douglas was in effect cut out of the decisional process, albeit over Justice White's written protest. White believed that only Congress could remove a justice, and the Court, de facto, had informally removed one of their own.[32] Unlike McKenna's situation, no colleague dared to suggest he resign, since it was common knowledge that this advice would only be resented and had no chance of succeeding.

Douglas's legendary independence did not abate in his final months on the Court, nor did it do so in the time following his eventual retirement. Consequently, the present system of life tenure has much to commend it. No other approach is more likely to effectively protect the independence of the justices and their unique role in American government than the arrangements now in existence. Procedures that have worked tolerably well for over two centuries should not be casually set aside in the absence of an overwhelming case for change, which does not now exist. Still, as the Court's more recent history suggests, there are certain incremental changes that would improve the status quo, and they can and should be implemented by the justices themselves.

Ghostwriters of the Law

In recent years the justices have delegated more and more of their work to their law clerks. This increase in the use of staff affects, of course, all of the justices, not merely those who are infirm or who have diminished capabilities. But elderly justices with diminished energy and those who have become ill are most likely to rely heavily on staff assistance and do less by themselves.

The burdensome task of writing opinions—engaged in by all earlier generations of justices—has been substantially discarded. Largely gone is the possibility that a justice will have a change of mind on an issue because the opinion "won't write." Consequently, the opinions—which are increasingly lengthy, bureaucratic in tone, and relentlessly modeled on the law review style of writing that emphasizes repetition, documentation, and factual detail—tell us less and less about the capabilities of individual justices and what they actually think about controversial issues. In addition, a justice's office can continue to produce product even though a justice may be largely incapacitated, if he or she is willing to delegate most of the work to the law clerks. Illness or incapacitation does not necessarily result in lessened productivity. Consequently, the increasingly important role of the law clerks may make it difficult to implement peer group controls, since the work of a justice's office continues almost as if on automatic pilot, whether or not he or she is functioning normally.

This disengagement of the justices from the crafting of opinions—so important to earlier generations of American judges—means that the give-and-take in conference sessions and among offices becomes an empty gesture. This trend is unfortunate, because there is evidence suggesting that when the judicial process works best, arguments are advanced, engaged, and either found persuasive or rejected.[33] Minds can be changed when cases elicit serious argument. But when staffers do much of the intellectual work previously expected of justices, there is less chance that justices will alter their positions because of legal argument, either from petitioners or from other justices. The ablest judicial craftsmen, like Judge Learned Hand or the second Justice Harlan, attached significance to the presentation of a persuasive rationale justifying the conclusion in each opinion.[34] Justice Antonin Scalia reflected this concern when he expressed disappointment that there were seldom real debates among the justices; there was instead merely a statement of views.[35]

This problem of excessive delegation has emerged because of congressional willingness to provide more and more law clerks for the justices. The chief justice now has five law clerks, and the other justices each have four. Stanley Reed once said the difference between his years as solicitor general and those as a justice was the absence, as a justice, of a staff to whom he could delegate; a justice had to do more of his own work.[36] As late as Justice Reed's tenure, the justices had only one or two law clerks and were obliged to do most of their own work. As total staffs have grown to seven (four law clerks, two secretaries, and a messenger), the institutional norms have changed to encourage ever more delegation. Justices remain responsible for their votes and thus have become increasingly similar to legislators. The analogy is still incomplete, because at least most justices maintain some degree of control by editing their opinions, but the trend toward opinions written by committee is unmistakable and can only be reversed by an unlikely congressional determination to reduce the number of law clerks or for the Court to deliberately reduce their role in the decision-making process.

With the proliferation of law clerks and their use of personal computers, the justices no longer reflect Louis Brandeis's dictum that they are respected "because [they] are almost the only people in Washington who do their own work."[37] This loss of an important tradition has had a negative impact on the competence of the institution. Opinions have become office products. Thus when Justice Brennan in his later years talked not of "Brennan opinions" but opinions from "the Brennan office," he recognized how the advancing years affected him personally. By using the liberal law clerks selected for him by past law clerks, Thurgood Marshall was able to delegate much of what went on in his office.[38] The conservative think tanks have provided law clerks who offer skilled assistance for Clarence Thomas, much as the government bureaucracy provided him with speechwriters during his chairmanship of the Equal Employment Opportunity Commission.

Why does this matter? No one doubts that in decided cases the votes do reflect the general ideological sentiments of the justice. However, it does matter very much, because there is an important distinction between voting and intellectually working an issue through by studying briefs and writing the opinion, or at least some of it.[39] If this approach is not taken, the difficulties of the case are not engaged by the person charged with the responsibility to decide, the complexities of the issues and arguments are delegated or avoided, and there should be diminished confidence in the results as this pathology becomes known over time to the general public.[40] At present, as Bernard Schwartz has concluded, "The greatest deficiency in the Supreme Court's decision process has been the increasing delegation—if not abdication—of key elements of the deciding function to the law clerk corps within the Court."[41] The law clerks have assumed the principal responsibility for determining which cases should be heard by the Court, and they write virtually all of the opinions. It is uncertain to what degree the justices maintain any involvement with opinion writing, although there are still some, like John Paul Stevens and Antonin Scalia, who exercise substantial control over what is issued from their offices.[42]

If too many justices have become editors rather than authors, the public has a right to know how ably they perform this lessened responsibility and how much editorial work is passed on to their staff. Even in the state courts (as in California, where professionals are permanently retained to write opinions) the truly able judges—like Roger Trayner—always precisely detailed the outline of the opinion and assumed responsibility for the final editing. The object always is to avoid a situation where conclusions are reached without the intellectual effort traditionally regarded as a major check on judicial irresponsibility. When Benjamin Cardozo discussed the art of judging in *The Nature of the Judical Process* in 1921, it is inconceivable that he could have anticipated the rise of what Justice Douglas—referring to the law clerks—once critically described as the "Junior Supreme Court."[43] The art of judging is not delegable.

Three Ways to Improve the Status Quo

"The behavior of the Court at any time," Joseph Tanenhaus once observed, "is the product of three factors—the external, the institutional, and the personal."[44] Three proposals, each reflecting one of these factors, if adopted would further strengthen the case for leaving life tenure for the justices alone. Each proposal, to be effective, requires only that the justices themselves adopt and abide by them.

The first proposal, concerning an external factor that would improve the status quo, would be for the Court to respond to the public interest in and concern for the health of each justice by being more forthcoming about the topic. The Court's record on this matter is far from deplorable, but it could be significantly improved. The Court has been too reticent about medical problems. One encounter between Chief Justice Rehnquist and reporters covering the Court was described this way:

> In this session, right after one of the justice's illnesses, [one of the reporters] asked the chief if they [the justices] could make some kind of accommodation to tell us when they're hospitalized. He did it in a very deferential tone. Rehnquist just flipped out. His whole expression changed. And he called us vultures. "You people are really vultures when it comes to that sort of thing." Rehnquist just blew up at us. The sessions are off the record and we're not supposed to repeat them. It was a very strange thing, and it just shows the depth of feeling about the thing.[45]

A second proposal, concerning the institutional factor, would be to delimit the role of the law clerks. Much has already been made of the harm done by present practices to the institutional integrity of the Court in the area of decision making, but an equally important concern should now be reemphasized. One of the reasons for maintaining the status quo on retirement practices is that the chief justices have managed to exert peer group pressure quite effectively. Unfortunately, the law clerk cadre weakens this check by insulating a justice from peer group criticism. If the work of a disabled justice's office continues as if nothing is wrong, it becomes arguably more difficult to focus concern within the Court about what actually may be a very serious situation.

A possible solution is to pool the law clerks, requiring of them loyalty to the institution rather than to individual justices. As at present, a new group would be recruited annually so that the importance or influence of individual clerks would not be exaggerated. The community of law clerks then becomes merely another resource, which—to be utilized—must be subject to detailed instruction and supervision. For most justices this format should present no extraordinary burden. Under a law clerk pool arrangement each justice must be more directly involved with what he or she wishes to have done. The clerks will have been chosen through an institutional process, not by individual justices, and they will not necessarily be familiar with the detailed constitutional views of the justice to whom they are temporarily assigned. At present, the clerks are often described as ardent supporters of their justices; unfortunately, they also may become equally fierce opponents of those justices who take contrary views.[46]

This deplorable combat attitude would change; increased loyalty to the institution, not individual justices, would be expected. Such a proposal may require that fewer cases be decided, that the opinions be shorter, and that there be fewer concurrences and dissents because significantly greater involvement in the decision-making process will again be required of Court members. Requirements such as these are hardly too much to expect of the Court. As one of Justice Black's former clerks has written:

> When the President of the United States appoints and the Senate of the United States confirms a Justice of the Supreme Court, the operation is not intended to result in turning over any serious responsibility to untried boys. The ghost writer may be a necessary evil in the White House, in the Senate, or in the cabinet, but nothing in the Court's situation requires the ghost to walk in that marble palace. The tradition is overwhelmingly against it.[47]

A third proposal, which concerns the personal factor, is that justices should exercise some measure of self-awareness and generally leave the Court while still in good health, usually by their mid-seventies, although the age might properly be extended if medical science continues to lengthen average life spans. This proposal should become an informal institutional tradition, and to a degree it already has. Of the three most recent justices to extend their tenure into their eighties, only Justice Marshall was clearly unable to function satisfactorily in his last years. Justice Marshall's situation was not revealed to the public. One reporter explained why:

> A story that should have been written but hasn't been by me or anyone else is that Justice Marshall doesn't seem to do much work, seems to leave it largely to his clerks to write his opinions, seems unprepared in oral arguments, and in general is old and past his prime—isn't really a very active participant in the Court's processes, and therefore there is a legitimate question that somebody like him ought to retire. That story hasn't been written at all for a variety of reasons. It's sort of hard to prove it in a journalistically satisfying way. A lot of it rests on rumor and impression, which is widespread. I think one reason it hasn't been

written is that he is the first black justice in the history of the Supreme Court. He's a nice man; he's a man with a great and distinguished career. I'm not going to be the first journalist who decides to make his career as a hatchet meister by questioning Thurgood Marshall's competence. He's a nice, distinguished old man. What would you accomplish by writing about him being a doting, noncontributing member? It's not as if he is the secretary of defense and handling the nuclear button. He's largely voting the same way he's always voted, and his opinions are not badly written because they're written by very competent clerks. That's a story—I can imagine a real hot, exposé-oriented journalist thinking it's an outrage that somebody hasn't exposed Marshall. But I frankly don't think it's an outrage.[48]

Hugo Black remained intellectually vigorous until toward the end of his tenure, as did Harry Blackmun, who in his eighties visited law schools and chatted amiably with students and faculty while appearing entirely fit. Justice Brennan remained sufficiently active in his eighties to have Court watchers remark on his continuing ability to forge controlling coalitions in important cases. Nonetheless, even though he was not seriously impaired by the mild stroke he experienced in 1990, Brennan acted quickly to terminate his active service.

The absence of any recent deaths among sitting justices suggests a willingness shared by most of them to leave while still in good health. Such a tradition should be firmly established and encouraged within the Court in the years ahead. However, should the justices prove increasingly reluctant to leave at or about age seventy-five, a modernized variation of President Roosevelt's 1937 Court reform proposal might be worthy of consideration. Hopefully it will not be necessary, but something further may be required if the justices become disinclined to internalize an informal policy of voluntary retirement.

Removed from the politics of the Depression era, some modification of the Court might meet with acceptance from Congress and the general public if the impression becomes widespread that justices are retaining office longer than they should. There is nothing in the Constitution mandating a nine-member Court. Congress set the membership of the first Court at six, President Jefferson added another justice in 1807, the number increased to nine in 1837, and President Lincoln added a tenth in 1863. In 1869 President Grant stabilized the Court at nine, and there it has remained ever since.

President Roosevelt's unsuccessful Court plan permitted the appointment of up to six new justices. An additional justice could be appointed for each sitting justice who reached the age of seventy, which meant the Court could have reached a total membership of fifteen. There were other elements to the plan, but the new justices were the most controversial aspect.[49] That the proposal failed was no surprise: Roosevelt, usually the most adept of politicians, made an initial mistake by dissembling as to the reasons for the change in his February 5 message to Congress. He indicated that the Court was behind in its work, that aging justices could not maintain an adequate and necessary workload. Chief Justice Charles Evans Hughes sent a letter to Senator Burton K. Wheeler, who chaired the Senate Judiciary Committee hearings, emphatically and persuasively denying this allegation.

The real problem was that the justices, who individually had grave reservations about all or part of Roosevelt's New Deal legislation, had been only too active in declaring most of it unconstitutional. The president's miscalculation required him to address the nation in a fireside chat on March 9, in which he candidly indicated that the Court was out of touch with the wishes of the executive and legislative branches of government. He warned of a "quiet crisis" that was nonetheless making it impossible to engineer the economic recovery he and the Congress had promised the country.

But the people had not been prepared for a major restructuring of the judiciary. Moreover, Roosevelt had acted in this matter without strong support from many members of his own party in Congress, including the Senate majority leader, Joseph Robinson, and even his own vice president, John Nance Garner, who was once seen holding his nose with his thumb down while discussing the bill.[50] To many institutional conservatives of both parties, the Court was seen as less a menace than a savior. Just as the country had recoiled when Theodore Roosevelt had earlier advocated the recall of federal judges by popular vote, so now there appeared to be no stomach for what was perceived as a radical reform of the Supreme Court. The votes for change were simply not there.

The Court-packing plan did have important and persuasive defenders among some of the Democrats in Congress, including Hugo Black and Sherman Minton. Although defeated, Roosevelt's proposal was taken seriously when it was proposed. Would a modified Court reform plan, less threatening to the Court, find acceptance now? If seventy-five was substituted for seventy as the age for the appointment of additional members, and if the proposal included a cap of eleven rather than fifteen, would the plan be viewed as the institutional threat it was thought to be in 1937?

Perhaps not. A Court of eleven would be similar to the ten that composed the Civil War Court. If passed by Congress, such a proposal might seldom, if ever, be invoked if the justices adopted an informal retirement rule. Its very presence, however, would serve as a reminder that Congress and the president believe that justices should voluntarily remove themselves from office by age seventy-five and that a refusal to do so could bring about another appointment.

The purpose of such legislation would not be to encourage a change in policy; rather, unlike the 1937 plan, the purpose would be to lessen the Court's dependence on aging members of whatever political persuasion. Such a proposal admittedly would be largely symbolic, since at most only two justices could be added to the present Court of nine, but symbols are often important.[51] Justice Frankfurter was surely correct when he once emphatically insisted that "we live by symbols."[52] Such legislation would further ensure that justices understand that life tenure, like all public responsibilities, should not be abused.

APPENDIX A
WHO ASKED JUSTICE GRIER TO RESIGN?

Problems of credibility abound for the biographer. There is no documentary evidence that Justice Stephen J. Field either led or participated in a delegation charged with urging resignation on an ailing Justice Robert C. Grier in 1869. The source for Field's participation comes from Charles Evans Hughes, who repeated a story he said he had heard from John Marshall Harlan. The evidence is based on oral tradition. Hughes reported the following:

I heard Justice Harlan tell of the anxiety which the Court had felt because of the condition of Justice Field. It occurred to the other members of the Court that Justice Field had served on a committee which waited upon Justice Grier to suggest his retirement, and it was thought that recalling that to his memory might aid him to decide to retire. Justice Harlan was deputized to make the suggestion. He went over to Justice Field, who was sitting alone on a settee in the robing room apparently oblivious of his surroundings, and after arousing him gradually approached the question, asking if he did not recall how anxious the Court had become with respect to Justice Grier's condition and the feeling of the other justices that in his own interest and in that of the Court he should give up his work. Justice Harlan asked if Field did not remember what had been said to Justice Grier on that occasion. The old man listened, gradually became alert and finally, with his eyes blazing with the old fire of youth, he burst out: "Yes! And a dirtier day's work I never did in my life!" That was the end of the effort of the brethren of the Court to induce Justice Field's retirement; he did resign not long after.

Published on page 76 of Hughes's 1928 book, *The Supreme Court and the United States,* this famous anecdote has been repeated many times by constitutional scholars. However, an article by Charles Alan Wright has cast doubt on its authenticity, because there is in fact no known documentary evidence suggesting that Field participated in any meeting with Grier (see "Authenticity of 'A Dirtier Day's Work' Quote In Question," *The Supreme Court Historical Society Quarterly* 13.4 [Winter 1990]: 6–7). There is only the oral tradition.

The available documentary evidence may be found in Charles Fairman's monumental contribution to the Oliver Wendell Holmes Devise History of the Supreme Court, *Reconstruction and Reunion, 1864–88,* part 1, vol. 6 (1971), on pages 725–31. On November 17, George Harding, described by Fairman as "an able Philadelphia lawyer with excellent political connections," wrote to Joseph Bradley, soon to take a seat on the Court himself:

Called on Judge Grier saw Mrs. Beck [a daughter] & him for an hour. They are moving on to Capitol Hill—He feels his oats & doesnt talk of resigning. I sounded him but he wouldnt respond to my touch. I saw Swayne—Nelson, & Davis—They are greatly exercised at his not resigning—They declared they were going to crowd him about Dec 1 '69. He sleeps on the bench, drops his head down & looks very badly. Congress will also crowd him if he dont resign—. . . .

Nelson, Davis & Swayne are loud in calling for you & they mutter at Grier saying how long—how long—

It is supposed that Mrs. Smith [Grier's other daughter] & Mrs. Beck support Grier in his wish to remain on the bench with a view to maintain their social status another winter in Washington—The Court are provoked at this—much of their time being spent in canvassing the subject.

It seems clear enough that Chief Justice Salmon P. Chase and the senior associate, Justice Samuel Nelson, paid a call on Grier approximately three weeks later. One of Grier's two married daughters, Mrs. Sarah Grier Beck, confirmed this meeting in a letter to George Harding dated December 9, 1869:

The Chief & Judge Nelson waited on Pa this mor'n. to ask him to resign saying that the politicians are determined to oust him, & if he don't, they will repeal the law giving the retiring salaries.

Pa told them if they wished him to resign he would do so, to take
effect the 1" of Feb.

What do you say to all this? Do you think he ought to do so?

Excuse this rapid scribble—

At this time Grier probably lived with his daughter while the Court was in
session, returning to Philadelphia when the term was completed. His health
was precarious, as was known by all. He could scarcely walk and admitted
that he could only "write with difficulty, even with a pencil."

Mrs. Beck's letter accurately indicates what happened. Grier did resign in
December, effective as of February 1, 1870. However, it cannot be inferred
from the letter whether this was the only exchange on the subject of resignation between Grier and members of the Court prior to December 9, or,
given Grier's tendency to vascillate, whether there were any meetings subsequent to that date. He again may have become uncertain about the future
and required further encouragement from his colleagues in order to carry
through with his resignation. Or he may not have.

Only Mrs. Beck's letter of December 9 remains to throw light on who
actually called on her father. Should the letter be read to mean that only
Chase and Nelson talked with her father on this topic? Although there is the
outside possibility that others were present even if she was not and she merely
repeated what her forgetful father recounted to her about his visitors when
she returned home, it is more likely from the tone of the letter that she either
was at the meeting or acted as the justice's greeter when Chase and Nelson
appeared. If these assumptions are correct, there are two possibilities left,
which the documentary evidence does not foreclose.

First, there may have been other calls at the home, either before or after
December 9, left unrecorded by correspondence. Second, there may have
been words spoken at the Capitol while the Court was about its business
(either before or after the formal sessions on the bench) when the matter of
Grier's retirement was raised, however informally. Even though he was the
junior associate, it is inconceivable that Field either was indifferent or unwilling to participate in such conversations as may have taken place. Everything
that is known about Field suggests that he would be the last man to with-
draw from controversy, especially when the chief justice, the senior associate,
David Davis (himself a gifted persuader), and Noah H. Swayne were "greatly
exercised" about the need for Grier to leave.

To conclude that only Chase and Nelson spoke to Grier about the desir-
ability of his resignation, though possible, requires one to suppose that be-

cause Mrs. Beck mentioned only one meeting and only those two justices, nothing else happened and no one else said a word to Grier about resigning. Perhaps such a thing occurred, but for this supposition to be true, a high degree of reticence on the part of some ordinarily unreserved people must be assumed, rather unrealistically. And of course there is other evidence to be considered: the story Harlan told Hughes.

How reliable is the "Yes! And a dirtier day's work I never did in my life!" anecdote? For one thing, it is double hearsay. Harlan's encounter with Field probably occurred sometime in the middle 1890s (Field resigned in April 1897, effective as of December so that he could establish a Court longevity record), and Hughes probably heard of it from Harlan sometime between when he joined the Court for the first time in 1910 and Harlan's death in 1911. Harlan retained his mental acuity until his death, so there is no reason to doubt his general accuracy. The credibility of Harlan's story is high because of the richness of detail it contains; he was recounting institutional history of the sort relished by insiders. Of course, it may have been distorted in small particulars, but at issue here is Hughes's credibility. Importance should fairly be attached to the fact that Charles Evans Hughes obviously believed the story, and he was no mean judge of men and events. Moreover, knowing what is known about Hughes inspires confidence that he got it right from Harlan.

Where, then, does the evidence lead? Several conclusions seem to follow. First, there is no documentary evidence corroborating Hughes's "A dirtier day's work" anecdote. Second, for the anecdote to be judged entirely apocryphal, for it to have no meaning at all, one must assume either Harlan or Hughes falsified it. A motive for this action is entirely lacking. There is, however, a high circumstantial probability that in some manner Field, perhaps along with others, separately or in a group, expressed to Grier the belief that he should step aside. Third, there is no way, unless told by her father, that Mrs. Beck could have known what took place at the Capitol (which is where Harlan later confronted Field). The interaction Field refers to may have been informal and almost incidental in order to spare Grier's feelings, which appears to be what happened when Harlan approached Field, who was sitting on a "settee" in the "robing room."

When the documentary evidence and the oral tradition are both examined, the following scenario seems likely. At some point Field spoke to Grier and to his other colleagues on the Court and at that time expressed the desire that Grier step down. In his old age Field might have regarded those words, those expressions, as a "dirty day's work," thus inadvertently assigning himself (the junior associate) an improbable and misleading importance in the whole affair. In short, it is the centrality Field assumes in the story that is the problem, not the recitation of what happened between Grier and his colleagues. Justice Grier remains, after all, the first justice in Court history "forced" from the bench by his colleagues.

APPENDIX B
AGE AND TENURE OF JUSTICES

During the first period (Table 1, this appendix), the average age of the Court only twice fell below fifty (in 1790 and 1812) and never exceeded sixty-eight. This tendency reflected the relative youthfulness of many of the revolutionaries who assumed and held for many years the principal positions of government. Nonetheless, the turnover on the early Court was so high that it was not until 1861 that the average tenure reached twenty.

The remaining years of the nineteenth century (Table 2) found the Court's average age stabilizing in the sixties, with no years above or below that norm. Only eight of the thirty-five years covered showed an average age of sixty-five or older. During this time the average tenure for the Court never exceeded thirteen years.

Beginning with the twentieth century (Table 3), the average age of the Court equaled or exceeded sixty-five for thirty-one of the thirty-seven years included in the period. Two of those years included an average age of seventy and seventy-one. Despite the aging of the Court, the average tenure still did not exceed fifteen, and that average was reached only in 1909.

The Roosevelt appointments, beginning with Hugo L. Black in 1937, resulted in a dramatic lowering of the average tenure on the Court in the contemporary period (Table 4). Beginning with an average tenure of fifteen in 1937, this high average was again reached by 1967, with the 1930s appointees Hugo Black and William O. Douglas still serving. However, beginning in 1939, the average age on the Court reached or exceeded sixty-five only four times, reflecting the youthfulness of the Roosevelt appointees. The average age exceeded seventy once, in 1937, when the "Old Court" was still very much intact.

As Table 5 indicates, the most recent pattern shows the Court on average becoming older. Five of the years include an average age of seventy or older, and eighteen years show a Court averaging sixty-five or older. Moreover, average tenure has increased, with ten years indicating an average of fifteen years or more.

*Average Age and Tenure of Supreme Court Justices**

Table 1, 1789–1864

Year	Average Age	Average Tenure	Year	Average Age	Average Tenure
1789	51	1	1819	56	14
1790	49	2	1820	57	15
1791	52	3	1821	58	16
1792	53	4	1822	58	16
1793	52	4	1823	59	16
1794	53	5	1824	59	17
1795	54	6	1825	60	18
1796	53	5	1826	60	16
1797	54	6	1827	60	17
1798	55	7	1828	61	18
1799	53	6	1829	61	18
1800	53	6	1830	60	15
1801	52	6	1831	61	16
1802	53	7	1832	62	17
1803	54	8	1833	63	18
1804	53	8	1834	64	19
1805	54	9	1835	59	14
1806	55	10	1836	56	8
1807	52	8	1837	56	8
1808	53	9	1838	57	8
1809	54	10	1839	58	9
1810	55	11	1840	59	10
1811	50	8	1841	60	11
1812	49	7	1842	61	12
1813	50	8	1843	62	13
1814	51	9	1844	62	13
1815	52	10	1845	61	12
1816	53	11	1846	61	9
1817	54	12	1847	61	9
1818	55	13	1848	62	10

Table 1 *continued*

Year	Average Age	Average Tenure	Year	Average Age	Average Tenure
1849	63	11	1857	65	16
1850	64	12	1858	66	17
1851	65	13	1859	67	18
1852	64	13	1860	68	19
1853	61	12	1861	68	20
1854	62	13	1862	66	15
1855	63	14	1863	63	13
1856	64	15	1864	64	14

Table 2, 1865–1899

Year	Average Age	Average Tenure	Year	Average Age	Average Tenure
1865	60	10	1883	62	9
1866	61	11	1884	63	10
1867	62	12	1885	64	11
1868	62	11	1886	65	12
1869	63	12	1887	66	13
1870	61	9	1888	66	13
1871	62	10	1889	66	13
1872	63	11	1890	65	13
1873	62	8	1891	64	11
1874	62	9	1892	63	9
1875	63	10	1893	63	9
1876	64	11	1894	61	9
1877	65	12	1895	62	10
1878	64	11	1896	63	11
1879	65	12	1897	64	12
1880	66	13	1898	62	9
1881	63	11	1899	63	10
1882	61	8			

Table 3, 1900–1936

Year	Average Age	Average Tenure	Year	Average Age	Average Tenure
1900	65	11	1902	67	13
1901	66	12	1903	65	10

Year	Average Age	Average Tenure	Year	Average Age	Average Tenure
1904	66	11	1921	67	11
1905	67	11	1922	68	12
1906	66	12	1923	66	9
1907	67	13	1924	67	10
1908	68	14	1925	68	11
1909	69	15	1926	66	10
1910	66	11	1927	67	10
1911	63	9	1928	68	11
1912	61	7	1929	69	12
1913	62	8	1930	68	12
1914	63	9	1931	69	13
1915	62	9	1932	67	11
1916	63	10	1933	68	11
1917	65	9	1934	69	12
1918	66	10	1935	70	13
1919	67	11	1936	71	14
1920	68	12			

Table 4, 1937–1968

Year	Average Age	Average Tenure	Year	Average Age	Average Tenure
1937	72	15	1953	64	11
1938	68	12	1954	64	11
1939	63	9	1955	65	11
1940	61	8	1956	66	12
1941	61	6	1957	63	10
1942	58	6	1958	64	11
1943	57	7	1959	62	10
1944	58	8	1960	63	11
1945	59	6	1961	64	12
1946	57	6	1962	60	10
1947	58	7	1963	61	11
1948	59	8	1964	62	12
1949	60	9	1965	63	13
1950	61	8	1966	64	14
1951	62	9	1967	65	15
1952	63	10	1968	65	14

Table 5, 1969–1998

Year	Average Age	Average Tenure	Year	Average Age	Average Tenure
1969	66	15	1985	71	16
1970	65	14	1986	72	17
1971	66	14	1987	70	16
1972	62	10	1988	68	15
1973	63	11	1989	69	16
1974	64	12	1990	70	17
1975	65	13	1991	67	15
1976	64	10	1992	63	13
1977	64	11	1993	63	11
1978	65	12	1994	64	12
1979	66	13	1995	61	10
1980	67	14	1996	62	11
1981	69	15	1997	63	12
1982	68	13	1998	64	13
1983	69	14			
1984	70	15			

*These data were compiled by the author in accordance with criteria established by Robert Scigliano, ed., *The Courts: A Reader in the Judicial Process* (Boston: Little, Brown, 1962), 107. The data for 1938–1961 were compiled by Scigliano.

APPENDIX C
WHERE ARE THEY BURIED?

George A. Christensen published an article in 1983 entitled "Here Lies the Supreme Court: Gravesites of the Justices" in the *Yearbook* of the Supreme Court Historical Society, in which he located all of the gravesites and provided precise addresses so tourists and other interested persons can find the cemeteries. Enough time has passed so that by now some roads may have changed or been renumbered; nonetheless, this source of additional information is invaluable for those who wish to visit the gravesites. More recently, Lee Epstein, Jeffrey A. Segal, Harold J. Spaeth, and Thomas G. Walker have included a table of the gravesites in their *Supreme Court Compendium.*

Three of the justices have been the subject of some confusion regarding their burial sites, although documentary evidence in each case reveals where they are now buried. According to cemetery records, Lucius Q. C. Lamar was disinterred on October 22, 1894, from Riverside Cemetery in Macon, Georgia, and moved to St. Peter's Cemetery in Oxford, Mississippi. Some uncertainty has also surrounded the whereabouts of Henry Baldwin, whose burial in Oak Hill Cemetery in the Georgetown area of Washington, D.C., is documented. No documentary evidence exists of any subsequent transfer to Greendale Cemetery in Meadville, Pennsylvania, where his wife is buried. Although both of their names are inscribed on the tombstone, his name is a memorial rather than a grave marker. He remains at Oak Hill Cemetery.

No justice met a more gruesome death than William Johnson, who died of shock while on the operating table. He well knew he might not survive an elective cancer surgery undertaken at a time when anesthesiology was unavailable to patients. At one time it was thought that Johnson's body had disappeared after his funeral in New York City while temporarily stored in a church awaiting shipment back to Charleston, South Carolina. However, cemetery records at St. Philip's Church in Charleston indicate the justice was eventually buried there as he had planned, and his burial plot is clearly recorded. His monument, now weathered and with the words barely legible, is in the center of the West Cemetery along the south wall.

Nine of the justices are buried at Arlington; four are at Rock Creek, and three are at Oak Hill, both located in Washington, D.C. Four are in Cambridge, Massachusetts, at Mount Auburn Cemetery. No justice has been buried west of Boulder, Colorado. Louis D. Brandeis, John H. Clarke, Abe Fortas, Felix Frankfurter, and Wiley B. Rutledge were cremated.

Below are the many different gravesites or cemeteries in which the justices are interred.

Baldwin, Henry	Oak Hill Cemetery Washington, D.C.
Barbour, Philip P.	Congressional Cemetery Washington, D.C.
Black, Hugo L.	Arlington National Cemetery Arlington, Va.
Blair, John, Jr.	Bruton Parish Church Williamsburg, Va.
Blatchford, Samuel	Green Wood Cemetery Brooklyn, N.Y.
Bradley, Joseph P.	Mount Pleasant Cemetery Newark, N.J.
Brandeis, Louis D.	University of Louisville Law School Louisville, Ky.
Brennan, William J., Jr.	Arlington National Cemetery Arlington, Va.
Brewer, David J.	Mount Muncie Cemetery Leavenworth, Kans.
Brown, Henry B.	Elmwood Cemetery Detroit, Mich.
Burger, Warren E.	Arlington National Cemetery Arlington, Va.
Burton, Harold H.	Highland Park Cemetery Cleveland, Ohio
Butler, Pierce	Calvary Cemetery St. Paul, Minn.

Byrnes, James F.	Trinity Cathedral Graveyard Columbia, S.C.
Campbell, John A.	Green Mount Cemetery Baltimore, Md.
Cardozo, Benjamin N.	Cypress Hills Cemetery Brooklyn, N.Y.
Catron, John	Mount Olivet Cemetery Nashville, Tenn.
Chase, Salmon P.	Spring Grove Cemetery Cincinnati, Ohio
Chase, Samuel	St. Paul's Cemetery Baltimore, Md.
Clark, Tom C.	Restland Memorial Park Dallas, Texas
Clarke, John H.	Lisbon Cemetery Lisbon, Ohio
Clifford, Nathan	Evergreen Cemetery Portland, Maine
Curtis, Benjamin R.	Mount Auburn Cemetery Cambridge, Mass.
Cushing, William	Family Cemetery Scituate, Mass.
Daniel, Peter V.	Hollywood Cemetery Richmond, Va.
Davis, David	Evergreen Memorial Cemetery Bloomington, Ill.
Day, William R.	West Lawn Cemetery Canton, Ohio
Douglas, William O.	Arlington National Cemetery Arlington, Va.
Duvall, Gabriel	Family estate Prince George's County, Md.
Ellsworth, Oliver	Palisado Cemetery Windsor, Conn.
Field, Stephen J.	Rock Creek Cemetery Washington, D.C.
Fortas, Abe	Cremated, no interment
Frankfurter, Felix	Mount Auburn Cemetery Cambridge, Mass.

Fuller, Melville W.	Graceland Cemetery Chicago, Ill.
Goldberg, Arthur J.	Arlington National Cemetery Arlington, Va.
Gray, Horace	Mount Auburn Cemetery Cambridge, Mass.
Grier, Robert C.	West Laurel Hill Cemetery Bala-Cynwyd, Pa.
Harlan, John Marshall I	Rock Creek Cemetery Washington, D.C.
Harlan, John Marshall II	Emmanuel Church Cemetery Weston, Conn.
Holmes, Oliver W., Jr.	Arlington National Cemetery Arlington, Va.
Hughes, Charles E.	The Woodlawn Cemetery Bronx, N.Y.
Hunt, Ward	Forest Hill Cemetery Utica, N.Y.
Iredell, James	Hayes Plantation Edenton, N.C.
Jackson, Howell E.	Mount Olivet Cemetery Nashville, Tenn.
Jackson, Robert H.	Mapel Grove Cemetery Frewsburg, N.Y.
Jay, John	Family cemetery Rye, N.Y.
Johnson, Thomas	Mount Olivet Cemetery Frederick, Md.
Johnson, William	St. Philip's Churchyard Chalreston, S.C.
Lamar, Joseph R.	Summerville Cemetery Augusta, Ga.
Lamar, Lucius Q. C.	St. Peter's Cemetery Oxford, Miss.
Livingston, H. Brockholst	Trinity Church Churchyard New York, N.Y.
Lurton, Horace	Greenwood Cemetery Clarksville, Tenn.

Marshall, John — Shockoe Hill Cemetery
Richmond, Va.

Marshall, Thurgood — Arlington National Cemetery
Arlington, Va.

Matthews, Stanley — Spring Grove Cemetery
Cincinnati, Ohio

McKenna, Joseph — Mount Olivet Cemetery
Washington, D.C.

McKinley, John — Cave Hill Cemetery
Louisville, Ky.

McLean, John — Spring Grove Cemetery
Cincinnati, Ohio

McReynolds, James C. — Glenwood Cemetery
Elkton, Ky.

Miller, Samuel — Oakland Cemetery
Keokuk, Iowa

Minton, Sherman — Holy Trinity Catholic Cemetery
New Albany, Ind.

Moody, William H. — Byfield Parish Churchyard
Georgetown, Mass.

Moore, Alfred — St. Philip's Churchyard
Southport, N.C.

Murphy, Frank — Our Lady of Lake Huron Cemetery
Harbor Beach, Mich.

Nelson, Samuel — Lakewood Cemetery
Cooperstown, N.Y.

Paterson, William — Albany Rural Cemetery
Menands, N.Y.

Peckham, Rufus W. — Albany Rural Cemetery
Menands, N.Y.

Pitney, Mahlon — Evergreen Cemetery
Morristown, N.J.

Powell, Lewis F. — Hollywood Cemetery
Richmond, Va.

Reed, Stanley F. — Maysville Cemetery
Maysville, Ky.

Roberts, Owen J. — St. Andrew's Cemetery
West Vincent, Pa.

Rutledge, John	St. Michael's Cemetery Charleston, S.C.
Rutledge, Wiley B.	Green Mountain Cemetery Boulder, Colo.
Sanford, Edward T.	Greenwood Cemetery Knoxville, Tenn.
Shiras, George, Jr.	Allegheny Cemetery Pittsburgh, Pa.
Stewart, Potter	Arlington National Cemetery Arlington, Va.
Stone, Harlan F.	Rock Creek Cemetery Washington, D.C.
Story, Joseph	Mount Auburn Cemetery Cambridge, Mass.
Strong, William	Charles Evans Cemetery Reading, Pa.
Sutherland, George	Cedar Hill Cemetery Suitland, Md.
Swayne, Noah H.	Oak Hill Cemetery Washington, D.C.
Taft, William H.	Arlington National Cemetery Arlington, Va.
Taney, Roger B.	St. John the Evangelist Cemetery Frederick, Md.
Thompson, Smith	Poughkeepsie Cemetery Poughkeepsie, N.Y.
Todd, Thomas	Frankfort Cemetery Frankfort, Ky.
Trimble, Robert	Paris Cemetery Paris, Ky.
Van Devanter, Willis	Rock Creek Cemetery Washington, D.C.
Vinson, Fred M.	Pinehill Cemetery Louisa, Ky.
Waite, Morrison	Woodlawn Cemetery Toledo, Ohio
Warren, Earl	Arlington National Cemetery Arlington, Va.

Washington, Bushrod	Family vault Mount Vernon, Va.
Wayne, James M.	Laurel Grove Cemetery Savannah, Ga.
White, Edward D.	Oak Hill Cemetery Washington, D.C.
Whittaker, Charles E.	Calvary Cemetery Kansas City, Mo.
Wilson, James	Christ Churchyard Philadelphia, Pa.
Woodbury, Levi	Harmony Grove Cemetery Portsmouth, N.H.
Woods, William B.	Cedar Hill Cemetery Newark, Ohio

NOTES

CHAPTER 1. WHY DO THEY LEAVE OR STAY?

1. See, e.g., David J. Danelski, *A Supreme Court Justice Is Appointed* (New Haven: Yale University Press, 1964), and Henry J. Abraham, *Justices and Presidents: A Political History of Appointments to the Supreme Court,* 3d ed. (New York: Oxford University Press, 1992).

2. U.S. Const., art. 3, sec. 1.

3. Cited in Walter F. Murphy and C. Herman Pritchett, eds., *Courts, Judges, and Politics,* 2d ed. (New York: Random House, 1974), 189. The impeachment provision applicable to all federal judges sitting on constitutional courts is found in U.S. Const., art. 2, sec. 4, which provides: "The President, Vice-President and all civil officers of the United States, shall be removed from Office on Impeachment for, and Conviction of, Treason, Bribery, or other high Crimes and Misdemeanors."

4. James F. Watts Jr., "William Moody," in Leon Friedman and Fred L. Israel, eds., *The Justices of the United States Supreme Court, 1789–1978: Their Lives and Major Opinions* (New York: Chelsea House, 1978), 3:1821.

5. See the discussion of the act in Kermit L. Hall, ed., *The Oxford Companion to the Supreme Court of the United States* (New York: Oxford University Press, 1992), 475.

6. Lawrence H. Larsen, "Observations on One Hundred Years of Federal Judging in Western Missouri District Court," in John R. Wunder, ed., *Law and the Great Plains: Essays on the Legal History of the Heartland* (Westport, Conn.: Greenwood Press, 1996), 146.

7. Elder Witt, ed., *Congressional Quarterly's Guide to the U.S. Supreme Court,* 2d ed. (Washington, D.C.: Congressional Quarterly Press, 1990), 657.

8. Since 1989 justices who have retired to senior status must perform some actual judicial duties in order to qualify for pay increases. They must certify that in three months they have accomplished service equivalent to that achieved by an active justice in twelve months. See Lee Epstein, Jeffrey A. Segal, Harold J. Spaeth, and Thomas G. Walker, eds., *The Supreme Court Compendium: Data, Decisions and Developments* (Washington, D.C.: Congressional Quarterly Press, 1994), 36–37. The authors provide a synopsis of each of the statutes affecting retirements and resignations through the 1989 change affecting senior status.

9. U.S. Const., art. 3, sec. 1. See *Booth v. U.S.,* 291 U.S. 339 (1934). See also Hall, 227–28.

10. *Kansas City Star,* 29 June 1991.

11. Glendon Schubert, "Aging, Conservatism, and Judicial Behavior," *Micropolitics* 3 (1983): 135, where cohort analysis is employed. Although Schubert acknowl-

edges operational difficulties inherent in the project, the data suggest a relationship between aging and conservatism.

12. Neal E. Cutter and John R. Schmidhauser, "Age and Political Behavior," in Diana S. Woodruff and James E. Birren, eds., *Aging: Scientific Perspectives and Social Issues* (New York: D. Van Nostrand, 1975), 374.

13. "Age Found Not to Reduce Intelligence as Believed," Kansas City Times, 1 March 1984.

14. Ibid.

15. Richard A. Posner, *Aging and Old Age* (Chicago: University of Chicago Press, 1994), 67–70.

16. Jerrold M. Post and Robert S. Robins, *When Illness Strikes the Leader: The Dilemma of the Captive King* (New Haven: Yale University Press, 1993); Robert E. Gilbert, *The Mortal Presidency: Illness and Anguish in the White House* (New York: Basic Books, 1992).

17. The revelation that French president François Mitterrand concealed from the public that his prostate cancer had spread throughout his body, even though he was aware of this condition six months after he took office in 1981, met with widespread disapproval. Mitterrand maintained the deception until his death at age seventy-nine on January 8, 1996. He was often ill, sometimes could not function, and lied about the reasons why he was absent. See Jim Hoagland, "The Fraudulent François Mitterrand," Kansas City Star, 23 January 1996.

18. Robert W. Calvert, "Mandatory Retirement of Judges," in Glenn R. Winters and Richard A. Hanson, eds., *Selected Readings: Judicial Discipline and Removal* (Chicago: American Judicature Society, 1973), 42.

19. James M. McPherson, *Battle Cry of Freedom: The Civil War Era* (New York: Oxford University Press, 1988), 714.

20. Occasionally party and ideology may operate to encourage retirement, as probably happened in the cases of Byron White (party) and Harry Blackmun (ideology). White, a Democrat, left when a Democratic president would select his replacement, and Blackmun, a Republican, left when he knew an ideologically agreeable Democratic president (whom he had known for a number of years through annual retreats) would choose his successor.

21. See Terry Eastland, "While Justice Sleeps," *National Review*, 21 April 1989, 24–26. Eastland quotes Justice Brennan as having once said that "a disabled Justice is almost as bad as one you disagree with."

22. James F. Simon, *Independent Journey: The Life of William O. Douglas* (New York: Harper and Row, 1980), 451.

23. David W. Maxey, "The Translation of James Wilson," *Journal of Supreme Court History: 1990 Yearbook of the Supreme Court Historical Society*, 28.

24. Hadley Arkes, *The Return of George Sutherland: Restoring a Jurisprudence of Natural Rights* (Princeton: Princeton University Press, 1994).

CHAPTER 2. THE ANTEBELLUM COURT, 1789–1864

1. See Charles Fairman, "The Retirement of Federal Judges," *Harvard Law Review* 51 (1938): 405.

2. See Table 1 in David N. Atkinson, "Bowing to the Inevitable: Supreme Court Deaths and Resignations, 1789–1864," *Arizona State Law Journal* (1982): 616.

3. George Pellew, *John Jay* (1890; reprint, New York: Chelsea House, 1980), 301.

4. Ibid., 311.

5. Leon Friedman, "John Rutledge," in Leon Friedman and Fred L. Israel, eds., *The Justices of the United States Supreme Court 1789–1978: Their Lives and Major Opinions* (New York: Chelsea House, 1978), 1:44–45.

6. Ibid., 1:46.

7. Ibid.

8. Ibid.

9. See Richard H. Barry, *Mr. Rutledge of South Carolina* (New York: Duell, Sloan, and Pearce, 1942), 351.

10. Friedman and Israel, 1:48.

11. Ibid.

12. Griffith J. McRee, *Life and Correspondence of James Iredell: One of the Associate Justices of the Supreme Court of the United States* (New York: D. Appelton, 1857), 2:527.

13. Ibid., 528.

14. Edward S. Delaplaine, *The Life of Thomas Johnson: Member of the Continental Congress, First Governor of the State of Maryland, and Associate Justice of the United States Supreme Court* (New York: F. H. Hitchcock, 1927), 508.

15. Ibid., 509.

16. Fred L. Israel, "John Blair, Jr.," in Friedman and Israel, 1:115.

17. Ibid.

18. See Robert G. McCloskey, "Introduction," in McCloskey, ed., *The Works of James Wilson* (Cambridge: Harvard University Press, 1967), 1:2–6, 17, 23, 24.

19. Ibid.

20. Charles Page Smith, *James Wilson: Founding Father, 1742–1798* (1956; reprint, Westport, Conn: Greenwood Press, 1973), 380.

21. Benjamin Rush, *The Autobiography of Benjamin Rush*, ed. G. Corner (Princeton: Princeton University Press, 1948), 237.

22. Smith, 380.

23. Ibid., 384.

24. McRee, 2:380.

25. Ibid., 534.

26. Henry Flanders, *The Lives and Times of the Chief Justices of the Supreme Court of the United States* (Philadelphia: Lippincott, 1875), 2:238.

27. Ibid., 239.

28. Ibid., 247–48. Ellsworth recognized the relationship between gout and kidney stones before the importance of uric acid in the blood was understood in the progression of both diseases. See W. S. C. Copeman, *A Short History of the Gout and the Rheumatic Diseases* (Berkeley: University of California Press, 1964), 106–7.

29. He wrote: "I know you will be much disappointed at my not returning this fall; but the gravel and the gout in my kidneys, which constantly afflict me, forbid my undertaking a voyage in a cold and boisterous season of the year" (William Garrott Brown, The Life of Oliver Ellsworth [1905; reprint, New York: Da Capo Press, 1970], 302).

30. Flanders, 2:258–59.

31. D. Grier Stephenson Jr., "The Judicial Bookshelf," *Journal of Supreme Court History: 1994 Yearbook of the Supreme Court Historical Society*, 154.

32. Ibid.

33. McRee, 2:583.

34. James Buchanan, "Alfred Moore," in Clare Cushman, ed., *The Supreme Court*

Justices: Illustrated Biographies, 1789–1993 (Washington, D.C.: Congressional Quarterly Press, 1993), 59.

35. Michael Kraus, "William Paterson," in Friedman and Israel, 1:173.

36. John E. O'Connor, *William Paterson: Lawyer and Statesman, 1745–1806* (New Brunswick, N.J.: Rutgers University Press, 1979), 273.

37. Ibid., 276.

38. Ibid., 278.

39. Smith, 376.

40. Arthur P. Rugg, "William Cushing," *Yale Law Journal* 30 (1920): 141.

41. Charles Warren, *The Supreme Court in United States History*, rev. ed. (Boston: Little, Brown, 1935), 1:400.

42. Elder Witt, ed., *Congressional Quarterly's Guide to the U.S. Supreme Court*, 2d ed. (Washington, D.C.: Congressional Quarterly Press, 1990), 807.

43. James Haw, "Samuel Chase," in Cushman, 45.

44. William. W. Story, ed., *The Life and Letters of Joseph Story* (1851; reprint, Freeport, N.Y.: Books for Libraries Press, 1971), 2:422.

45. Ibid., 2:499.

46. Fred L. Israel, "Robert Trimble," in Friedman and Israel, 1:518.

47. Ibid.

48. G. Edward White, with Gerald Gunther, *The Marshall Court and Cultural Change, 1815–1935*, abridged ed. (New York: Oxford University Press, 1991), 354.

49. Ibid., 251.

50. Ibid., 257.

51. Witt, 809–10.

52. Donald G. Morgan, *Justice William Johnson, the First Dissenter: The Career and Constitutional Philosophy of a Jeffersonian Judge* (Columbia: University of South Carolina Press, 1954), 182.

53. White, 343.

54. Ibid., 277–78 n. 76.

55. Ibid., 281.

56. Irving Dilliard, "Gabriel Duvall," in Friedman and Israel, 1:427.

57. Ibid.

58. Ibid.

59. Carl Brent Swisher, *Roger B. Taney* (New York: Macmillan, 1961), 311–12.

60. White, 326.

61. See Herbert Alan Johnson, "John Marshall," in Friedman and Israel, 1:285–304.

62. Flanders, 2:534–35.

63. David G. Loth, *Chief Justice Marshall and the Growth of the Republic* (1949; reprint, New York: Greenwood Press, 1970), 380.

64. Albert J. Beveridge, *The Life of John Marshall* (Boston: Houghton Mifflin, 1919), 4:586.

65. Jean Edward Smith, *John Marshall: Definer of a Nation* (New York: Henry Holt and Company, 1996), 523. Smith persuasively counters the myth that Marshall was indolent. His easygoing manners sometimes masked reality, as the chief justice always rose at first light and did a day's work before noon. He was thereafter free during the afternoon and evening to pursue other interests, among which was his fondness for Madeira. Marshall was a famous imbiber of Madeira, but there appears to be no evidence of cirrhosis of the liver. In any event, only rarely does a tumor develop in the liver as a result of cirrhosis. And benign liver tumors, whenever they occur, are very rare; they are usually malignant. See Charles B. Clayman, ed., *The*

American Medical Association Family Medical Guide, 3d ed. (New York: Random House, 1994), 526.

66. Warren, 1:814.

67. Allan B. Magruder, *John Marshall* (1898; reprint, New York: AMS Press, 1972), 280.

68. Story, 2:348–49.

69. White, 302.

70. This diagnosis was suggested by Robert G. Seddig. See Kermit L. Hall, ed., *The Oxford Companion to the Supreme Court of the United States* (New York: Oxford University Press, 1992), 60.

71. Hampton L. Carson, *The History of the Supreme Court of the United States, with Biographies of All the Chief and Associate Justices* (1902; reprint, New York: B. Franklin, 1971), 2:281.

72. Gerald T. Dunne, *Justice Joseph Story and the Rise of the Supreme Court* (New York: Simon and Schuster, 1970), 425.

73. Ibid., 426.

74. Ibid., 347–51.

75. Story, 2:547. Dunne, 430, believes the "violent stricture" was probably a heart attack.

76. Dunne, 347–51.

77. R. Kent Newmyer, *Supreme Court Justice Joseph Story: Statesman of the Old Republic* (Chapel Hill: University of North Carolina Press, 1985), 381.

78. Frank Otto Gatell, "John McKinley," in Friedman and Israel, 1:777.

79. 60 U.S. (19 How.) 393 (1857).

80. Don E. Fehrenbacher, *The Dred Scott Case: Its Significance in American Law and Politics* (New York: Oxford University Press, 1978), 316–19.

81. Benjamin Robbins Curtis, ed., *A Memoir of Benjamin Robbins Curtis, LL.D., with Some of His Professional and Miscellaneous Writings* (1879; reprint, New York: Da Capo Press, 1970), 447–48.

82. See Francis P. Weisenburger, *The Life of John McLean: A Politician on the United States Supreme Court* (1937; reprint, New York: Da Capo Press, 1971), 216–17.

83. Erwin C. Surrency, *History of the Federal Courts* (New York: Oceanna Publications, 1987), 295.

84. William Gillette, "John A. Campbell," in Friedman and Israel, 2:936.

85. David M. Silver, *Lincoln's Supreme Court* (Champaign: University of Illinois Press, 1956), 12.

86. Ibid.

87. Burnet Anderson, "John A. Campbell," in Cushman, 165.

88. Gillette, 2:939.

89. Samuel Tyler, *Memoir of Roger Brooke Taney, LL.D., Chief Justice of the Supreme Court of the United States* (1872; reprint, New York: Da Capo Press, 1970), 457.

90. Swisher, 454.

91. Ibid., 575–76.

92. Ibid., 577.

93. Ibid., 578.

94. Warren, 2:389, quoting *Diary of Gideon Welles,* for 14 October and 26 November 1864.

95. Silver, 186–87.

96. Swisher, 581–82, quoting New York Tribune, 14 October 1864.

97. Ibid. 581.
98. Warren, 2:395–96.
99. Carson C. Hathaway, "At Last a Home for the Supreme Court," *New York Times Magazine*, 26 September 1926.
100. As Justice William Johnson wrote to Jefferson on 10 December 1822: "While I was on our state-bench I was accustomed to delivering seriatim opinions in our appellate court, and was not a little surprised to find our Chief Justice in the Supreme Court delivering all the opinions in cases in which he sat, even in some instances when contrary to his own judgment and vote. But I remonstrated in vain; the answer was he is willing to take the trouble and it is a mark of respect to him. I soon however found out the real cause. Cushing was incompetent. Chase could not be got to think or write—Patterson [*sic*] was a slow man and willingly declined the trouble, and the other two judges you know are commonly estimated as one judge" (Morgan, 181–82).

CHAPTER 3. CIVIL WAR TO CENTURY'S END, 1865–1899

1. See Alfred A. Kelly, Winfred A. Harbison, and Herman Belz, *The American Constitution: Its Origins and Development*, 6th ed. (New York: W. W. Norton, 1983), 373–418; Jonathan Lurie, *Law and the Nation, 1865–1912* (New York: Knopf, 1983), 27–42; and Carl Brent Swisher, *American Constitutional Development*, 2d ed. (New York: Houghton Mifflin, 1954), 389–452.
2. Thomas Carlyle, *Past and Present* (New York: C. Scribner's Sons, 1918), 311.
3. *Dred Scott v. Sandford*, 19 How. (60 U.S.) 393 (1857).
4. Charles Warren, *The Supreme Court in United States History* (Boston: Little, Brown, 1926), 2:318.
5. The chief justice had not assigned him opinions for the two terms prior to his death in deference to his physical weaknesses, although all were agreed that his mind and will remained clear and strong. Alexander A. Lawrence, *James Moore Wayne: Southern Unionist* (1943; reprint, Westport, Conn.: Greenwood Press, 1970), 213.
6. Charles Fairman, *Reconstruction and Reunion 1864–88, The Oliver Wendell Holmes Devise History of the Supreme Court of the United States*, part 1, vol. 6 (New York: Macmillan, 1971), 146–47.
7. Charles Fairman, *Mr. Justice Miller and the Supreme Court 1862–1890* (Cambridge: Harvard University Press, 1939), 164.
8. On October 9, 1866, at the age of seventy-two, he had suggested to the chief justice, "If I could have a *room in the Capitol* on the *level* of our court room, so as not to be compelled to '*get up the stairs*' I could attend to my duty at Washington as usual, if my health continues." This astonishing proposal was gently rebuffed. See Fairman, *Reconstruction and Reunion 1864–88,* 83.
9. Fairman, *Miller,* 164.
10. Chief Justice Chase understandably ignored Grier's mental decline in his official description of what was apparently a stroke that Grier suffered in 1867, two years before he resigned. Chase remembered that "partial paralysis had impaired his ability to move [his lower limbs] with strength, and to depend upon them. While not affecting the brain at all, or the muscles of the upper part of his frame, it was observed by him at a later date, that the shock did affect his power to use his hand in writing, and to consult with facility the heavy books of the law" (75 U.S. vii [1870]).
11. Fairman, *Miller,* 164.

12. *Hepburn v. Griswold*, 75 U.S. (8 Wall.) 603 (1870).

13. Burnett Anderson, "Robert C. Grier," in Clare Cushman, ed., *The Supreme Court Justices: Illustrated Biographies, 1789–1993* (Washington, D.C.: Congressional Quarterly Press, 1993), 155.

14. Fairman, *Reconstruction and Reunion 1864–88*, 729.

15. See Appendix A.

16. Fairman, *Reconstruction and Reunion 1864–88*, 677–775.

17. Merlo Pusey, "The Court Copes with Disability," in *Yearbook 1979, Supreme Court Historical Society*, 65.

18. Ibid.

19. Fairman, *Reconstruction and Reunion 1864–88*, 719.

20. Warren, 2:319.

21. Willard King, *Lincoln's Manager, David Davis* (Cambridge: Harvard University Press, 1960), 284.

22. Ibid.

23. New York Times, 8 May 1873.

24. Charles Fairman, "The Retirement of Federal Judges," *Harvard Law Review* 51 (1938): 419–20.

25. 83 U.S. (16 Wall.) 36 (1873).

26. *Bradwell v. Illinois*, 83 U.S. (16 Wall.) 130 (1873).

27. Jacob W. Schuckers, *The Life and Public Services of Salmon Portland Chase* (1874; reprint, New York: Da Capo Press, 1970), 622.

28. Ibid.

29. John Niven, *Salmon P. Chase: A Biography* (New York: Oxford University Press, 1995), 449.

30. New York Times, 8 May 1873.

31. King, 287.

32. Ibid.

33. Fairman, "Retirement of Federal Judges," 421.

34. King, 288.

35. Ibid., 302.

36. New York Times, 27 June 1886.

37. Theron G. Strong, *Landmarks of a Lawyer's Lifetime* (New York: Dodd, Mead, 1914), 28.

38. Ibid.

39. Fairman, *Miller*, 382.

40. Ibid., 383.

41. Burnett Anderson, "Noah H. Swayne," in Cushman, 175.

42. Fairman, *Miller*, 382.

43. C. Peter Magrath, *Morrison R. Waite: The Triumph of Character* (New York: Macmillan, 1963), 261.

44. Ibid.

45. Fairman, *Miller*, 374.

46. Ibid., 378.

47. Ibid.

48. Ibid.

49. Thomas E. Baynes Jr., "William B. Woods," in Cushman, 225.

50. Fairman, *Miller*, 391.

51. Magrath, 309.

52. Ibid., 309–10.

53. Ibid., 310.

54. See Felix Frankfurter, *The Commerce Clause Under Marshall, Taney and Waite* (1937; reprint, Chicago: Quadrangle, 1964), 74–114. See also Robert J. Steamer, *Chief Justice: Leadership and the Supreme Court* (Columbia: South Carolina University Press, 1986), 97–158.

55. Magrath, 310–11.

56. Fairman, *Miller,* 379–80.

57. New York Times, 11 October 1890.

58. Leon Friedman, "Joseph P. Bradley," in Leon Friedman and Fred L. Israel, eds., *The Justices of the United States Supreme Court 1789–1978: Their Lives and Major Opinions* (New York: Chelsea House, 1978), 2:1199.

59. Wirt Armistead Cate, *Lucius Q. C. Lamar, Secession and Reunion* (Chapel Hill: University of North Carolina Press, 1935), 515.

60. Ibid., 516.

61. Ibid., 518.

62. James B. Murphy, *L. Q. C. Lamar: Pragmatic Patriot* (Baton Rouge: Louisiana State University Press, 1973), 269.

63. Cate, 519.

64. Michael Kammen, *A Machine That Would Go of Itself: The Constitution in American Culture* (New York: Knopf, 1986), 197.

65. *Pollock v. Farmers' Loan & Trust Co.,* 157 U.S. 429; 158 U.S. 601 (1895).

66. Carl Brent Swisher, *Stephen J. Field: Craftsman of the Law* (1930; reprint, Chicago: University of Chicago Press, 1969), 440.

67. Ibid., 442–43.

68. *Pollock v. Farmers' Loan & Trust Co.,* 157 U.S. 429, 586 (1895).

69. Charles Evans Hughes, *The Supreme Court of the United States* (New York: Columbia University Press, 1928), 75–76. This famous anecdote, related by Harlan to Hughes, has been disputed. See Appendix A.

70. History sometimes furnishes interesting contrasts. When Justice Hugo L. Black's son, Hugo Jr., told his father—who was lying desperately ill at the Bethesda Naval Hospital—that he was within six months of Field's longevity record and that if he retired before he died his wife's insurance policy would be substantially reduced, Justice Black's reply was: "That does not make *any* difference! I *can't* serve" (Hugo L. Black and Elizabeth Black, *Mr. Justice and Mrs. Black: The Memoirs of Hugo L. Black and Elizabeth Black* [New York: Random House, 1986], 277–78).

71. 75 U.S. (8 Wall.) 603 (1870).

72. Fairman, *Miller,* 388.

73. Fairman, "The Retirement of Federal Judges," 425.

74. Logan Clendening, *The Human Body* (New York: Alfred A. Knopf, 1927), 384.

CHAPTER 4. THE COURT IN PROSPERITY AND DEPRESSION,
1900–1936

1. Memorandum, 10 November 1924, William Howard Taft Papers, Manuscript Division, Library of Congress. The memorandum is reprinted in Walter F. Murphy and C. Herman Pritchett, eds., *Courts, Judges, and Politics: An Introduction to the Judicial Process,* 2d ed. (New York: Random House, 1974), 218.

2. Willard L. King, *Melville Weston Fuller: Chief Justice of the United States 1888–*

1910 (New York: Macmillan, 1950; reprint, Chicago: University of Chicago Press, 1967), 133.

3. Louis Filler, "Horace Gray," in Leon Friedman and Fred L. Israel, eds., *The Justices of the United States Supreme Court 1789–1978: Their Lives and Major Opinions* (New York: Chelsea House, 1978), 2:1388.

4. New York Times, 16 September 1902.

5. Henry J. Abraham, *Justices and Presidents: A Political History of Appointments to the Supreme Court,* 3d ed. (New York: Oxford University Press, 1992), 163.

6. New York Times, 3 August 1924.

7. 163 U.S. 537 (1896). It is unfortunate that Justice Brown's work is not more widely known, because he was something of a centrist at the time he served and was not as conservative as, for example, Justice David Brewer. He has been described as one who was within the "broadly *liberal* tradition" of American politics. See Arnold M. Paul, *Conservative Crisis and the Rule of Law: Attitudes of Bar and Bench, 1887–1895* (Ithaca, N.Y.: Cornell University Press, 1960), 84–88.

8. New York Times, 6 December 1903.

9. Or "Secretary," as the first law clerk was called when he was hired by Justice Gray in 1882.

10. New York Times, 6 December 1903.

11. New York Times, 9 March 1906.

12. Ibid.

13. New York Times, 5 September 1913.

14. New York Times, 24 October 1909.

15. New York Times, 25 October 1909.

16. Robert B. Highsaw, *Edward Douglass White: Defender of the Conservative Faith* (Baton Rouge: Louisiana State University Press, 1981), 181.

17. New York Times, 28 October 1909.

18. Richard Skolnik, "Rufus Peckham," in Friedman and Israel, 3:1703.

19. New York Times, 29 March 1910.

20. Ibid.

21. *Standard Oil Co. v. U.S.,* 221 U.S. 1 (1911).

22. Michael J. Brodhead, *David J. Brewer: The Life of a Supreme Court Justice, 1837–1910* (Carbondale: Southern Illinois University Press, 1994), 183–84.

23. King, 309.

24. Ibid., 302–3. At a later time, Justice Felix Frankfurter reacted similarly when there was a good deal of media speculation about him retiring in favor of John Marshal Harlan prior to Harlan's own appointment in 1955. Like Fuller, he resented it.

25. Ibid.

26. Ibid.

27. New York Times, 5 July 1910.

28. New York Times, 8 July 1910.

29. New York Times, 9 July 1910.

30. King, 310.

31. Ibid., 335.

32. Moody was the prosecutor in the Lizzie Borden ax murder. Although unsuccessful, he conducted a vigorous and able prosecution.

33. James F. Watts Jr., "William Moody," in Friedman and Israel, 3:1816.

34. Jeffrey O'Connell and Thomas E. O'Connell, "Book Review," *St. Louis Uni-*

versity Law Journal 37 (1992): 178. Based on the symptoms described in Frederick Bernays Weiner, *The Life and Judicial Career of William Henry Moody,* 92–105, the O'Connells offer chronic inflammatory polyneuropathy as the most likely diagnosis. This condition is a variant of Guillain-Barré syndrome, which they point out is itself a variant of amyotrophic lateral sclerosis (Lou Gehrig's disease). The Weiner manuscript is on file at the Harvard Law School Library (available on microfilm) and was written by Weiner, later a distinguished civil liberties lawyer, while still a student at Harvard Law School. He prepared the study for Professor Felix Frankfurter's course on federal jurisdiction in the spring of 1930.

    35. Watts, 3:1821. Moody actually retired at full pay, all of which was agreed to prior to his retirement. See New York Times, 5 October 1910.

    36. Ibid.

    37. John Marshall Harlan to Horace Lurton, 8 July 1910, Horace H. Lurton Papers, Manuscript Division, Library of Congress.

    38. Watts, 3:1821.

    39. New York Times, 12 July 1917.

    40. Ibid.

    41. New York Times, 14 October 1911.

    42. Justice Harlan described his situation on that occasion in a letter to Justice Lurton: "I came back from my last year's vacation in good condition; but about the first day of December the grip came back upon me, and until within the past three or four weeks I have not felt to be myself by a good deal. The result is, that I have not done as much work here this winter as I ordinarily do, although I have done enough to prevent the impression gaining ground that I am too old to work. But I hope that cannot be said for a good many years to come. My sickness this winter struck me in some vital parts, and I have not yet entirely recovered. But I feel that this summer's vacation will make me all right again. My doctor advises me to take no more work than is absolutely essential. Indeed, he has said that if I could be absolutely without work for some months, it would put me in such condition that I might expect a long lease of life to come. Nevertheless, I am well enough to meet any emergency that may arise in the business in my circuit" (John Marshall Harlan to Horace H. Lurton, May 4, 1903, Lurton Papers).

    43. New York Times, 15 October 1911.

    44. Ibid.

    45. Although reported in the newspapers, one of Harlan's biographers, Loren P. Beth, believes the words may never have been spoken. If they were, Beth described them as "a fitting last remark by a man who had always practiced the courtly manners of an earlier era" (*John Marshall Harlan: The Last Whig Justice* [Lexington: University Press of Kentucky, 1992], 190). Mrs. Harlan's memoirs make no mention of these last words. See Tinsley E. Yarbrough, *Judicial Enigma: The First Justice Harlan* (New York: Oxford University Press, 1995), 238 n. 108.

    46. Louis Filler, "John M. Harlan," in Friedman and Israel, 2:1293.

    47. New York Times, 16 October 1911.

    48. New York Times, 18 October 1911.

    49. William R. Day to Horace H. Lurton, 17 October 1911, Lurton Papers.

    50. See Filler, 2:1293, for a discussion of Harlan's reputation following his death. Justice Brewer's quip that Harlan "retires at eight with one hand on the Constitution and the other on the bible, safe and happy in a perfect faith in justice and righteousness" has often been repeated, as have Justice Holmes's references to him as "old Harlan" and the "last of the tobacco-spitting judges."

51. Oliver Wendell Holmes to Sir Frederick Pollock, 5 April 1919, in Mark De Wolfe Howe, ed., *The Holmes-Pollock Letters* (Cambridge: Harvard University Press, 1946), 2:7–8.

52. New York Times, 13 July 1914.

53. William Howard Taft to Horace H. Lurton, 26 January 1914, Lurton Papers. Justice Lurton was himself a Democrat, although as the letter assumes, one who was entirely comfortable with Taft Republicanism.

54. William R. Day to Horace H. Lurton, 19 February 1914, Lurton Papers.

55. James F. Watts Jr., "Horace H. Lurton," in Friedman and Israel, 3:1863.

56. New York Times, 14 July 1914.

57. Clarinda H. Lamar, *The Life of Joseph Rucker Lamar, 1857–1916* (New York: Putnam, 1926), 269.

58. Ibid., 272.

59. Ibid.

60. Ibid., 276–77.

61. Alexander M. Bickel and Benno C. Schmidt Jr., *The Judiciary and Responsible Government 1910–21, The Oliver Wendell Holmes Devise History of the Supreme Court of the United States* (New York: Macmillan, 1984), 9:398.

62. Ibid., 396–97.

63. James F. Watts Jr., "Edward Douglass White," in Friedman and Israel, 3:1656.

64. In a note Taft sent Harding after his interview, he told the president that "*many times in the past the Chief Justice had said he was holding the office for me and that he would give it back to a Republican administration.*" Taft paraphrased what he had written to the president in a letter to his wife. See Henry F. Pringle, *The Life and Times of William Howard Taft: A Biography* (New York: Farrar and Rinehart, 1939), 2:955.

65. Ibid., 1657.

66. In a letter to Sir Frederick Pollock on May 18, Justice Holmes described the situation: "The poor old boy is the object of nothing but sympathy just now. He has stuck to his work (I think unwisely) in the face of illness—cataracts on his eyes that have blinded one of them, and very great deafness. But he has gone to the hospital and was to have an operation performed at 11:30 A.M. today, I was told (not on his eyes). I hope that it is not serious but feel no assurance till I hear the result. His infirmities have made the work harder for others, and I imagine that he has suffered much more than he has told" (Highsaw, 187).

67. New York Times, 16 May 1921.

68. Clarke considered McReynolds a "lazy man" who "continued to the end living by the legal standards of his law school days." (Carl Wittke, "Mr. Justice Clarke in Retirement," *Western Reserve Law Review* 1 [1949]: 28, 34).

69. Alpheus Thomas Mason, *Brandeis: A Free Man's Life* (New York: Viking Press, 1946), 536.

70. David M. O'Brien, *Storm Center: The Supreme Court in American Politics*, 3d ed. (New York: W. W. Norton, 1993), 164.

71. He was critical of the Court's "necessity of spelling out reasons for the obvious" and assured them he was returning to "the old time freedom of my neighbors from restraint and the happiness of being able to do and say just what I please" (Hoyt Landon Warner, *The Life of Mr. Justice Clarke: A Testament to the Power of Liberal Dissent in America* [Cleveland: Western Reserve University Press, 1959], 113–14).

72. Ibid., 114.

73. New York Times, 10 September 1922.

74. Warner, 204.

75. Ibid., 184.

76. Ibid. This group consisted of businessmen, lawyers, and a general. One could confidently predict that in this setting the justice would receive much attention.

77. New York Times, 23 March 1945.

78. John H. Clarke to Willis Van Devanter, 20 May 1937, Willis Van Devanter Papers, Manuscript Division, Library of Congress. Henry D. Williams of the New York City Bar wrote Justice Van Devanter: "On one of my voyages abroad I met former Justice John H. Clarke, and he told me that the work of a justice of the Supreme Court was so engrossing that he found he was not able to do it, and therefore resigned" (Henry D. Williams to Willis Van Devanter, 24 May 1937, Van Devanter Papers).

79. Warner, 204. One of his friends held an Episcopal Church memorial service for him in Youngstown when his ashes arrived there in transit to the grave site, which was clearly contrary to his wishes.

80. The small-statured Day had two big, strapping sons who Justice Holmes referred to as "blocks off the old chip."

81. New York Times, 10 July 1923.

82. Fred L. Israel, "Mahlon Pitney," in Friedman and Israel, 3:2004.

83. Ibid.

84. New York Times, 22 September 1922.

85. New York Times, 31 October 1922.

86. New York Times, 5 December 1922.

87. New York Times, 17 December 1922.

88. New York Times, 10 December 1924.

89. Mathew McDevitt, *Joseph McKenna, Associate Justice of the United States* (1946; reprint, New York: Da Capo Press, 1974), 202.

90. James F. Watts Jr., "Joseph McKenna," in Friedman and Israel, 3:1735.

91. McDevitt, 228.

92. Alpheus Thomas Mason, *William Howard Taft: Chief Justice* (New York: Simon and Schuster, 1964), 214.

93. Murphy and Pritchett, 217.

94. Ibid., 219

95. Watts, 3:1735.

96. New York Times, 21 November 1926.

97. David Burner, "Edward Terry Sanford," in Friedman and Israel, 3:2204.

98. New York Times, 9 March 1930.

99. Ibid.

100. Pringle, 2:967.

101. Ibid., 1072

102. Ibid., 1077.

103. New York Times, 7 January 1930.

104. New York Times, 8 January 1930.

105. New York Times, 4 February 1930.

106. Although he had not served ten continuous years on the Supreme Court, Taft was eligible for retirement at full pay because of a bill passed the year before that extended retirement benefits to those who had served ten or more years on the federal bench and had reached the age of seventy. Since Taft had previously served

as a judge on the U.S. Court of Appeals for the Sixth Circuit, he qualified for a full pension. New York Times, 4 February 1930.

107. Taft believed Stone had "definitely ranged himself with Brandeis and with Holmes" (Alpheus Thomas Mason, "William Howard Taft," in Friedman and Israel, 3:2119).

108. New York Times, 4 February 1930.

109. Liva Baker, *The Justice from Beacon Hill: The Life and Times of Oliver Wendell Holmes* (New York: HarperCollins, 1991), 629.

110. Apparently a group of justices had suggested to Chief Justice Hughes that the time had come for Holmes to step down. He had difficulty getting onto the bench and sometimes had to be helped, he seemed slower in conference, and even Brandeis reluctantly agreed it was best he resign. Holmes accepted the suggestion without the slightest argument. Baker, 629.

111. New York Times, 13 January 1932. "Old age, Holmes said, was like a fierce dog that came into the room with you and grew and grew until it filled the whole room" (Sheldon M. Novick, *Honorable Justice: The Life of Oliver Wendell Holmes* [Boston: Little, Brown, 1989], 364).

112. New York Times, 30 January 30.

113. Baker, 642.

114. New York Times, 2 March 1935.

115. New York Times, 3 March 1935.

116. New York Times, 5 March 1935.

117. William R. Day to Horace H. Lurton, 25 Dec. 1903, Lurton Papers.

118. 182 U.S. 1 (1901).

119. 182 U.S. 244 (1901).

120. Although Puerto Rico was not considered "foreign," neither was it considered a "state" within the Constitution. In all, some fourteen cases comprised what became known as the *Insular* cases, which collectively dealt with the application of the Constitution to foreign territories. See Kermit L. Hall, ed., *The Oxford Companion to the Supreme Court of the United States* (New York: Oxford University Press, 1992), 433.

121. 188 U.S. 321 (1903). Known as the *Lottery* case, the decision acknowledged the existence of a federal equivalent to the state police power.

122. 193 U.S. 197 (1904). The Sherman Antitrust Act was applied to stock ownership.

123. 198 U.S. 45 (1905). "Liberty of contract" was used to invalidate a New York law regulating hours of labor.

124. 256 U.S. 232 (1921). The case is important because it signaled a willingness to ignore what the states might chose to do in their party primaries. A series of racially discriminatory policies were thereafter adopted in many states.

125. Taft rationalized his nomination of Lurton by suggesting, in a letter to Circuit Judge John W. Warrington of Cincinnati, that "the consideration of age ought to weigh much less heavily in a case where a man has reached his ripest judicial power and is able by reason thereof to take his place on the bench and begin writing opinions there as if he had always been there." (Daniel S. McHargue, "President Taft's Appointments to the Supreme Court," *Journal of Politics* 12 [1950]: 483).

126. Pringle, 1:529–30. Of course, Taft's comments no doubt reflect his impatience to revamp the Court. Still, his assessment of the justices, however harsh, is probably not inaccurate.

CHAPTER 5. FROM ROOSEVELT TO WARREN, 1937–1968

1. Elder Witt, ed., *Congressional Quarterly's Guide to the U.S. Supreme Court,* 2d ed. (Washington, D.C.: Congressional Quarterly Press, 1990), 657.

2. New York Times, 19 May 1937.

3. See David N. Atkinson, "Minor Supreme Court Justices: Their Characteristics and Importance," *Florida State University Law Review* 3 (1975): 354.

4. For a discussion of his subsequent judicial service, see Charles Evans Hughes, "Proceedings in Memory of Mr. Justice Van Devanter," 316 U.S. vvi–xvi (1942). Following his retirement, he was to say characteristically, "I am still a judge" (Francis Biddle, "Proceedings in Memory of Mr. Justice Van Devanter," 316 U.S. xxxvii [1942]).

5. New York Times, 7 July 1937.

6. Ibid.

7. Ibid.

8. New York Times, 19 May 1937.

9. David T. Pride, "Willis Van Devanter," in Clare Cushman, ed., *The Supreme Court Justices: Illustrated Biographies, 1789–1993* (Washington, D.C.: Congressional Quarterly Press, 1993), 315.

10. New York Times, 6 January 1938.

11. Ibid.

12. Joel F. Paschal, *Mr. Justice Sutherland: A Man Against the State* (Princeton: Princeton University Press, 1951), 234.

13. This is the judgment of his biographer; see Paschal, 233.

14. Justice Cardozo's work on the Supreme Court has received much less attention than his accomplishments while on the New York Court of Appeals. For evaluation of some of his Supreme Court decisions, see David N. Atkinson, "Mr. Justice Cardozo: A Common Law Judge on a Public Law Court," *California Western Law Review* 17 (1981): 257; "Mr. Justice Cardozo and the New Deal: An Appraisal," *Villanova Law Review* 15 (1969): 68; and "Mr. Justice Cardozo on the Supreme Court: State and Federal Taxation," *Houston Law Review* 5 (1967): 254.

15. Andrew L. Kaufman, *Cardozo* (Cambridge: Harvard University Press, 1998), 195. A physician who examined Cardozo the following year concluded later that he eventually lived longer than reasonably could have been expected, given the available treatment in those years. The justice took nitroglycerine tablets to relieve the symptoms of angina, and according to his last law clerk, Joseph Rauh, he took them more frequently than his doctors thought advisable. See ibid., 486.

16. New York Times, 19 July 1938. Following this heart attack, Chief Justice Hughes modified his usual opinion assignment practice and began to have Cardozo's opinion assignments delivered on Sunday morning instead of the customary Saturday evening following the conference of the Court. See Kaufman, 481.

17. George S. Hellman, *Benjamin N. Cardozo: American Judge* (New York: McGraw-Hill, 1940), 299–300.

18. Ibid., 308.

19. Ibid., 311.

20. Kaufman, 567.

21. New York Times, 10 July 1938.

22. Ibid.

23. Ibid.

24. Richard Polenberg, *The World of Benjamin Cardozo: Personal Values and the Judicial Process* (Cambridge: Harvard University Press, 1997), 238.

25. Ibid.

26. New York Times, 27 January 1938.

27. Alpheus Thomas Mason, *Brandeis: A Free Man's Life* (New York: Viking Press, 1946), 633.

28. New York Times, 14 February 1939.

29. Mason, 634.

30. New York Times, 19 February 1939.

31. New York Times, 4 June 1939.

32. Mason, 635.

33. Leonard Baker, *Brandeis and Frankfurter: A Dual Biography* (New York: Harper and Row, 1984), 372–73.

34. Merlo J. Pusey, *Charles Evans Hughes* (New York: Macmillan, 1951), 2:784.

35. It was expected that he would remain in the hospital for a week or ten days. See New York Times, 18 August 1939.

36. New York Times, 23 September 1939.

37. New York Times, 3 October 1939.

38. New York Times, 23 January 1941.

39. Ibid.

40. George A. Christensen, "Here Lies the Supreme Court: Gravesites of the Justices," *Yearbook 1983, Supreme Court Historical Society*, 20.

41. The illness is described in Pusey, 782–84.

42. Ibid., 785–86.

43. Ibid., 786.

44. Ibid., 786–87.

45. Charles Evans Hughes, *The Autobiographical Notes of Charles Evans Hughes*, ed. David Danelski and Joseph S. Tulchin (Cambridge: Harvard University Press, 1973), 324.

46. Justice Robert H. Jackson wrote Justice Frankfurter from Nuremberg, Germany, on June 19, 1946, that "Black, as you and I know, has driven Roberts off the bench and pursued him after his retirement." Justice Jackson was not, of course, a disinterested party. See David N. Atkinson, "Justice Sherman Minton and Behavior Patterns Inside the Supreme Court," *Northwestern University Law Review* 69 (1974): 723 n. 21.

47. Erwin Griswold, "Owen J. Roberts as a Judge," *University of Pennsylvania Law Review* 104 (1955): 348–49.

48. New York Times, 3 May 1945.

49. But he practiced law under a special set of self-imposed restrictions and would not personally appear in any court. See Griswold, 349.

50. Felix Frankfurter, "Mr. Justice Roberts," *University of Pennsylvania Law Review* 104 (1955): 312. Justice Roberts entrusted this memoranda to Justice Frankfurter with the understanding that it would be published at the latter's discretion.

51. Roger K. Newman, *Hugo Black: A Biography* (New York: Pantheon, 1994), 322–23. Justice Douglas wrote to Yale law professor Fred Rodell that "Frankfurter got Roberts to believe that new judges were scheming behind his back, giving stories to the press, and playing politics. While he was doing this to Roberts, he was saying behind Roberts' back 'I would hate to be Roberts. I couldn't sleep nights if I were. I would think his conscience would keep him awake—the way he votes.'"

52. Melvin I. Urofsky, *Felix Frankfurter: Judicial Restraint and Individual Liberties* (Boston: Twayne Publishers, 1991), 87.

53. Alpheus Thomas Mason, *Harlan Fiske Stone: Pillar of the Law* (New York: Viking Press, 1956), 765–69.

54. Jay S. Bybee, "Owen J. Roberts," in Cushman, 366–70.

55. Mason, *Stone,* 800.

56. Ibid.

57. Ibid., 802.

58. Ibid., 806. Justice Burton also recorded the events in his diary: "The Chief Justice had repeated himself just a little in his oral dissent . . . , but looked all right. However, when it came his turn to give 3 opinions for the Court at 1:40, he was unable to speak or collect his papers. Justice Black signaled for immediate adjournment. The Court rose at once. Justices Black and Reed helped the Chief to the robing room. He walked about not thinking or speaking clearly. He lay down there. The Marshal called (the doctor) from the Capitol. He reported good pulse and pressure but some blood circulation indigestion. . . . The rest of the Justices (except Justice Murphy) had lunch as usual and returned to the bench at 2:30. Justice Black presiding announced 'in the temporary absence of the Chief Justice' the three cases which (the) Chief had been authorized to announce. . . . We then proceeded with the regular business" (Burton Diary, 22 April 1946, Harold H. Burton Papers, Manuscript Division, Library of Congress).

59. Justice William O. Douglas once discussed this matter with the author and a small group of students at the University of Missouri–Kansas City, 13 April 1970, explaining why the Court reconvened. Justice Frankfurter was instrumental in getting the justices back on the bench, because he quickly realized, as Douglas said, that "you can't cast a dead man's vote." A delay would have caused the loss of important unannounced work in which the chief justice had participated during the term. No opinions are finalized until they are announced from the bench.

60. *United States v. Bethlehem Shipbuilding Co.,* 315 U.S. 289 (1942).

61. James F. Byrnes, *Speaking Frankly* (New York: Harper, 1947), 12–13.

62. Ibid., 13.

63. David Robertson, *Sly and Able: A Political Biography of James F. Byrnes* (New York: W. W. Norton, 1994), 315.

64. Ibid.

65. Ibid., 17–18.

66. Byrnes, 18.

67. Mason, *Stone,* 705–14; William Pettit, "Justice Byrnes and the United States Supreme Court," *South Carolina Law* Quarterly 6 (1954): 423 n. 4.

68. James F. Byrnes, *All in One Lifetime* (New York: Harper, 1958), 155.

69. Justice Byrnes declared that he would not resign from the Supreme Court to accept any office during peacetime, but during a war he could not decline a request from the commander in chief. See New York Times, 4 October 1942.

70. See J. Woodford Howard Jr., *Mr. Justice Murphy: A Political Biography* (Princeton: Princeton University Press, 1968), 458.

71. Ibid. Some of his relatives put a different perspective on the summer's events: "[They] saw a Greek-like tragedy being played as the head of a romantic clan found himself, estranged at home and unable to arrange a wedding in suitable glory in the Manila Cathedral, with no place to save pride but a hospital in Detroit. And in the familiar Murphy manner, a few kinsmen believed he was dying of a broken heart."

72. After Justice Murphy's death, it was disclosed that his entire estate was worth $2,100, and he owed $1,600 to his hotel in Washington.

73. Howard, 458.

74. Ibid., 459–60.

75. New York Times, 20 July 1949. The day before his death, Justice Murphy had gone for an automobile ride, which he seemed to have enjoyed.

76. See Fowler V. Harper, *Justice Rutledge and the Bright Constellation* (Indianapolis: Bobbs-Merrill, 1965), 335 (quoting Irving Brant).

77. Ibid., 336–37. Although unidentified, the writer is almost certainly Justice Douglas.

78. Irving Brant, "Mr. Justice Rutledge—The Man," *Iowa Law Review* 35 (1950): 564–65.

79. New York Times, 29 August 1949.

80. New York Times, 11 September 1949.

81. New York Times, 8 September 1953.

82. New York Times, 10 September 1953.

83. New York Times, 11 September 1953.

84. 347 U.S. 483 (1954).

85. Eugene C. Gerhart, *America's Advocate: Robert H. Jackson* (Indianapolis: Bobbs-Merrill, 1958), 468.

86. New York Times, 8 September 1956.

87. Frances H. Rudko, *Truman's Court: A Study in Judicial Restraint* (Westport, Conn.: Greenwood Press, 1988), 114.

88. Atkinson, "Justice Sherman Minton," 737. "He did not pretend to be—no, let's be truthful and say he was clearly not—a scholar, yet he was smart and sharp. If he had been a lunkhead like Vinson or Reed or Burton, do not fear, I would say so" (from a 20 October 1967 letter from one of Sherman Minton's law clerks to the author).

89. New York Times, 8 September 1956.

90. Rudko, 114.

91. Author's interview with Chief Justice Earl Warren in Washington, D.C., 31 January 1968.

92. Rudko, 114.

93. Atkinson, "Justice Sherman Minton," 720.

94. Ibid.

95. Rudko, 114.

96. David N. Atkinson, "Sherman Minton," in Cushman, 435.

97. His correspondence with Justice Frankfurter is laced with highly partisan political comments and personal concerns, as when he wrote Frankfurter, "When I got home I wondered how you were but in reading the paper I came across one of your characteristic retorts courteous to counsel & I knew you were alright!" (Sherman Minton to Felix Frankfurter, 1 April 1959, Felix Frankfurter Papers, Manuscript Division, Library of Congress).

98. Although his son could not recall exactly when the conversion took place, he did remember that the time interval before the justice's death was "appreciable" (correspondence, Dr. Sherman Minton Jr. to the author, 17 June 1991).

99. Correspondence, Mary Anne Minton Callanan to the author, 18 June 1991.

100. New York Times, 1 February 1957.

101. New York Times, 4 April 1980.

102. Ibid.
103. John D. Fassett, *New Deal Justice: The Life of Stanley Reed of Kentucky* (New York: Vantage Press, 1994), 627.
104. Ibid.
105. Ibid.
106. John D. Fassett, "Stanley Reed," in Cushman, 385.
107. Fassett, *Life of Stanley Reed*, 642.
108. Burton Diary, 7 June 1958, Burton Papers.
109. David N. Atkinson, "Justice Harold H. Burton and the Work of the Supreme Court," *Cleveland State Law Review* 27 (1978): 76.
110. Burton Diary, 13 June 1958, Burton Papers.
111. Ibid., 17 July 1958. It was at this meeting with Justice Burton and Attorney General Rogers that President Eisenhower expressed his dissatisfaction with Chief Justice Earl Warren and Justice William J. Brennan, who had succeeded Justice Minton, and expressed pleasure over Justice Tom Clark's present opinions. Justice Burton and Attorney General Rogers urged President Eisenhower to consider Potter Stewart. The president expressed concern over Stewart's age, which was only forty-three.
112. Ibid., 19 September 1958.
113. 358 U.S. 1 (1958).
114. Burton Diary, 26 September 1958, Burton Papers. The press incorrectly reported that the other justices were not aware of his intention to retire until his 2 October letter to Chief Justice Warren. See New York Times, 14 October 1958.
115. Mary Frances Berry, *Stability, Security, and Continuity: Mr. Justice Burton and Decision-Making in the Supreme Court* (Westport, Conn.: Greenwood Press, 1978), 228. Burton wrote a total of ten opinions and participated in sixty-six cases.
116. Burton Diary, 18 June 1957, Burton Papers.
117. After leaving the Court, Justice Whittaker was willing to speak frankly about his difficulties. See Judith Cole, "Mr. Justice Charles Evans Whittaker: A Case Study in Judicial Recruitment and Behavior" (master's thesis, University of Missouri–Kansas City, 1972), 156. This work was based on interviews with the justice, his law clerks, and many persons who were close to him. See also Craig A. Smith, "Charles Evans Whittaker, Associate Justice of the Supreme Court" (master's thesis, University of Missouri–Kansas City, 1997). Smith's thesis is likewise based on interviews with law clerks, friends and acquaintances of the justice, and interviews with the Whittaker sons. He additionally had access to the Charles E. Whittaker Papers in the custody of the family. Both studies are rich in primary source material.
118. Cole, 115.
119. Author's interview with Justice Charles E. Whittaker, Kansas City, 18 September 1969. The justices vote now in the same order in which they express their views, with the most senior justice speaking and then voting first. See Henry J. Abraham, *The Judicial Process*, 6th ed. (New York: Oxford University Press, 1993), 196 n. 124.
120. Cole, 150.
121. Ibid., 149.
122. Ibid.
123. Ibid., 148.
124. Ibid.
125. Ibid., 153.
126. 369 U.S. 186 (1962).

127. Unease with some colleagues and indecision about the cases have been the usual explanations for what happened, but these were problems he contended with from the very beginning of his service. See Bernard Schwartz, *Super Chief: Earl Warren and His Supreme Court—A Judicial Biography* (New York: New York University Press, 1983), 427–28, and Stephen L. Wasby, *The Supreme Court in the Federal Judicial System*, 4th ed. (Chicago: Nelson-Hall Publishers, 1993), 91. More likely, as his son Kent (also a lawyer) suggested, the depression that forced him to resign was precipitated by three factors: first, his inability to delegate more to his law clerks made it difficult for him to accommodate the sheer volume of work on the Supreme Court; second, the absence of a "philosophy of governance" that could be relied on to assist in deciding cases meant that he confronted most cases on an entirely ad hoc basis; and third, his education and modest beginnings continued to be a source of embarrassment to him, resulting in an inferiority complex that he was never entirely able to surmount. See Smith, 76. Medication may have further complicated his situation. His doctors plied him with an extraordinary cornucopia of drugs, and one wonders about the interactive effects. His personal correspondence with his doctor, in which he complained about the side effects of these prescriptions, indicates that in 1957, prior to his breakdown, he was taking Neurosene, Thorazine, Ultran, and Desbutol (a combination of the drugs Desoxyn and Nembutal). As Smith notes, "Thorazine is currently used to control the manic type of manic-depression; Desoxyn, a methamphetamine, is used to control attention deficit disorder and obesity; and Nembutal, an addictive sedative, treats insomnia" (103 n. 68).

128. Author's interview with Dr. C. Keith Whittaker, in Kansas City, Missouri, 27 August 1996. Another son, Kent, recalled that the nervous breakdown occurred sometime around 1937 and lasted for about a month. See Smith, 29.

129. Author's interview with Dr. C. Keith Whittaker.

130. Ibid.

131. Ibid.

132. Cole, 157. This was his son Kent's estimate.

133. Wolferman's Restaurant, which was between 11th and 12th Streets, on the west side of Main Street, no longer exists. The justice presided as the "autocrat" of the "Lawyers' Table," which was a large corner table in the restaurant's Tiffin Room. He ate there while a practicing lawyer, discontinued the lunches during his tenure on the federal bench because of his concern that it would be inappropriate to dine regularly with other lawyers, but happily resumed regular dining upon his return to Kansas City following his retirement.

134. Smith, 166.

135. Cole., 156.

136. Garson Kanin, "Trips to Felix," *Atlantic Monthly,* March 1964, 57.

137. New York Times, 6 April 1962. His doctor attributed the collapse to "a transient episode of acute cerebroriasculor insufficiency."

138. Kanin, 58.

139. New York Times, 7 April 1962. This was the medical opinion on the day of the stroke.

140. New York Times, 1 May 1962. The announcement that he would be back for the October term seemed optimistic.

141. Kanin, 61.

142. New York Times, 30 August 1962.

143. Kanin, 60.

144. Baker, 491.

145. Ibid.

146. Ibid., 491–92.

147. New York Times, 21 July 1965.

148. New York Times, 25 July 1965.

149. Kansas City Times, 20 January 1990.

150. Emily Field Van Tassel, "Justice Arthur J. Goldberg," in Jennifer M. Lowe, ed., *The Jewish Justices of the Supreme Court Revisited: Brandeis to Fortas* (Washington, D.C.: Supreme Court Historical Society, 1994), 96.

151. Bruce Allen Murphy, *Fortas: The Rise and Ruin of a Supreme Court Justice* (New York: Morrow, 1988), 169.

152. Ibid., 170, citing Bill Moyers as a source.

153. David Stebenne, *Arthur J. Goldberg: New Deal Liberal* (New York: Oxford University Press, 1996), 348–51.

154. Daniel Patrick Moynihan, "Letters to the Editor," *New York Times Book Review*, 24 November 1996, 4.

155. Kathleen Shurtleff, "Arthur J. Goldberg," in Cushman, 470.

156. Kansas City Times, 20 January 1990.

157. New York Times, 1 March 1967.

158. Carl T. Rowan, *Dream Makers, Dream Breakers: The World of Justice Thurgood Marshall* (Boston: Little, Brown, 1993), 297.

159. New York Times, 14 June 1977.

160. Newman, 619.

CHAPTER 6. THE CONTEMPORARY PERIOD, 1969–1998

1. New York Times, 27 June 1968.

2. Senator Sam Ervin contended that since Chief Justice Warren had not retired and would not retire until his successor had been confirmed, there was no vacancy to fill. See Robert Shogan, *A Question of Judgment: The Fortas Case and the Struggle for the Supreme Court* (Indianapolis: Bobbs-Merrill, 1972), 161.

3. Whereas President Eisenhower allegedly called the Warren appointment the "biggest damfool mistake I ever made," President Johnson assessed Warren as the "greatest Chief Justice of them all" (New York Times, 23 June 1969).

4. G. Edward White, *Earl Warren: A Public Life* (New York: Oxford University Press, 1982), 315. The usual practice was, if the retired justice did not hear lower court cases, to have the law clerks reassigned to the chief justice, who then allocated their time. It was this custom that Warren refused to allow.

5. Ibid., 320–24.

6. Ibid., 325.

7. Ibid.

8. Bernard Schwartz, *Super Chief: Earl Warren and His Supreme Court—A Judicial Biography* (New York: New York University Press, 1983), 769–70.

9. *United States v. Nixon*, 418 U.S. 683 (1974).

10. Schwartz, 772.

11. The detailed circumstances surrounding Justice Fortas's resignation are recounted in Bruce Allen Murphy, *Fortas: The Rise and Ruin of a Supreme Court Justice* (New York: William Morrow, 1988), 545–77. See William Lambert, "Fortas: A Question of Ethics," *Life*, 9 May 1969, 32.

12. Shogan, 191.

13. Ibid., 263, 279–82. Justice Fortas sent a detailed accounting of his activities

to Chief Justice Warren on the day of his resignation. No criminal statute was at any time violated, according to Attorney General John Mitchell.

14. Ibid., 249.

15. Ibid., 258–59.

16. Clark Clifford, with Richard Holbrooke, *Counsel to the President: A Memoir* (New York: Random House, 1991), 558–59.

17. Ibid., 559.

18. *U.S. News and World Report*, 26 May 1969: 33.

19. Laura Kalman, *Abe Fortas: A Biography* (New Haven: Yale University Press, 1990), 400–401.

20. New York Times Co. v. United States, 403 U.S. 713 (1971).

21. Hugo L. Black Jr., *My Father: A Remembrance* (New York: Random House, 1975), 248.

22. The disease affects elderly persons and is characterized by throbbing headaches as well as ocular symptoms. Loss of sight in an eye, if this occurs, may be irreversible.

23. Black, 250.

24. Ibid., 263.

25. Ibid., 256.

26. Ibid., 263, 264. Justice Black blamed his condition on failing vision. "I'll tell you something, son," he said. "If I could see, I could exercise. And if I could exercise, I could have ten more good years and wouldn't be in this desperate condition."

27. Ibid., 266.

28. George A. Christensen, "Here Lies the Supreme Court: Gravesites of the Justices," *Yearbook 1983, Supreme Court Historical Society,* 25.

29. Black, 257–58.

30. Ibid., 260.

31. New York Times, 19 and 24 September 1971.

32. New York Times, 17 September 1971.

33. Black, 261.

34. Tinsley E. Yarbrough, *John Marshall Harlan: Great Dissenter of the Warren Court* (New York: Oxford University Press, 1992), 334.

35. Ibid.

36. New York Times, 2 January 1975.

37. New York Times, 4 January 1975.

38. New York Times, 16 February 1975.

39. New York Times, 26 March 1975.

40. Ibid.

41. Ibid.

42. *Time,* 24 November 1975, 69.

43. New York Times, 8 July 1975. He had done this previously when thrown from a horse and nearly killed in October 1949; at that time he sent his votes back to Justice Black.

44. James F. Simon, *Independent Journey: The Life of William O. Douglas* (New York: Harper and Row, 1980), 448–49.

45. New York Times, 13 September 1975.

46. Bob Woodward and Scott Armstrong, *The Brethren: Inside the Supreme Court* (New York: Simon and Schuster, 1979), 389.

47. Ibid., 390–91.

48. Ibid., 391–92.

49. *Time,* 24 November 1975, 69–70.

50. Simon, 453.

51. William O. Douglas, *The Court Years, 1939–1975: The Autobiography of William O. Douglas* (New York: Random House, 1980).

52. Gil Kujovich, "Potter Stewart," in Clare Cushman, ed., *The Supreme Court Justices: Illustrated Biographies, 1789–1993* (Washington, D.C.: Congressional Quarterly Press, 1993), 460.

53. John C. Jeffries, Jr. *Justice Lewis F. Powell Jr.: A Biography* (New York: Scribner's, 1994), 542.

54. Kansas City Times, 7 December 1985.

55. Kansas City Star, 26 June 1995.

56. From Chief Justice Burger's letter to President Reagan, dated 17 June 1986. See New York Times, 18 June 1986.

57. Ibid.

58. Ibid.

59. See John A. Jenkins, "A Candid Talk with Justice Blackmun," *New York Times Magazine,* 20 February 1983, for a frank critical view of Chief Justice Burger's administrative limitations from someone who knew the chief justice from the age of five.

60. New York Times, 18 June 1986.

61. Kansas City Star, 1 November 1995.

62. Kansas City Star, 9 November 1995.

63. Ibid.

64. Jeffries, 397.

65. Ibid., 539.

66. Ibid., 543.

67. Ibid., 546.

68. Des Moines Register, 21 July 1990.

69. Legal Times, 30 June 1986.

70. The affirmative action case is *Metro Broadcasting, Inc. v. FCC,* 497 U.S. 547 (1990); the flag burning cases are *U.S. v. Eichman,* 496 U.S. 310 (1990) and *Texas v. Johnson,* 491 U.S. 397 (1989).

71. Los Angeles Times, 22 July 1990.

72. Los Angeles Times, 21 July 1990.

73. Ibid.

74. Kim Isaac Eisler, *A Justice for All: William J. Brennan Jr. and the Decisions That Transformed America* (New York: Simon and Schuster, 1993), 280.

75. Kansas City Star, 29 July 1997.

76. 410 U.S. 113 (1973).

77. Kansas City Star, 30 July 1997.

78. Kansas City Star, 28 June 1991.

79. Kansas City Star, 2 October 1991.

80. Kansas City Star, 8 September 1991.

81. 428 U.S. 153.

82. Michael D. Davis and Hunter R. Clark, *Warrior at the Bar, Rebel on the Bench* (New York: Carol Publishing, 1992), 350.

83. Ibid., 3.

84. Timothy M. Phelps and Helen Winternitz, *Capitol Games: Clarence Thomas, Anita Hill, and the Story of a Supreme Court Nomination* (New York: Hyperion, 1992), 150.

85. Ibid., 4.

86. Ibid., 4–5.

87. Ibid., 7–8.

88. Carl T. Rowan, *Dream Makers, Dream Breakers: The World of Justice Thurgood Marshall* (Boston: Little, Brown, 1993), 408.

89. 501 U.S. 808 (1991).

90. New York Times, 25 January 1993.

91. Clarence Page, "Marshall Gave It All He Had," Kansas City Star, 1 July 1991.

92. New Orleans Times-Picayune, 20 March 1993.

93. Ibid.

94. Dennis J. Hutchinson, *The Man Who Once Was Whizzer White: A Portrait of Justice Byron R. White* (New York: Free Press, 1998), 408–9.

95. Hutchinson, 432.

96. Kansas City Times, 21 July 1987.

97. Ibid.

98. Kansas City Star, 9 November 1993.

99. Ibid.

100. Kansas City Star, 7 April 1994.

101. Ibid.

102. Edward Lazarus, *Closed Chambers: The First Eyewitness Account of the Epic Struggles Inside the Supreme Court* (New York: Random House, 1998), 156–57.

103. The case was almost certainly the one involving "Letty Lynton," *Sheldon v. Metro-Goldwyn Pictures Corp.*, 309 U.S. 390 (1940). Author's interview with Justice Stanley F. Reed, Washington, D.C., 23 January 1968.

104. See *Palmer v. Thompson*, 403 U.S. 217 (1971), a 5 to 4 decision where Justice Blackmun's vote was influenced by what was said in oral argument.

105. Robert J. Steamer, *Chief Justice: Leadership and the Supreme Court* (Columbia: University of South Carolina Press, 1986), 25.

106. Roger K. Newman, *Hugo Black: A Biography* (New York: Pantheon, 1994), 597.

107. Hugo L. Black and Elizabeth Black, *Mr. Justice and Mrs. Black: The Memoirs of Hugo L. Black and Elizabeth Black* (New York: Random House, 1986), 229 (diary entry of Wednesday, August 6). Thereafter, Mrs. Black regularly encouraged her husband to retire.

108. *New York Times v. United States*, 403 U.S. 713 (1971).

109. Author's conversation with William O. Douglas, Kansas City, Missouri, 14 April 1970.

110. Woodward and Armstrong, 157.

111. Ibid., 361.

112. Lawrence K. Altman, "A Justice's Health: What Is Private?" New York Times, 4 January 1982.

113. Ibid.

114. Lawrence K. Altman, "Drug Rehnquist Used Carries Strict Warning," New York Times, 7 January 1982. Altman cites 1980 data indicating that Placidyl was implicated in 5,000 hospitalizations and 300 accidental and suicidal deaths for that year. It induces sleep and has some muscle-relaxing properties. Rehnquist apparently used it for insomnia.

115. So important that they have become the subject of popular fiction. See Brad

Meltzer, *The Tenth Justice* (New York: Rob Weisbach Books, 1997). Meltzer's theme of the improper disclosure by a clerk was anticipated by the real-life leak attending *Roe v. Wade*, 410 U.S. 113 (1973). See Woodward and Bernstein, 237–38.

116. Lazarus, 446–47.

CHAPTER 7. WHEN SHOULD JUSTICES LEAVE?

1. Richard A. Posner, *Aging and Old Age* (Chicago: University of Chicago Press, 1995), 195. The implication is that aging justices would be backward looking, which Judge Posner notes is not necessarily something to be criticized. This tendency, to the extent it exists, may provide a "balance-wheel function" to politics, in which courts and judges reduce the "amplitude of swings in public policy."

2. Although sometimes vigorously criticized by the academic community, the Vinson Court exercised judicial restraint in a way that defused public criticism of their decisions. See C. Herman Pritchett, *Civil Liberties and the Vinson Court* (Chicago: University of Chicago Press, 1954).

3. Glendon Schubert, *The Constitutional Polity* (Boston: Boston University Press, 1970), 127.

4. Ibid., 129.

5. The public reception to the broadcast was favorable. Black's wife repeatedly remarked in her diary about the positive correspondence he received from around the country and the supportive comments from friends and colleagues. See Hugo L. Black and Elizabeth Black, *Mr. Justice and Mrs. Black: The Memoirs of Hugo L. Black and Elizabeth Black* (New York: Random House, 1986), 209–10.

6. For a discussion sympathetic to the thesis that the issues changed rather than Justice Black, see Tinsley E. Yarbrough, *Mr. Justice Black and His Critics* (Durham, N.C.: Duke University Press, 1988), 17–18.

7. When the author visited with him in 1968, he at once said he had spent much of the morning reading his old Senate speeches attacking the Supreme Court during the battle over the "Court-packing" plan. The same thing was happening again: the Court was acting without constitutional authority. He took a typed manuscript from his desk drawer (later published as *A Constitutional Faith*), held it up, and said he was going to explain his position in some lectures he had agreed to give. "Judges like power!" he exclaimed. He saw that tendency as the main problem. While discussing the recent wiretapping decision in which he had dissented (*Katz v. U.S.*, 389 U.S. 347 [1967]), Justice Black became quite animated when he insisted that the Constitution did not ban the seizure of intangible objects: "You've got to grab it. You can't seize it [under the Fourth Amendment] if you can't grab it." He was most emphatic. The justice was alert, engaged, had excellent recall, and clearly was not in the least "senile." Only the harsh glare of several powerful fluorescent floor lamps grouped around his desk provided evidence of his failing eyesight. But Justice Black, skilled politician that he remained, pulled his chair away from his desk and directed me toward a seat removed some distance from the discomfort of the lights. Author's interview with Justice Hugo L. Black, Washington, D.C., 22 January 1968.

8. Justice White observed in a 1996 interview that "every time a new justice comes to the Supreme Court, it's a different court. You sit there and for two or three years you say to yourself: 'This person is voting much differently than his predecessor'" (Dennis J. Hutchinson, *The Man Who Once Was Whizzer White: A Portrait of Justice Byron R. White* [New York: Free Press, 1998], 467).

9. For example, positive cue taking existed between John Marshall and Bushrod Washington, Holmes and Brandeis in Holmes's last years, Harlan and Whittaker, Black and Douglas until the last years, Brennan and Marshall, and, more recently, Scalia and Thomas. The illustrations of personal conflicts that may have lead to negative cues are many. They would include most famously McReynolds and Brandeis, Frankfurter and Douglas, and Black and Jackson. See Phillip J. Cooper, *Battles on the Bench: Conflict Inside the Supreme Court* (Lawrence: University Press of Kansas, 1995).

10. See, e.g., Charles Evans Hughes, *The Supreme Court of the United States* (New York: Columbia University Press, 1928), 75–76. The list would include Justices Grier, Field, McKenna, and Holmes.

11. Ibid., 76–77.

12. Theodore L. Becker, *American Government: Past, Present, Future* (Boston: Allyn and Bacon, 1976), 484.

13. Benjamin F. Wright, Book Review, *Harvard Law Review* 56 (1942): 487.

14. See A. A. Berle Jr., "Elected Judges—or Appointed?" *New York Times Magazine*, 11 December 1955, 26.

15. Both William Riker and Robert A. Dahl have presented variations of this argument. See William Riker, *Democracy in the United States*, 2d ed. (New York: Macmillan, 1965), 266–67; and Robert A. Dahl, "Decision-Making in a Democracy: The Supreme Court as a National Policy-Maker," *Journal of Public Law* 6 (1957): 279, where Dahl argues that the Supreme Court is indeed usually very much a part of the majority political coalition and is not a special protector of minority rights.

16. Jonathan D. Casper, "The Supreme Court and National Policy Making," *American Political Science Review* 70 (1976): 53–54.

17. Walter F. Murphy and Joseph Tanenhaus, *The Study of Public Law* (New York: Random House, 1972), 35. The point may be illustrated by two highly publicized decisions against a president: *United States v. Nixon*, 418 U.S. 683 (1974); and *New York Times Co. v. United States*, 403 U.S. 713 (1971).

18. Alexis de Tocqueville, *Democracy in America* (Oxford: Oxford University Press, 1946), 97.

19. See, e.g. Riker, 269.

20. *The Federalist or The New Constitution: Papers by Alexander Hamilton, James Madison, and John Jay* (Norwalk, Conn.: Heritage Press, 1945), 530.

21. Ibid.

22. James Boswell, *The Life of Samuel Johnson LL.D.* (Norwalk, Conn.: Heritage Press, 1993), 2:162.

23. Henry F. Pringle, *The Life and Times of William Howard Taft: A Biography* (New York: Farrar and Rinehart, 1939), 2:956.

24. "I want you to start exercising and watch your diet," Thomas told a friend, "so you'll be around when I step down from the Court in 2034. They can say what they want to say, but I'm going to be making law for a long time" (Jeffrey Rosen, "Moving On," *New Yorker*, 29 April and 6 May 1996, 73).

25. Robert Kramer and Jerome A. Barron, "The Constitutionality of Removal and Mandatory Retirement Procedures for the Federal Judiciary," in Glenn R. Winters and Richard A. Hanson, eds., *Selected Readings: Judicial Discipline and Removal* (Chicago: American Judicature Society, 1973), 58.

26. Ibid.

27. Owen J. Roberts, speech to the Association of the Bar of the City of New

York, December 11, 1948, cited in Elder Witt, ed., *Congressional Quarterly's Guide to the U.S. Supreme Court,* 2d ed. (Washington, D.C.: Congressional Quarterly Press, 1990), 761.

28. For an explanation of why all Supreme Court justices, and not merely the "great" ones, are important, see David N. Atkinson, "Minor Supreme Court Justices: Their Characteristics and Importance," *Florida State University Law Review* 3 (1975): 348.

29. Posner, 194.

30. Walter F. Murphy, *Elements of Judicial Strategy* (Chicago: University of Chicago Press, 1964), 84.

31. Bob Woodward and Scott Armstrong, *The Brethren: Inside the Supreme Court* (New York: Simon and Schuster, 1979), 367. Justice White's letter of 20 October 1975 is reprinted in Hutchinson, 463. Interestingly enough, White took this occasion to state his preference for a mandatory retirement age, set by a constitutional amendment. But since the Constitution was otherwise, he objected to how his colleagues treated Douglas. White's biographer, however, notes that the impeachment power is not necessarily compromised when five justices vote to rehear a case, regardless of their motives.

32. John C. Jeffries Jr., *Justice Lewis F. Powell Jr.: A Biography* (New York: Scribner's, 1994), 417–18.

33. J. Woodford Howard Jr., "On the Fluidity of Judicial Choice," *American Political Science Review* 62 (1968): 43.

34. See Gerald Gunther, *Learned Hand: The Man and the Judge* (New York: Alfred A. Knopf, 1994), 290–91.

35. Henry J. Abraham, *The Judical Process,* 6th ed. (New York: Oxford University Press, 1993), 195.

36. Author's interview with Justice Stanley F. Reed, Washington, D.C., 23 January 1968.

37. Bernard Schwartz, *Decision: How the Supreme Court Decides Cases* (New York: Oxford University Press, 1996), 48.

38. "He didn't write anything my year," one clerk told reporter David Savage. The next year's clerk said the same thing. See David G. Savage, *Turning Right: The Making of the Rehnquist Supreme Court* (New York: John Wiley, 1992), 73.

39. Justice William O. Douglas once told the author, when asked if he had been surprised by Sherman Minton's "conservative" voting record on the Court after a "liberal" political career in the Senate and White House, that he was not at all surprised. He explained that politicians can vote a party line, but when one is on the Court, an issue must be thought through without the comforting aid of a party line. He used wiretapping as an example. A senator might support a position against excessive wiretapping if that is the position taken at the time by his party, but all of that is lost when one goes on the Court. Author's interview with Justice William O. Douglas, Washington, D.C., 30 January 1968.

40. See Joseph Goldstein, *The Intelligible Constitution: The Supreme Court's Obligation to Maintain the Constitution as Something We the People Can Understand* (New York: Oxford University Press, 1992), 125, where Goldstein suggests that there be a final review conference free of law clerks to ensure that the justices know the issues they are deciding and to "mitigate some of the untoward effects on opinion-writing of the bureaucratization of the Court."

41. Schwartz, 257.

42. Ibid., 259–60. Specific reference is made to Justices Stevens and Scalia in Mary

Ann Glendon, *A Nation Under Lawyers: How the Crisis in the Legal Profession Is Transforming American Society* (Cambridge: Harvard University Press, 1994), 146. The law clerks read briefs, brief the arguments, and prepare draft opinions. As Glendon concludes, "The assignment of such tasks to staff attorneys and law clerks is the equivalent of replacing an experienced surgeon with a resident or intern after the patient is anesthetized" (145).

43. Schwartz, 257.

44. Joseph Tanenhaus, "Supreme Court Attitudes Toward Federal Administrative Agencies, 1947–1956—An Application of Social Science Methods to the Study of the Judicial Process," *Vanderbilt Law Review* 14 (1961): 482–83.

45. Richard Davis, *Decisions and Images: The Supreme Court and the Press* (Englewood Cliffs, N.J.: Prentice Hall, 1994), 125.

46. Cooper, 74. For a description of the disfunctional pettiness encouraged by the present system, see Edward Lazarus, *Closed Chambers: The First Eyewitness Account of the Epic Struggles Inside the Supreme Court* (New York: Random House, 1998), 261–75.

47. John P. Frank, *Marble Palace: The Supreme Court in American Life* (New York: Alfred A. Knopf, 1968), 117.

48. Davis, 127.

49. For example, fifty new federal judges were to be added to the lower courts, constitutional appeals were to be expedited directly to the Supreme Court, government attorneys were to be heard before lower courts could issue injunctions against a congressional act in situations where the act was argued to be unconstitutional, and district court judges were to be periodically assigned to those jurisdictions where backlogs had developed. These were proposals that were far less controversial than the personnel changes projected for the Supreme Court.

50. Leonard Baker, *Back to Back: The Duel Between FDR and the Supreme Court,* (New York: Macmillan, 1967), 14.

51. This proposal would not, of course, correct a situation where a justice younger then seventy-five became disabled and refused to retire, nor would it go so far as Justice Roberts's mandatory retirement proposal. But it would acknowledge that people of a certain age—as a general proposition—become less able to perform their work satisfactorily, become more susceptible to serious illnesses likely to impair their job performance, and are less likely to reflect the views of the currently elected branches of government than younger appointees. When democratically determined public policies that directly affect the nation are at issue, it is not unreasonable to expect that those who exercise judicial review over what is done by the president and Congress be part of the present, not the past. This point was central to President Roosevelt's critique of the 1930s Supreme Court.

52. The phrase appears in his opinion for the Court in *Minersville School District v. Gobitis,* 310 U.S. 586, 596 (1940). Justice Frankfurter found the expression in Oliver Wendell Holmes's equivocal speech on John Marshall, reprinted in Richard A. Posner, ed., *The Essential Holmes: Selections from the Letters, Speeches, Judicial Opinions, and Other Writings of Oliver Wendell Holmes Jr.* (Chicago: University of Chicago Press, 1992), 208.

SELECTED BIBLIOGRAPHY

BOOKS

Abraham, Henry J. *The Judicial Process.* 5th ed. New York: Oxford University Press, 1986.

———. *The Judicial Process.* 6th ed. New York: Oxford University Press, 1993.

———. *Justices and Presidents: A Political History of Appointments to the Supreme Court.* 3d ed. New York: Oxford University Press, 1992.

Aichele, Gary J. *Oliver Wendell Holmes Jr.: Soldier, Scholar, Judge.* Boston: Twayne Publishers, 1989.

Arkes, Hadley. *The Return of George Sutherland: Restoring a Jurisprudence of Natural Rights.* Princeton: Princeton University Press, 1994.

Baker, Leonard, *Back to Back: The Duel Between FDR and the Supreme Court.* New York: Macmillan, 1967.

———. *Brandeis and Frankfurter: A Dual Biography.* New York: Harper and Row, 1984.

———. *John Marshall: A Life in Law.* New York: Collier Books, 1974.

Baker, Liva. *Felix Frankfurter.* New York: Coward-McCann, 1969.

———. *The Justice from Beacon Hill: The Life and Times of Oliver Wendell Holmes.* New York: HarperCollins, 1991.

Ball, Howard, and Phillip J. Cooper. *Of Power and Right: Hugo Black, William O. Douglas, and America's Constitutional Revolution.* New York: Oxford University Press, 1992.

Barry, Richard H. *Mr. Rutledge of South Carolina.* New York: Duell, Sloan and Pearce, 1942.

Becker, Theodore L. *American Government: Past, Present, Future.* Boston: Allyn and Bacon, 1976.

Berry, Mary Frances. *Stability, Security, and Continuity: Mr. Justice Burton and Decision-Making in the Supreme Court.* Westport, Conn.: Greenwood Press, 1978.

Beth, Loren P. *John Marshall Harlan: The Last Whig Justice.* Lexington: University Press of Kentucky, 1992.

Beveridge, Albert J. *The Life of John Marshall.* 4 vols. Boston: Houghton Mifflin, 1919.

Bickel, Alexander M., and Benno C. Schmidt Jr. *The Judiciary and Responsible Government 1910–21. The Oliver Wendell Holmes Devise History of the Supreme Court of the United States.* Vol. 9. New York: Macmillan, 1984.

Black, Hugo. *A Constitutional Faith.* New York: Alfred A. Knopf, 1969.

Black, Hugo L., and Elizabeth Black. *Mr. Justice and Mrs. Black: The Memoirs of Hugo L. Black and Elizabeth Black.* New York: Random House, 1986.

Black, Hugo L., Jr. *My Father: A Remembrance.* New York: Random House, 1975.

Blue, Frederick J. *Salmon P. Chase, A Life in Politics.* Kent, Ohio: Kent State University Press, 1987.

Boswell, James. *The Life of Samuel Johnson LL.D.* 3 vols. Norwalk, Conn.: Heritage Press, 1993.

Brodhead, Michael J. *David J. Brewer: The Life of a Supreme Court Justice, 1837–1910.* Carbondale: Southern Illinois University Press, 1994.

Brown, William Garrott. *The Life of Oliver Ellsworth.* 1905. Reprint. New York: Da Capo Press, 1970.

Byrnes, James F. *All in One Lifetime.* New York: Harper, 1958.

———. *Speaking Frankly.* New York: Harper, 1947.

Carp, Robert A., and Ronald Stidham. *Judicial Process in America.* 4th ed. Washington, D.C.: Congressional Quarterly Press, 1998.

Carson, Hampton L. *The History of the Supreme Court of the United States, with Biographies of All the Chief and Associate Justices.* 2 vols. 1902. Reprint. New York: B. Franklin, 1971.

Cate, Wirt Armistead. *Lucius Q. C. Lamar: Secession and Reunion.* Chapel Hill: University of North Carolina Press, 1935.

Clayman, Charles B., ed. *The American Medical Association Family Medical Guide.* 3d ed. New York: Random House, 1994.

Clendening, Logan. *The Human Body.* New York: Alfred A. Knopf, 1927.

Clifford, Clark, with Richard Holbrooke. *Counsel to the President: A Memoir.* New York: Random House, 1991.

Cooper, Philip J. *Battles on the Bench: Conflict Inside the Supreme Court.* Lawrence: University Press of Kansas, 1995.

Copeman, W. S. C. *A Short History of the Gout and the Rheumatic Diseases.* Berkeley: University of California Press, 1964.

Cray, Ed. *Chief Justice: A Biography of Earl Warren.* New York: Simon and Schuster, 1997.

Curtis, Benjamin Robbins. ed. *A Memoir of Benjamin Robbins Curtis, LL.D., with Some of His Professional and Miscellaneous Writings.* 1879. Reprint. New York: Da Capo Press, 1970.

Cushman, Clare. ed. *The Supreme Court Justices: Illustrated Biographies, 1789–1993.* Washington, D.C.: Congressional Quarterly Press, 1993.

Danelski, David J. *A Supreme Court Justice Is Appointed.* New Haven: Yale University Press, 1964.

Davis, Michael D., and Hunter R. Clark. *Warrior at the Bar, Rebel on the Bench.* New York: Carol Publishing, 1992.

Davis, Richard. *Decisions and Images: The Supreme Court and the Press.* Englewood Cliffs, N.J.: Prentice Hall, 1994.

Delaplaine, Edward S. *The Life of Thomas Johnson: Member of the Continental Congress, First Governor of the State of Maryland, and Associate Justice of the United States Supreme Court.* New York: F. H. Hitchcock, 1927.

Douglas, William O. *The Court Years, 1939–1975: The Autobiography of William O. Douglas.* New York: Random House, 1980.

Dunham, Allison, and Philip B. Kurland, eds. *Mr. Justice.* Rev. and enlarged ed. Chicago: University of Chicago Press, 1964.

Dunne, Finley Peter. *Mr. Dooley on ivrything and irvybody.* New York: Dover Publications, 1963.

Dunne, Gerald. T. *Hugo Black and the Judicial Revolution*. New York: Simon and Schuster, 1977.

———. *Justice Joseph Story and the Rise of the Supreme Court*. New York: Simon and Schuster, 1970.

Eisler, Kim Isaac. *A Justice for All: William J. Brennan Jr. and the Decisions That Transformed America*. New York: Simon and Schuster, 1993.

Epstein, Lee, Jeffrey A., Segal, Harold J. Spaeth, and Thomas G. Walker, eds. *The Supreme Court Compendium: Data, Decisions, and Developments*. Washington, D.C.: Congressional Quarterly Press, 1994.

Fairman, Charles. *Mr. Justice Miller and the Supreme Court, 1862–1890*. Cambridge: Harvard University Press, 1939.

———. *Reconstruction and Reunion 1864–88. The Oliver Wendell Holmes Devise History of the Supreme Court of the United States*. Part 1. vol. 6. New York: Macmillan, 1971.

———. *Reconstruction and Reunion 1864–88. The Oliver Wendell Holmes Devise History of the Supreme Court of the United States*. Part 2, vol. 7. New York: Macmillan, 1987.

Fassett, John D. *New Deal Justice: The Life of Stanley Reed of Kentucky*. New York: Vantage Press, 1994.

Fehrenbacher, Don E. *The Dred Scott Case: Its Significance in American Law and Politics*. New York: Oxford University Press, 1978.

Ferrell, Robert H. *Ill-Advised: Presidential Health and Public Trust*. Columbia: University of Missouri Press, 1992.

Fine, Sidney. *Frank Murphy: The Washington Years*. Ann Arbor: University of Michigan Press, 1984.

Flanders, Henry. *The Lives and Times of the Chief Justices of the Supreme Court of the United States*. 2 vols. Philadelphia: Lippincott, 1875.

Frank, John P. *Justice Daniel Dissenting: A Biography of Peter V. Daniel, 1784–1860*. Cambridge: Harvard University Press, 1964.

———. *Marble Palace: The Supreme Court in American Life*. New York: Alfred A. Knopf, 1968.

Frankfurter, Felix. *The Commerce Clause Under Marshall, Taney, and Waite*. 1937. Reprint. Chicago: Quadrangle, 1964.

Friedman, Leon, and Fred L. Israel, eds. *The Justices of the United States Supreme Court, 1789–1978: Their Lives and Major Opinions*. 4 vols. New York: Chelsea House, 1978.

Gerhard, Eugene C. *America's Advocate: Robert H. Jackson*. Indianapolis: Bobbs-Merrill, 1958.

Gilbert, Robert E. *The Mortal Presidency: Illness and Anguish in the White House*. New York: Basic Books, 1992.

Glendon, Mary Ann. *A Nation Under Lawyers: How the Crisis in the Legal Profession Is Transforming American Society*. Cambridge: Harvard University Press, 1994.

Goldstein, Joseph. *The Intelligible Constitution: The Supreme Court's Obligation to Maintain the Constitution as Something We the People Can Understand*. New York: Oxford University Press, 1992.

Gugin, Linda C., and James E. St. Clair. *Sherman Minton: New Deal Senator, Cold War Justice*. Indianapolis: Indiana Historical Society, 1997.

Gunther, Gerald. *Learned Hand: The Man and the Judge*. New York: Alfred A. Knopf, 1994.

Hall, Kermit L., ed. *The Oxford Companion to the Supreme Court of the United States.* New York: Oxford University Press, 1992.

Hamilton, Alexander, James Madison, and John Jay. *The Federalist or The New Constitution: Papers by Alexander Hamilton, James Madison, and John Jay.* Norwalk, Conn.: Heritage Press, 1945.

Harper, Fowler. *Justice Rutledge and the Bright Constellation.* Indianapolis: Bobbs-Merrill. 1965.

Hellman, George Sidney. *Benjamin N. Cardozo: American Judge.* New York: McGraw-Hill, 1940.

Highsaw, Robert B. *Edward Douglass White: Defender of the Conservative Faith.* Baton Rouge: Louisiana State University Press, 1981.

Howard, J. Woodford, Jr. *Mr. Justice Murphy; A Political Biography.* Princeton: Princeton University Press, 1968.

Howe, Mark De Wolfe. ed. *The Holmes-Pollock Letters.* 2 vols. Cambridge: Harvard University Press, 1946.

Hughes, Charles Evans. *The Autobiographical Notes of Charles Evans Hughes.* Edited by David J. Danelski and Joseph S. Tulchin. Cambridge: Harvard University Press, 1973.

———. *The Supreme Court of the United States.* New York: Columbia University Press, 1928.

Hutchinson, Dennis J. *The Man Who Once Was Whizzer White: A Portrait of Justice Byron R. White.* New York: Free Press, 1998.

Jeffries, John C., Jr. *Justice Lewis F. Powell Jr.: A Biography.* New York: Scribner's, 1994.

Kalman, Laura. *Abe Fortas: A Biography.* New Haven: Yale University Press, 1990.

Kammen, Michael. *A Machine That Would Go of Itself: The Constitution In American Culture.* New York: Alfred A. Knopf, 1986.

Kaufman, Andrew L. *Cardozo.* Cambridge: Harvard University Press, 1998.

King, Willard L. *Lincoln's Manager, David Davis.* Cambridge: Harvard University Press, 1960.

———. *Melville Weston Fuller: Chief Justice of the United States, 1888–1910.* 1950. Reprint. Chicago: University of Chicago Press, 1967.

Klinkhamer, Marie C. *Edward Douglass White: Chief Justice of the United States.* Washington, D.C.: Catholic University of America Press, 1943.

Lamar, Clarinda H. *The Life of Joseph Rucker Lamar, 1857–1916.* New York: Putnam, 1926.

Lawrence, Alexander A. *James Moore Wayne: Southern Unionist.* 1943. Reprint. Westport, Conn.: Greenwood Press, 1970.

Lazarus, Edward. *Closed Chambers: The First Eyewitness Account of the Epic Struggles Inside the Supreme Court.* New York: Random House, 1998.

Lewis, Walker. *Without Fear or Favor: A Biography of Chief Justice Roger Brooke Taney.* Boston: Houghton Mifflin, 1965.

Loth, David G. *Chief Justice Marshall and the Growth of the Republic.* 1949. Reprint. New York: Greenwood Press, 1970.

Lowe, Jennifer M., ed. *The Jewish Justices of the Supreme Court Revisited: Brandeis to Fortas.* Washington, D.C.: Supreme Court Historical Society, 1994.

Lurie, Jonathan. *Law and the Nation, 1865–1912.* New York: Knopf, 1983.

Magrath, C. Peter. *Morrison R. Waite: The Triumph of Character.* New York: Macmillan, 1963.

Magruder, Allan B. *John Marshall*. 1898. Reprint. New York: AMS Press, 1972.

Marke, Julius J., ed. *The Holmes Reader*. 2d ed. Dobbs Ferry, N.Y.: Oceanna Publications, 1964.

Mason, Alpheus Thomas. *Brandeis: A Free Man's Life*. New York: Viking Press, 1946.

———. *Harlan Fiske Stone: Pillar of the Law*. New York: Viking Press, 1956.

———. *William Howard Taft: Chief Justice*. New York: Simon and Schuster, 1964.

McCloskey, Robert G. *The American Supreme Court*. Chicago: University of Chicago Press, 1960.

———, ed. *The Works of James Wilson*. 2 vols. Cambridge: Harvard University Press, 1967.

McDevitt, Mathew. *Joseph McKenna: Associate Justice of the United States*. 1946. Reprint. New York: Da Capo Press, 1974.

McLean, Joseph E. *William Rufus Day: Supreme Court Justice from Ohio*. Baltimore: Johns Hopkins University Press, 1946.

McPherson, James M. *Battle Cry of Freedom: The Civil War Era*. New York: Oxford University Press, 1988.

McRee, Griffith J. *Life and Correspondence of James Iredell: One of the Associate Justices of the Supreme Court of the United States*. 2 vols. New York: D. Appleton, 1857.

Meltzer, Brad. *The Tenth Justice*. New York: Rob Weisbach Books, 1997.

Monaghan, Frank. *John Jay*. New York: Bobbs-Merrill, 1935.

Morgan, Donald G. *Justice William Johnson, the First Dissenter: The Career and Constitutional Philosophy of a Jeffersonian Judge*. Columbia: University of South Carolina Press, 1954.

Murphy, Bruce Allen. *Fortas: The Rise and Ruin of a Supreme Court Justice*. New York: William Morrow, 1988.

Murphy, James B. *L. Q. C. Lamar: Pragmatic Patriot*. Baton Rouge: Louisiana State University Press, 1973.

Murphy, Walter F. *Elements of Judicial Strategy*. Chicago: University of Chicago Press, 1964.

Murphy, Walter F., and C. Herman Pritchett, eds. *Courts, Judges, and Politics*. 2d ed. New York: Random House, 1974.

Murphy, Walter F., and Joseph Tanenhaus. *The Study of Public Law*. New York: Random House, 1972.

Newman, Roger K. *Hugo Black: A Biography*. New York: Pantheon, 1994.

Newmyer, R. Kent. *Supreme Court Justice Joseph Story: Statesman of the Old Republic*. Chapel Hill: University of North Carolina Press, 1985.

Niven, John. *Salmon P. Chase: A Biography*. New York: Oxford University Press, 1995.

Novick, Sheldon M. *Honorable Justice: The Life of Oliver Wendell Holmes*. Boston: Little, Brown, 1989.

O'Brien, David M. *Storm Center: The Supreme Court in American Politics*. 3d ed. New York: W. W. Norton, 1993.

O'Connor, John E. *William Paterson: Lawyer and Statesman, 1745–1806*. New Brunswick, N.J.: Rutgers University Press, 1979.

Paschal, Joel F. *Mr. Justice Sutherland: A Man Against the State*. Princeton: Princeton University Press, 1951.

Paul, Arnold M. *Conservative Crisis and the Rule of Law: Attitudes of Bar and Bench, 1887–1895*. Ithaca, N.Y.: Cornell University Press, 1960.

Pellew, George. *John Jay*. 1890. Reprint. New York: Chelsea House, 1980.

Phelps, Timothy M., and Helen Winternitiz. *Capitol Games: Clarence Thomas, Anita Hill, and the Story of a Supreme Court Nomination.* New York: Hyperion, 1992.

Polenberg, Richard. *The World of Benjamin Cardozo: Personal Values and the Judicial Process.* Cambridge: Harvard University Press, 1997.

Posner, Richard A. *Aging and Old Age.* Chicago: University of Chicago Press, 1995.

———, ed. *The Essential Holmes: Selections from the Letters, Speeches, Judicial Opinions, and Other Writings of Oliver Wendell Holmes Jr.* Chicago: University of Chicago Press, 1992.

Post, Jerrold M., and Robert S. Robins. *When Illness Strikes the Leader: The Dilemma of the Captive King.* New Haven: Yale University Press, 1993.

Pringle, Henry F. *The Life and Times of William Howard Taft: A Biography.* 2 vols. New York: Farran and Rinehart, 1939.

Pritchett, C. Herman. *Civil Liberties and the Vinson Court.* Chicago: University of Chicago Press, 1954.

Pusey, Merlo J. *Charles Evans Hughes.* 2 vols. New York: Macmillan, 1951.

Rehnquist, William H. *Grand Inquests: The Historic Impeachments of Justice Samuel Chase and President Andrew Johnson.* New York: Morrow, 1992.

Riker, William. *Democracy in the United States.* 2d ed. New York: Macmillan, 1965.

Robertson, David. *Sly and Able: A Political Biography of James F. Byrnes.* New York: W. W. Norton, 1994.

Rowan, Carl T. *Dream Makers, Dream Breakers: The World of Justice Thurgood Marshall.* Boston: Little, Brown, 1993.

Rudko, Frances H. *Truman's Court: A Study in Judicial Restraint.* Westport, Conn.: Greenwood Press, 1988.

Rush, Benjamin. *The Autobiography of Benjamin Rush.* Edited by G. Corner. Princeton: Princeton University Press, 1948.

Savage, David G. *Turning Right: The Making of the Rehnquist Supreme Court.* New York: John Wiley and Sons, 1992.

Schmidhauser, John R. *The Supreme Court: Its Politics, Personalities, and Procedures.* New York: Holt, Rinehart, and Winston, 1963.

Schubert, Glendon. *The Constitutional Polity.* Boston: Boston University Press, 1970.

Schuckers, Jacob W. *The Life and Public Services of Salmon Portland Chase.* 1874. Reprint. New York: Da Capo Press, 1970.

Schwartz, Bernard. *Decision: How the Supreme Court Decides Cases.* New York: Oxford University Press, 1996.

———. *A History of the Supreme Court.* New York: Oxford University Press, 1993.

———. *Super Chief: Earl Warren and His Supreme Court—A Judicial Biography.* New York: New York University Press, 1983.

Scigliano, Robert, ed. *The Courts: A Reader in the Judicial Process.* Boston: Little, Brown, 1962.

Shogan, Robert. *A Question of Judgment: The Fortas Case and the Struggle for the Supreme Court.* Indianapolis: Bobbs-Merrill, 1972.

Silver, David M. *Lincoln's Supreme Court.* Champaign: University of Illinois Press, 1956.

Simon, James F. *The Antagonists: Hugo Black, Felix Frankfurter, and Civil Liberties in Modern America.* New York: Simon and Schuster, 1989.

———. *Independent Journey: The Life of William O. Douglas.* New York: Harper and Row, 1980.

Smith, Charles Page. *James Wilson: Founding Father, 1742–1798.* 1956. Reprint. Westport, Conn.: Greenwood Press, 1973.

Smith, Jean Edward. *John Marshall: Definer of a Nation*. New York: Henry Holt, 1996.

Steamer, Robert J. *Chief Justice: Leadership and the Supreme Court*. Columbia: University of South Carolina Press, 1986.

Stebenne, David. *Arthur J. Goldberg: New Deal Liberal*. New York: Oxford University Press, 1996.

Story, William W., ed. *The Life and Letters of Joseph Story*. 2 vols. 1851. Reprint. Freeport, N.Y.: Books for Libraries Press, 1971.

Strong, Theron G. *Landmarks of a Lawyer's Lifetime*. New York: Dodd, Mead, 1914.

Stumpf, Harry P. *American Judicial Politics*. 2d ed. Upper Saddle River, N.J.: Prentice Hall, 1998.

Surrency, Erwin C. *History of Federal Courts*. New York: Oceanna Publications, 1987.

Swisher, Carl Brent. *American Constitutional Development*. 2d ed. New York: Houghton Mifflin, 1954.

———. *Roger B. Taney*. New York: Macmillan Company, 1935.

———. *Stephen J. Field: Craftsman of the Law*, 1930. Reprint. Chicago: University of Chicago Press, 1969.

———. *The Taney Period 1836-64. The Oliver Wendell Holmes Devise History of the Supreme Court of the United States*. Vol. 5. New York: Macmillan, 1974.

Tocqueville, Alexis de. *Democracy in America*. Oxford: Oxford University Press, 1946.

Tyler, Samuel. *Memoir of Roger Brooke Taney, LL.D., Chief Justice of the Supreme Court of the United States*. 1872. Reprint. New York: Da Capo Press, 1970.

Urofsky, Melvin I. *Felix Frankfurter: Judicial Restraint and Individual Liberties*. Boston: Twayne Publishers, 1991.

———, ed. *The Douglas Letters: Selections from the Private Papers of Justice William O. Douglas*. Bethesda, Md.: Adler and Adler, 1987.

———, ed. *The Supreme Court Justices: A Biographical Dictionary*. New York: Garland Publishing, 1994.

Warner, Hoyt Landon. *The Life of Mr. Justice Clarke: A Testament to the Power of Liberal Dissent in America*. Cleveland: Western Reserve University, 1959.

Warren, Charles. *The Supreme Court in United States History*. Rev. ed. 2 vols. Boston: Little, Brown, 1926.

Wasby, Stephen L. *The Supreme Court in the Federal Judicial System*. 4th ed. Chicago: Nelson-Hall Publishers, 1993.

Weisenburger, Francis P. *The Life of John McLean: A Politician on the United States Supreme Court*. 1937. Reprint. New York: Da Capo Press, 1971.

White, G. Edward. *Earl Warren: A Public Life*. New York: Oxford University Press, 1982.

———, with Gerald Gunther. *The Marshall Court and Cultural Change, 1815-1835*. Abridged ed. New York: Oxford University Press, 1991.

Winters, Glenn R., and Richard A. Hanson., eds. *Selected Readings: Judicial Discipline and Removal*. Chicago: American Judicature Society, 1973.

Witt, Elder., ed. *Congressional Quarterly's Guide to the U.S. Supreme Court*. 2d ed. Washington, D.C.: Congressional Quarterly Press, 1990.

Wood, Gertrude Sceery. *William Paterson of New Jersey, 1745-1806*. Fair Lawn, N.J.: Fair Lawn Press, 1933.

Woodruff, Diana S., and James E. Birren., eds. *Aging: Scientific Perspectives and Social Issues*. New York: D. Van Nostrand, 1975.

Woodward, Bob, and Scott Armstrong. *The Brethren: Inside the Supreme Court.* New York: Simon and Schuster, 1979.

Wunder, John R., ed. *Law and the Great Plains: Essays on the Legal History of the Heartland.* Westport, Conn.: Greenwood Press, 1996.

Yarbrough, Tinsley E. *John Marshall Harlan: Great Dissenter of the Warren Court.* New York: Oxford University Press, 1992.

———. *Judicial Enigma: The First Justice Harlan.* New York: Oxford University Press, 1995.

———. *Mr. Justice Black and His Critics.* Durham, N.C.: Duke University Press, 1988.

ARTICLES

Atkinson, David N. "Bowing to the Inevitable: Supreme Court Deaths and Resignations, 1789–1864." *Arizona State Law Journal* (1982): 615–40.

———. "Justice Harold H. Burton and the Work of the Supreme Court." *Cleveland State Law Review* 27 (1978): 69–84.

———. Justice Sherman Minton and Behavior Patterns Inside the Supreme Court." *Northwestern University Law Review* 69 (1974): 716–38.

———. "Minor Supreme Court Justices: Their Characteristics and Importance." *Florida State University Law Review* 3 (1975): 348–59.

———. "Mr. Justice Cardozo: A Common Law Judge on a Public Law Court." *California Western Law Review* 17 (1981): 257–85.

———. "Mr. Justice Cardozo and the New Deal: An Appraisal." *Villanova Law Review* 15 (1969): 68–82.

———. "Mr. Justice Cardozo on the Supreme Court: State and Federal Taxation." *Houston Law Review* 5 (1967): 254–73.

———. "The Problems of Disabled Justices: Supreme Court Deaths and Resignations: 1865–1900." *Drake Law Review* 38 (1989): 903–25.

———. "Retirement and Death on the United States Supreme Court: From Van Devanter to Douglas." *UMKC Law Review* 45 (1976): 1–27.

Biddle, Francis. "Proceedings in Memory of Mr. Justice Van Devanter." *United States Reports* 316 (1942): xxix.

Brant, Irving. "Mr. Justice Rutledge—The Man." *Iowa Law Review* 35 (1950): 544–65.

Casper, Jonathan D. "The Supreme Court and National Policy Making." *American Political Science Review* 70 (1976): 50–63.

Christensen, George A. "Here Lies the Supreme Court: Gravesites of the Justices." *Yearbook 1983, Supreme Court Historical Society,* 17–30.

Dahl, Robert A. "Decision-Making in a Democracy: The Supreme Court as a National Policy-Maker." *Journal of Public Law* 6 (1957): 279–95.

Danelski, David J. "A Supreme Court Justice Steps Down." *Yale Review* 54 (1965): 411–25.

Eastland, Terry. "While Justice Sleeps." *National Review,* 21 April 1989, 24–26.

Fairman, Charles. "The Education of a Justice: Justice Bradley and Some of His Colleagues." *Stanford Law Review* 1 (1949): 217–55.

———. "Mr. Justice Bradley's Appointment to the Supreme Court and the Legal Tender Cases." Parts 1 and 2. *Harvard Law Review* 54 (1941): 977–1034; 1128–55.

————. "The Retirement of Federal Judges." *Harvard Law Review* 51 (1938): 397–443.

————. "What Makes a Great Justice? Mr. Justice Bradley and the Supreme Court, 1870–1892." *Boston University Law Review* 30 (1950): 49–102.

Frankfurter, Felix. "Mr. Justice Roberts." *University of Pennsylvania Law Review* 104 (1955): 311–17.

Howard, J. Woodford, Jr. "On the Fluidity of Judicial Choice." *American Political Science Review* 63 (1968): 43–56.

Jenkins, John A. "A Candid Talk with Justice Blackmun." *New York Times Magazine,* 20 February 1983.

Kanin, Garson. "Trips to Felix." *Atlantic Monthly,* March 1964, 55–62.

Maxey, David W. "The Translation of James Wilson." *Journal of Supreme Court History: 1990 Yearbook of the Supreme Court Historical Society,* 29–43.

McHargue, Daniel S. "President Taft's Appointments to the Supreme Court." *Journal of Politics* 12 (1950): 478–510.

Moynihan, Daniel Patrick. "Letters to the Editor." *New York Times Book Review,* 24 November 1996.

O'Connell, Jeffrey, and Thomas E. O'Connell. "Book Review." *St. Louis University Law Journal* 37 (1992): 169–79.

Pettit, William. "Justice Byrnes and the United States Supreme Court." *South Carolina Law Quarterly* 6 (1954): 423–28.

Pusey, Merlo J. "The Court Copes with Disability." *Yearbook 1979, Supreme Court Historical Society,* 63–69, 100.

Rosen, Jeffrey. "Moving On." *New Yorker,* 29 April and 6 May 1996, 66–73.

Rugg, Arthur P. "William Cushing." *Yale Law Journal* 30 (1920): 128–44.

Schubert, Glendon. "Aging, Conservatism, and Judicial Behavior." *Micropolitics* 3 (1983): 135–79.

Stephenson, D. Grier, Jr. "The Judicial Bookshelf." *Journal of Supreme Court History: 1994 Yearbook of the Supreme Court Historical Society,* 147–70.

Tanenhaus, Joseph. "Supreme Court Attitudes Toward Federal Administrative Agencies, 1947–1956—An Application of Social Science Methods to the Study of the Judicial Process." *Vanderbilt Law Review* 14 (1961): 473–502.

Van Tassel, Emily Field. "Justice Arthur J. Goldberg." In *The Jewish Justices of the Supreme Court Revisited: Brandeis to Fortas,* ed. Jennifer M. Lowe, 81–102. Washington, D.C.: Supreme Court Historical Society, 1994.

Wittke, Carl. "Mr. Justice Clarke in Retirement." *Western Reserve Law Review* 1 (1949): 28–48.

Wright, Charles Alan. "Authenticity of 'A Dirtier Day's Work' Quote in Question." *Supreme Court Historical Society Quarterly* 13.4 (Winter 1990): 6–7.

UNPUBLISHED SOURCES

Court Papers

The Harold H. Burton Papers, Manuscript Division, Library of Congress.

The Felix Frankfurter Papers, Manuscript Division, Library of Congress.

The Horace H. Lurton Papers, Manuscript Division, Library of Congress.

The William Howard Taft Papers, Manuscript Division, Library of Congress.

The Willis Van Devanter Papers, Manuscript Division, Library of Congress.

Theses

Cole, Judith. "Mr. Justice Charles Evans Whittaker: A Case Study in Judicial Recruitment and Behavior." Master's thesis, University of Missouri–Kansas City, 1972.

Smith, Craig A. "Charles Evans Whittaker, Associate Justice of the Supreme Court." Master's thesis, University of Missouri–Kansas City, 1997.

Supreme Court Justice Interviews

Hugo L. Black
Tom C. Clark
William O. Douglas
John Marshall Harlan
Stanley F. Reed
Earl Warren
Charles E. Whittaker

INDEX